Frames of Memory after 9/11

Palgrave Macmillan Memory Studies

Series Editors: **Andrew Hoskins** and **John Sutton**

International Advisory Board: **Steven Brown,** University of Leicester, UK **Mary Carruthers,** New York University, USA **Paul Connerton,** University of Cambridge, UK **Astrid Erll,** University of Wuppertal, Germany **Robyn Fivush,** Emory University, USA **Tilmann Habermas,** University of Frankfurt am Main, Germany **Jeffrey Olick,** University of Virginia, USA **Susannah Radstone,** University of East London, UK **Ann Rigney,** Utrecht University, Netherlands

The nascent field of Memory Studies emerges from contemporary trends that include a shift from concern with historical knowledge of events to that of memory, from 'what we know' to 'how we remember it'; changes in generational memory; the rapid advance of technologies of memory; panics over declining powers of memory, which mirror our fascination with the possibilities of memory enhancement; and the development of trauma narratives in reshaping the past.

These factors have contributed to an intensification of public discourses on our past over the last thirty years. Technological, political, interpersonal, social, and cultural shifts affect what, how, and why people and societies remember and forget. This groundbreaking series tackles questions such as: What is 'memory' under these conditions? What are its prospects, and also the prospects for its interdisciplinary and systematic study? What are the conceptual, theoretical, and methodological tools for its investigation and illumination?

Andrea Hajek
NEGOTIATING MEMORIES OF PROTEST IN WESTERN EUROPE
The Case of Italy

Amy Holdsworth
TELEVISION, MEMORY AND NOSTALGIA

Jason James
PRESERVATION AND NATIONAL BELONGING IN EASTERN GERMANY
Heritage Fetishism and Redeeming Germanness

Sara Jones
THE MEDIA OF TESTIMONY
Remembering the East German Stasi in the Berlin Republic

Emily Keightley and Michael Pickering
THE MNEMONIC IMAGINATION
Remembering as Creative Practice

Amanda Lagerkvist
MEDIA AND MEMORY IN NEW SHANGHAI
Western Performances of Futures Past

Philip Lee and Pradip Ninan Thomas *(editors)*
PUBLIC MEMORY, PUBLIC MEDIA AND THE POLITICS OF JUSTICE

Erica Lehrer, Cynthia E. Milton and Monica Eileen Patterson *(editors)*
CURATING DIFFICULT KNOWLEDGE
Violent Pasts in Public Places

Oren Meyers, Eyal Zandberg and Motti Neiger
COMMUNICATING AWE
Media, Memory and Holocaust Commemoration

Anne Marie Monchamp
AUTOBIOGRAPHICAL MEMORY IN AN ABORIGINAL AUSTRALIAN
COMMUNITY
Culture, Place and Narrative

Katharina Niemeyer *(editor)*
MEDIA AND NOSTALGIA
Yearning for the Past, Present and Future

Margarita Saona
MEMORY MATTERS IN TRANSITIONAL PERU

Anna Saunders and Debbie Pinfold *(editors)*
REMEMBERING AND RETHINKING THE GDR
Multiple Perspectives and Plural Authenticities

V. Seidler
REMEMBERING DIANA
Cultural Memory and the Reinvention of Authority

Bryoni Trezise
PERFORMING FEELING IN CULTURES OF MEMORY

Evelyn B. Tribble and Nicholas Keene
COGNITIVE ECOLOGIES AND THE HISTORY OF REMEMBERING
Religion, Education and Memory in Early Modern England

Barbie Zelizer and Keren Tenenboim-Weinblatt *(editors)*
JOURNALISM AND MEMORY

Palgrave Macmillan Memory Studies
Series Standing Order ISBN   978–0–230–23851–0 (hardback)
                                    978–0–230–23852–7 (paperback)
                                    (outside North America only)

You can receive future titles in this series as they are published by placing a standing order. Please contact your bookseller or, in case of difficulty, write to us at the address below with your name and address, the title of the series and the ISBN quoted above.

Customer Services Department, Macmillan Distribution Ltd, Houndmills, Basingstoke, Hampshire RG21 6XS, England

---

Frames of Memory after 9/11

Culture, Criticism, Politics, and Law

Lucy Bond
University of Westminster, UK

First published 2015 by
PALGRAVE MACMILLAN

Palgrave Macmillan in the UK is an imprint of Macmillan Publishers Limited,
registered in England, company number 785998, of Houndmills, Basingstoke,
Hampshire RG21 6XS.

Palgrave Macmillan in the US is a division of St Martin's Press LLC,
175 Fifth Avenue, New York, NY 10010.

Palgrave Macmillan is the global academic imprint of the above companies
and has companies and representatives throughout the world.

Palgrave® and Macmillan® are registered trademarks in the United States,
the United Kingdom, Europe and other countries

ISBN 978-1-349-49439-2   ISBN 978-1-137-44010-5 (eBook)
DOI 10.1057/9781137440105

Library of Congress Cataloging-in-Publication Data

Bond, Lucy, 1983–
  Frames of memory after 9/11 : culture, criticism, politics, and law / Lucy Bond,
University of Westminster, UK.
    pages cm. — (Palgrave Macmillan memory studies)
  Includes bibliographical references.

  1. Collective memory—United States. 2. September 11 Terrorist Attacks, 2001.
  I. Title.
  HM1033.B66 2015
  909—dc23

                                                                    2014028338
A catalogue record for this book is available from the British Library.

A catalog record for this book is available from the Library of Congress.

For Mum, for everything.

Contents

Preface

Along the south-eastern perimeter of Arlington National Cemetery, just north of the Pentagon, runs the niche wall. From a distance, this long stretch of white marble seems simply to demarcate the boundary of America's second-largest graveyard. However, on closer inspection, the wall is revealed as a matrix of empty graves: blank plots awaiting the names and remains of their future occupants. Directly to the west of the niche wall stands the columbarium. Housing the ashes of soldiers who have died in international combat since 2001, as well as rows of vacant crematoria niches, this imposing series of arches creates a visual corridor from the recent past to present conflicts and the unknown (but all-too-predictable) future. Looking south, through the arches of the columbarium, reveals Arlington's memorial to (and graves of) those who died at the Pentagon on September 11, 2001. This hexagonal granite plinth commemorates Pentagon employees alongside the passengers and crew of American Airlines flight 77. To the east of the monument, divided from the cemetery by the busy thoroughfare of Washington Boulevard, is the Pentagon's own memorial to the attacks. Here, victims are remembered in a series of oblique 'benches', each set above its own reflecting pool.

Together, the 9/11 memorials and the columbarium offer a sad reminder of the brutal dawn of the twenty-first century. Their location in Arlington links these sites, and the events they memorialise, to the broader history of violence marked by the cemetery, emplotting them both figuratively and physically within the historical chronicle of the nation. The promise of new victims inherent in the empty graves indicates that Arlington's boundaries are not as fixed as they might appear; whilst the niche wall may define the spatial reach of the cemetery, it cannot delimit the number of deaths that will be claimed by military endeavours (strategised in the Pentagon across the road), or the number of casualties yet to be interred at the site. Its cavities constitute a porous and malleable future in which it seems all but certain that new losses will be inscribed. The wall demarcates the symbolic limits of Arlington as these haunting reminders of deaths-yet-to-come throw the heroic imaginary that abounds across the cemetery into sharp relief. Separated from the tourist trail by an expanse of empty land, the vacant graves destabilise the triumphalist rhetoric that characterises commemorative efforts elsewhere at the site – suggesting that, whilst the past can be reworked to portray America as the nation that 'hath Freedom claimed', and Arlington as the place 'Where Valor Rests',[1] the future remains a site of conceptual slippage, vulnerable to a volatile present.

As the national cemetery, Arlington sets strict limits upon the lives that are recognised as grievable within its boundaries. Only American losses are officially mourned here, yet, in their very absence, the casualties killed by US troops form a spectral presence throughout the cemetery. Whilst there is no place for them in the symbolic order of Arlington, their graves remain the unacknowledged double of the rows of white tombstones that stretch across the site, revealing Arlington's inescapable imbrication with distant places and people far beyond this Virginian terrain. In so doing, the cemetery exposes the permeability of memory: highlighting the fluidity of the temporal and spatial narratives we inhabit; testifying to the fact that our lives are consistently bound to those of invisible others; and exposing the present as a tightly folded concertina of other times and spaces. Visiting a site such as Arlington, we are subject to polychronic temporalities, comprised of the overlapping experiences of personal time (as the site relates to individual pasts and identities), collective time (as the cemetery plays upon broader familial, ethic, or social associations – such as an army regiment, a military campaign, or a veterans' organisation), national time (as Arlington reinforces American narratives of heroism and loss, and pays testament to the military history of the United States), and perhaps even global time (as it reflects moments of geopolitical fracture and conflict). The cemetery represents a topographical inscription of history. Its diverse areas mark a different event or series of events (from the Civil War to Vietnam, the assassination of John F. Kennedy to the Challenger and Columbia disasters). These memorials gesture far beyond the boundaries of Arlington – pointing across the borders of the United States, and even towards the very limits of the Earth's atmosphere.

Conceptualising the topography of Arlington in this manner affords a window onto the dynamics that shape the imaginative landscape of American memory. The cemetery is a political space, charged with preserving (and to some extent, constructing) a coherent impression of American history to be projected into the future. However, the past is not simply *there* in the present – it must be articulated in order to be made visible. The work of memory impels the continual remediation of historical events to suit the purposes of the present. This process takes place on many levels, requiring the interplay of multiple objects, texts, actions, and sites. At Arlington, the construction of memory involves the interaction of myriad commemorative *media,* including the graves, the tokens of remembrance that are left at them, the landscape in which they are set, the guidebooks that inform a visitor's journey across the site, the novels, DVDs, photographs, and postcards sold in the visitor's centre. The commemorative practices that take place at the cemetery emphasise that memory is a performative process, involving mourners, public figures, and tourists, witnessing and participating in rituals from the changing of the guard at the Tomb of the Unknown Soldier, to the ceremonial funereal honours given to those interred at the site, the placing of tributes on monuments and memorials, and the more profane purchasing of souvenirs in the site's shop. More broadly, our encounter with the cemetery is inflected by the diverse ways in which Arlington has been mobilised in local, national, and global culture over the course of its history.

Building upon this understanding of memory as a montage of myriad practices and media, this book examines the development of American memorial culture after September 11, 2001. I suggest that, whilst memories of 9/11 have taken diverse forms and served divergent agendas since 2001, certain *frames of memory* can be seen to inform the articulation of the attacks across cultural, critical, political, and juridical discourses. These templates manifest recurring representational paradigms that have been used to structure memories of diverse events and experiences by drawing them into familiar narrative patterns. Over the course of what follows, I highlight three frameworks that have proved particularly prominent in shaping the representation of the attacks in the American public sphere: the rhetoric of trauma; the American jeremiad; and analogical Holocaust memory. I trace these paradigms to their origins in American cultural history, interrogating the means by which such forms acquire hegemonic weighting as they are naturalised by their repetition over time. As I shall demonstrate, these frames of memory do not exist in isolation, but enter into dialogue with each other, sometimes in reinforcement, sometimes in discord.

Although the paradigms I investigate are by no means exhaustive (as the Conclusion will demonstrate, there have been many successful attempts to articulate significant counter-narratives in American memorial culture after 9/11), they have undoubtedly been instrumental in shaping patterns of commemoration across official, vernacular, and commercial memorial culture. This book seeks to destabilise this centralised approach to memory, opening the public sphere to a broader series of narratives and encouraging contesting perspectives to interact in a process of dialogic negotiation to encourage a *transcultural* reorientation of the memory of September 11 and its aftermath.

Acknowledgements

Much gratitude is due to the following individuals and institutions for their help in the realisation of *Frames of Memory after 9/11*. Firstly, thank you to the team at Palgrave Macmillan for all their hard work and expertise. Particular recognition must go to Felicity Plester and Chris Penfold for their invaluable guidance through the publication process, to the anonymous reviewer for their thoughtful comments, and to the series editors, Andrew Hoskins, John Sutton, and the editorial board for their faith in this project. Some of the material in this book has been published in different forms elsewhere, and I am very grateful to the editors and reviewers of the *Journal of American Studies, Culture, Theory and Critique,* and Walter de Gruyter for their feedback and advice. Enormous thanks are also due to Michael Rothberg and Robert Eaglestone for their incisive (and extensive) readers' reports, their ongoing help and encouragement, and their seminal contributions to memory and literary studies, which have been so influential in shaping my own thoughts.

The seeds of this book were sown during my time on the much-missed MA in Cultural Memory at the Institute of Germanic and Romance Studies (now the Institute for Modern Languages Research). This course changed my life personally and professionally. Thanks and so much more are due to Gill Rye, for her much-needed nurturing of us all, to Anna Phillips and Simon Bacon for their intelligence, wit, and willingness to engage in impassioned discussions over a bottle of wine (or two or three). The legacy of the MA endures in the Centre for the Study of Cultural Memory, which continues to host important and timely debates in the field – not least, the 2010 International Conference on Transcultural Memory, which was central to shaping my thinking on the global dimensions of memory. I am particularly grateful to Michael Rothberg, A. Dirk Moses, Astrid Erll, and Andrew Hoskins for their brilliant keynotes, to Susannah Radstone for her insightful comments as respondent, and to my co-organisers for all of their hard work.

My research would not have been possible without the kind sponsorship of the Arts and Humanities Research Council, who offered me the invaluable opportunity to study at the John W. Kluge Center in the Library of Congress as a British Research Council Fellow – thanks to Mariglynn and Geoff Edlins for making this an experience that I will never forget. I am also exceedingly grateful to the Department of English and Comparative Literature at Goldsmiths, University of London, for their generous contributions towards fieldtrips that were fundamental to the work of this project, and for providing such a stimulating environment in which to complete my Ph.D. Medals should be given to Christopher Lloyd and Helen Palmer, whose friendship and insight made the doctoral slog possible and, at times, even pleasurable! More recently, I have accrued a great debt to the staff and students of the Department of English, Linguistics, and Cultural Studies at the University of Westminster for the enthusiasm and inspiration they have provided over the past two years. Special mention must go to Alex Warwick, David Cunningham, John Beck, Leigh Wilson, Simon Avery, Georgina Colby, and Matt Charles for their encouragement and support.

Finally, then, to the people without whom I would be lost. To my friends and family who have tolerated innumerable discussions of catastrophic events at parties, birthdays, engagements, and weddings, when, I am sure, they would rather have been talking about anything else – I apologise! To Roanna Bond, Stephen Bond, and Sally and Tony Brzezicki – thank you all for your love, patience, and support over the past seven years. To my uncle, Martin, for his inspirational dedication to education (not to mention his enormous generosity, which made it possible for me to complete my research on this book) – you are much missed, every day. To Richard Crownshaw for his encyclopaedic knowledge of, and passion for, the field of memory studies – this book would not have been possible without your tireless guidance, loyalty, and kindness. To the amazing Jessica Rapson for accompanying me every step of the way – I owe you so much, and cannot imagine doing this without you. Finally, to Simon Brzezicki for our life together – you (and Potus!) brighten every day, even when I'm the most undeserving of creatures, and I do not have words to thank you enough.

Permissions

Earlier versions, reworked here, of Chapters 1, 2, and 3 were published, respectively, as:

- 2011. 'Compromised Critique: A Meta-critical Analysis of American Studies after 9/11'. *Journal of American Studies*, 45: 733–756.
- 2014. 'Types of Transculturality: Narrative Frameworks and the Commemoration of 9/11'. *The Transcultural Turn: Interrogating Memory*

Between and Beyond Borders, edited by Lucy Bond and Jessica Rapson, 61–81. Berlin: Walter de Gruyter.

- 2012. 'Intersections or Misdirections? Problematising Crossroads of Memory in the Commemoration of 9/11'. *Culture, Theory and Critique,* 53.2: 111–128.

I am very grateful for the permissions to republish these essays as reworked in *Frames of Memory after 9/11.* Particular thanks must go to Walter de Gruyter for their generosity in allowing me an exception to their procedural guidelines.

Introduction

1 Cultural memory in theory and practice

As has been widely documented,[1] the rise of memory as a body of cultural and critical interest can be loosely traced to a series of events that coalesced around the fall of Soviet Communism. These include the infamous historians' debate over the Holocaust in Germany and a related national commitment to *Vergangenheitsbewältigung*, or coming to terms with the past;[2] increasing concerns about the 'amnesiac' dimensions of both globalising capitalism and cultural postmodernism;[3] the heightened importance of identity politics in the late 1980s and 1990s; confrontations with the legacies of colonialism, fascism, and Apartheid; and an apparent decline in national affiliations and ideologies as a grounding for identity.[4] However, whilst these antecedents may point to a distinct, if diffuse, set of historical coordinates upon which to ground the recent interest in memory, subsequent developments have resulted in a rather amorphous, and arguably, indefinable field of study.

Kerwin Lee Klein asserts that memory has become 'the subject of any number of potential generalisations' (Klein 2000, 136), critiquing the emergence of an undifferentiated Western 'memory boom' in the academy and a concomitant cultural 'memory industry [that] ranges from the museum trade to the legal battles over repressed memory and on to the market for academic books and articles that invoke *memory* as a key word' (Klein 2000, 127). As Wulf Kansteiner suggests, memory may justifiably be labelled a 'slippery phenomenon' (Kansteiner 2002, 180), applied to individual psyches and collective institutions, academic and popular discourse, our own experiences, and our investment in the lives of others – a referent for both representations of the past and the objects that manifest them. Accordingly, Andreas Huyssen contends, 'memory is one of those elusive topics we all think we have a handle on. But as soon as we try to define it, it starts slipping and sliding, eluding attempts to grasp it either culturally, sociologically, or scientifically' (Huyssen 2003, 3).

Jeffrey Olick and Joyce Robbins argue that this hermeneutic fluidity is mirrored in memory's scholarly incarnation, labelling memory studies 'a nonparadigmatic, transdisciplinary, centreless enterprise' that has been approached 'from sociology, history, literary criticism, anthropology, psychology, art history, and political science, among other disciplines' (Olick and Robbins 1998, 105–6). Attempting to bring some conceptual clarity to this methodological opacity, Susannah Radstone asserts that 'what is at stake in studies of memory is the elaboration of the relationship between lived experience and the broader field of history [. . .] including within its purview questions of broad social forces and power relations that exceed those of relations between individuals' (Radstone 2005, 139).

Radstone's comments indicate that studies of memory negotiate the terms of the relationship between the individual and the collective, suggesting that remembrance exceeds the bounds of personal experience. Such a contention is not new: the idea of 'collective memory' found its first sustained exploration in the work of Maurice Halbwachs,[5] whose texts have informed the theoretical basis of much of the later work in the field. Insisting that 'individuals always use social frameworks when they remember', Halbwachs (1992, 185) argued that memory is structured by traditional patterns of narrative and language, encoding social norms in the very process of its articulation. In recent years, critics have taken up the task of clarifying and advancing Halbwachs's work. James Young substitutes Halbwachs's 'collective memory' for his own 'collected memory', arguing that the difference between the two is 'the difference between unified memory and unified meaning for many different types of memory' (Young 1993, xi). Young points to the dangers of homogenising cultures of remembrance by presuming that it is possible for individuals to assume each other's memories. Although he allows that social groups share – and construct – common sentiments about the past, he contends that memories remain the property of the individual, albeit mediated by, and subject to, the customs, beliefs, and traditions of the collective.

This attention to what one, following Young, might call 'the texture of memory' strongly informs the work of the two academics perhaps most responsible for carrying the theories of Halbwachs into the field of contemporary memory studies: Jan and Aleida Assmann. Distinguishing between commemorative media and memories themselves, Jan Assmann suggests that 'the term "memory" is *not a metaphor but a metonym* [italics in original] based on a material contact between a remembering mind and a reminding object' (Assmann 2008, 111). He draws further distinctions between 'cultural' and 'communicative' memory, arguing that cultural memory is 'exteriorized, objectified, and stored away in symbolic forms', and communicative memory 'lives in everyday interaction and communication' (Assmann 2008, 111).

Consequently, whilst cultural memory (in the form of artefacts, books, museums, memorials) is 'situation-transcendent' and 'may be transferred from one situation to another and transmitted from one generation to another', communicative memory 'is not formalised and stabilised by any forms of material symbolisation [. . .] and, for this very reason, has only a limited time depth, which normally reaches no farther back than eighty years, the time span of three interacting generations' (Assmann 2008, 111).

Faced with the rather rigid separation of cultural and communicative remembrance, a number of critics have sought to reconceptualise this binary in order to challenge the temporal and spatial limitations suggested by such theories of memory. Theorists such as Marianne Hirsch (1997), Alison Landsberg (2004), and E. Ann Kaplan (2005) contend that individuals may acquire 'memories' of (predominantly traumatic) events they themselves have not experienced through respective structures of 'postmemory', 'prosthetic memory', and 'media witnessing' that disconnect communicative memory from its intimate and experiential basis and allow the technologies of cultural memory to provide secondary or vicarious forms of remembrance. As recent critiques have argued,[6] such theses are problematic in a number of regards: firstly, they threaten to blur the distinction between subject and witness, allowing an over-identification with victims of historical atrocity that negates the specificity of their experience. Secondly, in their disconnection of an event from its context, they tend to dehistoricise memory. Thirdly, such modes of transmission rely heavily upon affective media that leave themselves open to sentimentalisation and appropriation.

These forms of secondary memory are not reliant on verbal or everyday structures of communication alone, but are heavily imbricated with the *technologies* of cultural memory. As Astrid Erll and Ann Rigney assert, memories do not simply inhere in cultures, rather 'the very concept of *cultural* [italics in original] memory is itself premised on the idea that memory can only become collective as part of a continuous process whereby memories are shared with the help of symbolic artefacts that mediate between individuals and, in the process, create communality across both space and time' (Erll and Rigney 2009, 1). Consequently, it is not only specific places (such as Auschwitz, Gettysburg, or Ground Zero) that constitute what Pierre Nora describes as *lieux de mémoire* (sites of memory),[7] but the constellation of diverse media relating to a specific event as they evolve over time. As Erll contends:

> events which are transformed into *lieux de memoire* are usually represented again and again, over decades or centuries, in different media. What is known about an event which has turned into a site of memory, therefore, seems to refer not so much to what one might cautiously call the 'actual event', but instead to a canon of existent medial constructions, to the narratives, images and myths circulating in a memory culture (Erll 2009, 111).

For Erll and Rigney, this 'canon' of memory is comprised of commemorative '"media" of all sorts – spoken language, letters, books, photos, films', each of which provides 'frameworks for shaping both experience and memory [. . .] in two, interconnected ways: as instruments for sense-making, they mediate between the individual and the world; as agents of networking, they mediate between individuals and groups' (Erll and Rigney 2009, 1).

Attempting to explicate the multidimensional nature of this process, Kansteiner argues that:

> we should conceptualize collective memory as the result of the interaction among three types of historical factors: the intellectual and cultural traditions that frame all our representation of the past, the memory makers who selectively adopt and manipulate these traditions, and the memory consumers who use, ignore, or transform such artifacts according to their own interests (Kansteiner 2002, 180).

Commemorative media in cultural circulation do not necessarily produce collective (or individual) memories. Inevitable disparities will arise between the intentions of the 'memory makers', the formal qualities of commemorative media, and the responses of the 'memory consumers' who purchase, visit, watch, or listen to these objects. Memory is thus the transient and intangible by-product of the interplay of these elements – premediated by the culture in which it is articulated, and repeatedly remediated by the form of its representation, the agenda behind its production, and the context of its consumption.

Such claims foreground the politics of memory, necessitating attention to the diverse ways in which the processes of production and reception described above are imbricated in and influenced by broader discourses at work in local, national, and even global cultures. Noting the repeated naturalisation of these dynamics in memory practice and theory, Radstone argues that greater attention must be paid to 'memory's mediation and articulation across and within the public sphere' (Radstone 2005, 134).[8] She asserts that, taken together:

> the terms mediation and articulation militate against any analysis of memory as reflective of or determined by the past, and against any notion that a text [. . .] constitutes an unproblematic reflection of memory. More than that, though, these terms together remind us that texts and practices are complexly related to the broader social formation in which their meanings are forged (Radstone 2005, 134–5).

Radstone conceives the public sphere as constituted by the contrasting interests of diverse groups and institutions, in which memory plays an important role in the battle for hegemony. By this reading, memory is far from the neutral reflection of the past, but a process under whose remit (social, economic, cultural, political) power may be gained or lost as the meaning (and 'ownership') of history is asserted, contested, reasserted, and recontested.[9]

Radstone draws important connections between the hegemonic practice of memory in the public sphere and the academic discipline of memory studies, contending that a lack of reflexivity on the latter's behalf has allowed the former to continue uncritiqued. She indicts a recent trend in memory studies that has led to the over-personalisation of the social and/or political dimensions of memory, contending that 'recent work on memory tends to demonstrate that what began as a radical questioning of the ways in which scholarship conceptualizes its worlds has hardened into a practice of reading in which the inner world [. . .] comes to be taken as "the" world' (Radstone 2005, 140). Kansteiner similarly condemns 'the metaphorical use of psychoanalytic and neurological terminology which misrepresents the social dynamics of collective memory as an effect and extension of individual, autobiographical memory' (Kansteiner 2002, 179), whilst Klein contends that the discipline of memory studies has been weakened by its subscription to these personalising paradigms, arguing that, as its terminology has been increasingly dominated by the 'new lexicon' inherited from psychoanalysis, 'memory work displaces the old hermeneutics of suspicion with a therapeutic discourse' that seeks to 're-enchant our relation with the world and pour presence back into the past' (Klein 2000, 141–5). Such concerns suggest that academic criticism must be conceived as a vital part of memorial practice – demanding reflexivity towards the role theory plays in mediating and articulating different understandings of the past. As this book will demonstrate, this awareness is particularly pertinent to the years following 9/11, which have seen a convergence between certain discourses emanating from the American academy and the master-narratives of the public sphere.

2 American memorial culture after 9/11

In the early twenty-first century, a number of critics have exhibited an anxiety about the future of memory. Whilst much of this ambivalence may be attributable to a general 'memory fatigue' (Huyssen 2003, 3) that has gripped certain sectors of the academy, the events of September 11 2001 inflected the field in a notable manner. Gavriel D. Rosenfeld argues that, following the attacks, 'new political, cultural, and social trends have emerged that may begin to erode memory's influence in the public sphere' (Rosenfeld 2009, 141). Rosenfeld's reasons for predicting the demise of the cultural and critical fascination with memory are two-fold: firstly, he contends that the 'working through' of difficult European legacies of atrocity (which preoccupied much of the early 'memory boom' in scholarship and the related cultural 'memory industry') has now been achieved; secondly, he suggests that the events of 9/11 have led to a revisiting of critical and political priorities and a concomitant sense that memory is 'a luxury that the new era of crisis can ill afford' (Rosenfeld 2009, 147).

These statements are problematic in a number of ways. Rosenfeld's characterisation of memory as a process aimed at working through the past suggests that the study and practice of memory are essentially dedicated to healing and redemption, and thus to closing down – rather than opening up – the historical record. By contrast, I suggest, memory-work necessarily remains an incomplete endeavour as new voices emerge from the margins of history and new experiences demand cultural, political, and critical accommodation and recognition. Rosenfeld further contends that attention to memory is 'something of a luxury made possible by the arrival of a comparatively secure, postideological world without major political threats to worry about or causes to pursue' (Rosenfeld 2009, 147). Conversely, I would argue, the empathic connections sought in the ethical study and practice of memory are urgently needed in a divisive and violent geopolitical climate. Finally, as this book will demonstrate, the dynamics of the American public sphere over the last thirteen years have not suggested memory fatigue, but on the contrary, brought commemoration to the forefront of public consciousness.

The relationship between the theory and practice of memory has assumed complex dynamics in the wake of 9/11. With a few notable exceptions,[10] leading theorists of memory have not published in detail on the commemoration of the attacks. This apparent ambivalence may be at least partially ascribable to a disjuncture between the current interests of memory studies and the particular character of much of the early commemorative practice pertaining to September 11.[11] Vered Vinitzky-Seroussi remarks that, in academic discourse 'over the last two decades or so, the preoccupation with the past has become less about a paradise lost and a nostalgia for heroic leaders than about skeletons in the closet and wrongdoing' (Vinitzky-Seroussi 2009, 3). Whilst the events of 9/11 and their aftermath may be argued to have manifested just the kind of 'moral trauma, disputes, tensions, and conflict' (Vinitzky-Seroussi 2009, 3) that Vinitzky-Seroussi defines as the foundational interests of memory studies, in the immediate aftermath of the attacks, both cultural and political discourses seemed broadly dedicated to lamenting the lost American paradise that the pre-attack era was presented, in retrospect, as having encompassed.

This neat division between the interests of practitioners and theorists is complicated by the fact that, since 9/11, commemorative narratives have displayed the distinct imprint of paradigms inherited from memory studies, often as the result of the direct intervention of critics themselves.[12] Memorial practitioners seem – consciously or unconsciously – to have internalised theoretical models of memory that both preceded and postdated the attacks. However, practitioners and theorists have recurrently displayed scant reflectiveness about the problematic ways in which such ideas may be mobilised and appropriated in the discourses of the public-political sphere, contributing to the emergence of a peculiarly homogenised and, arguably, hegemonic memorial culture.

Through its examination of the imbrication of culture, criticism, politics, and the law following 9/11, this book aims to restore a more balanced and reflexive relationship between the theory and practice of memory. The following chapters provide an overview of the commemoration of the attacks in the American public sphere from the immediate aftermath of September 11 2001 to the military commissions at Guantánamo Bay. Each foregrounds and interrogates a particular frame of memory that has shaped representations of 9/11 across multiple discursive spheres, from literature to law, media reportage to museum exhibits, political rhetoric to photographic memoirs. Whilst these case studies underscore the continuity of particular representational paradigms across the past thirteen years, it *is* possible to identify certain fluctuating dynamics in the practice and theory of memory within this period. As the following chronicle suggests, the commemoration of 9/11 can be loosely divided into five stages, each informed by different agendas and characterised by the emergence of distinctive memorative media. However, this timeline should not be read as definitive or absolute – these are, of course, not isolated developments, but overlapping movements.

The initial phase of commemoration took place in the immediate aftermath of the attacks and lasted until the invasion of Afghanistan in October 2001. This period might best be considered as one of spontaneous diversity, in which posters for the missing, candles, prayers, and many different tokens were left across New York City (centralised to some extent at sites like Union Square, but also deposited in shop windows, bridges, firehouses, parks, and other sites where the empty spaces in the skyline could be clearly glimpsed). These weeks also saw the first publications from what would later become *Portraits of Grief* (the series of obituaries published by *The New York Times*), and Internet activity proposing diverse designs for memorials at Ground Zero, the Pentagon, and Pennsylvania. In literary and critical culture, this period was defined by the swift publication of *The New Yorker* on 24 September 2001, offering a varied series of perspectives from critics and authors including John Updike, Jonathan Franzen, and Susan Sontag. The outrage that followed Sontag's (reasonable) suggestion that '[a] few shreds of historical awareness might help us understand what has just happened, and what may continue to happen' (Sontag 2001), marked the beginning of a more hostile and deterministic culture of memory, resistant to the multiplicity of perspectives that were seen in these early weeks.

This second period, lasting roughly from late 2001 to late 2004, saw a standardisation of many of the narratives in the public sphere as articulations of 9/11 coalesced around discourses of patriotism and freedom that accompanied the waging of war in Iraq and Afghanistan and the opening of the Pentagon memorial. It was during these years that the master-narratives to which this book responds (notions of American exceptionalism, heroism, and the sanctity of memory, coupled to the narrative of national trauma) were most clearly established. These ideas were evident in Libeskind's master plan for Ground Zero (analysed in Chapter 2), which exemplified the heavily emotive aspects of the commemorative climate at this time. The literary response in this period was largely, though not exclusively, focused upon poems, short stories, or children's books, several of which served an explicitly therapeutic purpose (see, for instance, Patel 2001; Roth 2001; Schnurr 2002), whilst many of the early critical responses to the attacks portrayed the events as a collective trauma, 'an event with no voice', to quote Laub (2003). In contrast to these highly personalised narratives, Michael Moore's (2004) controversial film *Fahrenheit 9/11* aimed to highlight the politicisation of the attacks and their aftermath.

These sentiments continued to inform the dominant thematic of the literary output of the third commemorative phase, which lasted from 2005 to President Obama's inauguration in January 2009. This period saw the first significant publication of full-length novels relating to the attacks (for instance, Foer 2006; DeLillo 2007; McInerney 2007; Auster 2008). With the exceptions of McCarthy (2006), Hamid (2007), and O'Neill (2008), the novels of this phase tend to reflect the personalised introspection of the early critical responses, doing little to change the discourse of the attacks (see Chapter 1). By contrast, it was in this stage that more nuanced and reflexive critical debate began to emerge from the American academy (see Simpson 2006; Rozario 2007; Sturken 2007; Faludi 2008). These accounts aimed to contextualise responses to the attacks within a broader cultural history and refute the politicised appropriation of the memory of 9/11. It was also during this period that the Bush Administration's popularity began to decline significantly after the disastrous handling of Hurricane Katrina in 2005 and the sentencing of the soldiers responsible for abuse in Abu Ghraib. This waning political support was accompanied by a concomitant depopularisation of the War on Terror. The memorial project at Ground Zero also began to flounder badly, as corporate interests seemed to marginalise commemorative concerns, and infighting between Libeskind and architect David Childs led to severe compromises to the master plan for the site.

With Obama's election in November 2008 (and his subsequent assumption of the presidential office in January 2009), a fourth phase of commemorative culture emerged. Alongside the gradual withdrawal of troops from Iraq (completed in December 2011), political activity in this period aimed to disassociate the White House from the increasingly chaotic construction process at Ground Zero, and tame some of the more polemic endeavours of the Bush Administration. September 11, which had been celebrated as 'Patriot Day' since 2002, was renamed 'National Day of Service and Remembrance', the Freedom Tower redesignated as 'One World Trade', and the War on Terror reclassified as the 'Overseas Contingency Operation'. This phase continued to witness critical academic reflections on the mediation and articulation of the attacks – notably Pease (2009) – and saw a decline in the number of novels addressing the events of September 11.

The tenth anniversary of the attacks saw the opening of the memorials at Ground Zero and Shanksville (although the latter site is not completed and, despite the opening of the National September 11 Museum in May 2014, the buildings that comprise the majority of the corporate redevelopment at Ground Zero, particularly One World Trade, are not yet operational) and the beginning of the final period of commemoration covered in this account. The media coverage of the anniversary ceremonies was notably more balanced in tone than in earlier years, with much mainstream commentary abandoning nationalist or partisan responses to reflect thoughtfully upon the events of the past decade. *The New Yorker* issued another special edition, without unpleasant backlash. By the end of 2011, there was undeniably a sense of 'closure' evident in attitudes towards 9/11 – a sentiment reinforced by Obama's (2012) State of the Union address, which appeared to draw a line under the '9/11 decade' following the killing of Osama bin Laden and the withdrawal of American troops from Iraq (although operations in Afghanistan are scheduled to continue into 2014). However, the recurrent controversies that have marked the pursuit of criminal justice during the military tribunals at Guantánamo Bay since 2012 (see Chapter 4) suggest that the memory of 9/11 remains an interruptive force in American culture. The attacks are still a highly emotive subject, and their legacy continues to inform both geopolitical relations and cultural and political discourses within the United States.

3 Frames of memory after 9/11

Examining the imbrication of culture, criticism, politics, and law in the aftermath of 9/11, this book understands the theory and practice of memory as transmedial, transdisciplinary, transhistorical, and transcultural phenomena in and through which representations of the past slip and flow between discourses. Whilst this formulation positions memory as an uncontainable property, I suggest that when appropriated and instrumentalised by the institutions of the public-political sphere, its conceptual leakage can become reifying rather than dynamic – closing down, instead of opening up, the experiences and perspectives encoded in commemorative culture. When certain frames of memory are naturalised as the normative means of structuring the articulation of particular events and experiences, the important dynamics that inform the production, circulation, and consumption of commemorative media are easily elided, producing what appear to be memorial masternarratives. Readings of the past can then appear homogenising rather than heterogeneous – static rather than fluid. Without sufficient reflexivity, tropes repeated across discourses can seem standardised, centralised, and institutionalised, bestowing memory with a centripetal quality that belies its centrifugal dynamism.

As W. T. J. Mitchell contends:

Every history is really two histories. There is the history of what actually happened, and there is the history of the perception of what happened. The first kind of history focuses on the facts and figures; the second concentrates on the images and words that define the framework within which those facts and figures make sense (Mitchell 2011, xii).

Conjoining the two planes of Mitchell's history, frames of memory are the representational schemata that provide a way of explaining, and containing, past events. Erll suggests that such paradigms manifest a means of encoding troubling occurrences, drawing upon 'traditional and strongly conventionalised genres [. . .] to provide familiar and meaningful patterns for experiences that would otherwise be hard to interpret' (Erll 2009, 148–9). These forms *premediate* memories of an event by enfolding them within recognisable cultural narratives. Accordingly, as Olick contends, 'images of the past are path-dependent', 'from the moment being remembered, present images are constantly being reproduced, revised, and replaced' (Olick 1999, 382) as both the memories of an event, and the frames through which they are articulated, evolve over time.

Olick suggests that 'images of the past depend not only on the relationship between past and present but also on the accumulation of previous such relationships and their ongoing constitution and reconstitution' (Olick 1999, 382). These relationships mediate the frames of memory, engendering what might be described, in Benjaminian terms, as their 'aura': 'the essence of all that is transmissible from its beginning, ranging from its substantive duration to its testimony to the history which it has experienced' (Benjamin 1968). This auratic *excess* ensures that the frames of memory are not neutral instruments, but often function as vehicles of normative preconceptions and conventions that shade and, to some extent, determine the shape of the memory articulated therein. They frequently encode particular ideological values that have been naturalised by their repetition over time. Treated reflexively, such dynamics need not necessarily be problematic (and can even be exploited to subversive effect), but when left uninterrogated, they can allow certain cultures of memory to be appropriated and mobilised in unfortunate, and often invisible, ways.

The commemoration of 9/11 has been structured by a series of frames with a long cultural history in the United States.[13] Whilst these paradigms have been utilised to articulate interpretations of the attacks that are informed by very different agendas, the homogenising consensus they project means that it is often difficult to distinguish one set of intentions and concerns from another. The cultural memory of 9/11 has thus generally appeared to exhibit an exemplary form of 'narrative coherence', to cite Paul Ricoeur (2004, 243), engendering 'a synthesis of the heterogeneous, in order to speak of the coordination between multiple events, or between causes, intentions, and also accidents within a single meaningful unity' (Ricoeur 2004, 243). In the wake of the attacks, certain theorists and practitioners of memory have lacked the requisite attention to this occlusion of difference. Elements of the American academy (particularly those working in memory and trauma studies) have demonstrated a concerning inattention to the ways the theoretical paradigms in which they have framed their responses to 9/11 are imbricated in (and even contribute to) the formation of hegemonic memorial culture.

This lack of reflexivity characterises the phenomenon that I define as *transcendental memory*. Transcendental cultures of memory exhibit a superficial standardisation of commemorative discourse, premised upon three key characteristics: firstly, a transdiscursive, transmedial, and transdisciplinary convergence of commemorative narratives around limited frames of memory; secondly, a thematic and structural elision of historicity (the erasure of historical specificity, the cancellation of difference between the past, present, and future, or the construction of atemporal narratives); thirdly, a redemptive or reparative orientation to commemoration. Transcendental memorial cultures tend to be intolerant of otherness; they acquire interpretative dominance by marginalising alternative perspectives, presenting an artificially homogenised reading of the past.

Against this master-narrative approach to memory, I suggest that *montaged* commemorative discourses offer a heterogeneous vision of history that does not seek to elevate any frame of memory above another. In an ideal rendering of such a culture, contrasting narratives would be able to coexist, forming a fluid and dialogic nexus of interpersonal memories that is tolerant of diversity and attentive to difference, both inside and outside national boundaries. Ideally, a montaged culture of memory would privilege history over myth, individuals over nations, and reflexivity over redemption. It would be able to trace affinities between disparate events without collapsing them into undifferentiated equation. Finally, it would remain alert to, and transparent about, the way in which the practice and theory of memory mediate and inflect the past, recognising the need for commemorative heterodoxy in which differing interpretations of events are held together in a proximal relationship, connecting at points of tension or accord.

The two forms of remembrance outlined above are not, of course, mutually exclusive. Transcendental narratives constitute elements of a montaged commemorative culture. The attempt at transcendence is unlikely to utterly erase divergent interpretations of the past from the public sphere, except – or perhaps, even – in the most totalitarian of regimes. Similarly, a truly montaged memorial culture will only ever exist in ideal form as practices of representation, technologies of articulation, and processes of commodification inevitably render some memories more visible than others. It would, therefore, be a mistake to read these two phenomena as dichotomously 'impure' and 'pure' modes of memory. Whilst montaged memory is perhaps less implicated within structures of power than transcendental memory (or rather, its diversity allows for a dispersal of hegemonic dominance), it should not be regarded as unmediated. Reflecting on the past from the perspective of the present will inevitably colour 'what was' with the shades of 'what is'. However, by opening up the public sphere to a greater variety of contesting voices, an increasingly montaged culture of memory might help to provide a more democratic way of imagining 'what will be' as we look – individually and collectively – towards the next period of the global twenty-first century.

Lest I lay myself open to the very charges of homogenisation I level at the discourses analysed herein, I should reiterate that my critique of American memorial culture after 9/11 is not intended to be exhaustive. There are, of course, many commemorative texts (across widely divergent media) that offer alternative perspectives on the attacks to those considered below. What follows is an attempt to outline some of the more prominent (and problematic) aspects of American memorial cultural over the past thirteen years. Finally, then, to an overview of the book:

Chapter 1

The first chapter interrogates the predominance of trauma as a frame of memory in literary culture, critical theory, media reportage, political rhetoric, and museal practice after 9/11. This commemorative paradigm designates the attacks as an incomprehensible, unrepresentable event, refusing to admit them as an object of historical knowledge. I analyse the paradigmatic nature of *9/11 trauma fiction*, considering texts aimed at adult, teenage, and child readerships from both 'popular' and 'literary' fiction to underline the standardisation of narratives across divergent genres and markets. I identify a lack of self-reflexivity in many of these novels, manifested in an uncritical recycling of paradigms inherited from canonical trauma theory, and a corresponding refusal to note the imbrication of these ideas with wider ideological discourses. I suggest that this uncritical approach has been replicated in the way many trauma theorists have approached the attacks, pointing to the emergence of a highly personalised body of scholarship that appears to have disavowed its ability to operate as a medium for critique. Finally, I interrogate the manner in which both of these discourses are imbricated with a hegemonic trauma culture that preceded 9/11 but intensified in its aftermath.

Chapter 2

The second chapter charts the re-emergence of triumphalist forms of national imagining in official (the speeches of George W. Bush, Libeskind's master plan for Ground Zero), vernacular (the national 9/11 flag, art exhibitions, and community projects), and commercial (souvenirs, photo books, and memorabilia) forums of remembrance. Locating 9/11 in the wider context of American memorial culture, I consider how preexisting memorial paradigms have been appropriated and remediated to define the representation of the attacks in the public-political realm. I contend that responses to 9/11 reflect an established 'culture of calamity' (Rozario 2007) reliant on moments of crisis to generate an image of a redemptive American future. I argue that this discourse has been manifested in the frame of memory that I describe as the *new American jeremiad*, demonstrating how the tropes of heroism, patriotism, and exceptionalism that characterise this "national symbolic" (Berlant 1991) parallel the political rhetoric emanating from the White House in the aftermath of September 11. Finally, I analyse the ways in which this discourse has inflected the troubled redevelopment process at Ground Zero over the past thirteen years.

Chapter 3

The third chapter critiques the convergence of the two discourses considered above in the repeated use of the Holocaust as an analogical frame of memory for 9/11. I suggest that commemorative tropes traditionally associated with the Holocaust have been remediated in the aftermath of the attacks to transform the anti-redemptive tenets of trauma theory into the celebratory paradigms associated with the new American jeremiad. I contend that this dialectic of trauma and triumphalism compromises counter-hegemonic narratives, neutering the force of their thrust by presenting them as echoing, and even reinforcing, the discourses of the public-political realm. I examine the prevalence of the Holocaust as a historical analogy for 9/11 in critical theory, cultural practice, and political rhetoric, tracing the roots of these discourses to trends preceding the attacks, most notably the 'Americanisation' of the Holocaust in official memorial culture, and the repeated use of the Holocaust in foreign policy rhetoric from the Cold War to the present day. In so doing, I critique recent theoretical innovations in memory studies that propose the genocide as the platform for a 'supranational' moral cosmopolitanism (Levy and Sznaider 2006), arguing that such interventions need to be more alert to the potential entanglement of their terms with political and military discourses.

Chapter 4

The final chapter examines the ways in which the frames of memory charted throughout this book have intersected in the American legal system after 9/11. As juridical rulings relating to the attacks have entered (in the case of the Guantánamo trials, have yet to enter) somewhat belatedly into the public sphere, US courts have struggled to impose a stable frame of memory upon 9/11. The master-narratives that have dominated the public sphere since September 11 (trauma, triumphalism, and a failed cosmopolitanism) have intersected in unexpected ways in legal discourse over the past thirteen years. This convergence of paradigms has not always proven conducive to the pursuit of juridical justice, leading to a concomitant destabilisation of these discourses and an overturning of legal protocol and precedent. In light of this understanding, I conclude by arguing that both memory and justice must be seen as multifaceted processes (perhaps never completed) rather than discrete acts, as the work of historical reckoning encompasses a wide variety of legal, political, cultural, and critical endeavours that ideally bring into constellation diverse and dissenting perspectives on the past, present, and future. Finally, then, I consider how the *transcendental* commemorative paradigms critiqued throughout this book might be reworked to accommodate a *montaged* culture of memory. In so doing, I draw attention to the counter-narratives that have been lost in the standardising discourses considered above.

1
American Trauma Culture after 9/11

In just sixteen words, Hernán Poza III (a former volunteer firefighter and, at the time of 9/11, a social worker in New York City) encapsulates the central tropes that have framed reactions to September 11 across multiple discursive realms: firstly, in media coverage and political rhetoric immediately following the attacks; secondly, in early critical theory; thirdly, and must enduringly, in the corpus of 9/11 trauma fiction, which forms the main focus of this chapter. Poza writes:

this is for history

this is overwhelming

this is not real

this is the new world
(Poza 2003, 19)

In his emphasis on the overwhelming nature of the attacks, Poza places the events in the territory of the incomprehensible and unrepresentable. Describing the 'unreal' spectacle that unfolded, he recalls the likeness between the images of September 11 and apocalyptic scenes from Hollywood blockbusters. In his suggestion that the attacks heralded the dawn of a new world, Poza reinforces the notion that 9/11 manifested a historical divide so trenchant that there could be no negotiation, no dialogue, between 'before' and 'after'. Poza's short stanza thus consolidates a representational template premised upon incomprehension, unreality, and rupture. However, it is my contention that the predominance of these concepts has prevented the realisation of his primary impression: the sense that 9/11 was 'for history'.

Taking literary representations of September 11 as its starting point, this chapter argues that much of the popular fiction relating to 9/11 exhibits a dehistoricising bent that eschews concentration on the geopolitical context and consequences of the attacks in favour of portrayals of disrupted domesticity.[1] Whilst a number of critics have commented upon this over-personalisation of the attacks,[2] I extend this analysis to interrogate the ways in which many of the most prominent 9/11 novels manifest an uncritical recycling of paradigms inherited from orthodox trauma theory. Critiquing the pervasiveness of trauma as a frame of memory, I examine how the concept has been framed and narrativised in the years since 2001, attending to its leakage between discursive realms and highlighting its political instrumentality. I suggest that, by failing to distinguish between different levels of traumatisation, or acknowledge alternative modes of response, memorial practitioners and theorists have unwittingly reinforced the impression of a collective, 'American', reaction to 9/11. This normative paradigm masks experiential differences, threatening to nationalise loss in problematic – and potentially appropriative – ways by collapsing diverse modes of response into an undifferentiated trauma culture.

1.1 Literature, memory, and trauma

Astrid Erll contends that literature might well be seen as the archetypal medium for the signification of memory – its 'symbol system', to be precise (Erll 2011a, 144). Literature is central to the study of memory for two key reasons: firstly, because literary texts do much to constitute the *content* of a culture's memory (reflecting upon and negotiating between differing interpretations of historic events); secondly, because, as it functions at a cultural level, the process of remembrance appears to mimic the *form* of literary texts in its attention to narrativisation, temporality, and genre. The meaning-making qualities of literature and memory are imbued with the ability to conjoin disparate times and places in a more-or-less coherent narrative. Accordingly, Hayden White suggests that our approach to the past is premised on the 'fantasy that real events are properly represented when they can be shown to display the formal coherency of a story' (White 1980, 8).

Literature and memory thus appear as entwined entities, dependent upon the organising qualities of narrative to structure and explicate lived experience, however reductively or imperfectly. As Paul Ricoeur (2004) has argued, temporality (or rather, the ability to structure time) is fundamental to the formal qualities of narrative, which assigns causality to historical events by construing a particular relationship between past, present, and future. Because literature and memory are selective, such causalities (and the temporal coordinates around which they are constructed) are contingent and contestable. Both forms of representation therefore involve processes of mediation that not only reflect existing attitudes to the past, but also help to generate new perspectives on history. This process occurs at the intersection of private and public realms – negotiating between individual and collective experiences, personal and political agendas.

Literature and memory draw upon pre-existing generic forms as a means of 'emplotting' (to use White's term) experience. Commonly understood, genres are conventionalised formats used to encode events and experiences, mediating them in a specific fashion to particular effect. When we remember, the manner in which we imagine events is informed by a body of cultural knowledge that individuals acquire through socialisation – customs, or traditions, passed through generations. As White argues, such structures render history familiar to us, 'providing the "meaning" of a story by identifying the *kind of story* that has been told. [. . .] Emplotment is the way by which a series of events fashioned into a story is gradually revealed to be the story of a particular kind' (White 1975, 7). Literature takes up such narrative patterns, shapes and transforms them, and feeds them back into a memory culture; however, literary genres do not only provide templates for the way we recall and relate our memories, these paradigms are also part of a culture's memory, preserved and revised over time. Such processes are particularly important in the aftermath of traumatic occurrences that appear to defy established categories of understanding.

As has been widely noted, Western interest in trauma as a psychological condition first developed seriously in the late nineteenth century.[3] Until this time, trauma (deriving from the Greek for 'wound') had predominantly been conceptualised as a physical impairment. In the 1800s, however, the term was redefined as a terminology in which to incorporate the various nervous 'shocks' that appeared to accompany the experience of modernity. Linking physical wounding to psychological damage caused by industrial accidents and railway disasters, neurologists identified a complex overlapping of internal and external disorders. Towards the end of the century, Jean-Martin Charcot's famous study of hysterics at the Salpêtrière in Paris connected trauma to disturbances of memory. Charcot's student, Pierre Janet, linked this idea to the concept of psychical disassociation, arguing that extreme events might produce a splitting in the self that engendered a 'new system of personality independent of the first' (Janet 1901, 492).

After taking a number of divergent approaches to trauma, Sigmund Freud (1914) developed this work via the concept of the 'repetition compulsion': the belated and obsessive return of past events not properly assimilated into memory; disturbing experiences that had been repressed (ineffectually) by the subject causing 'memories' from the unconscious to irrupt into the conscious mind. Following the First World War, Freud's work converged with growing attention to the phenomenon of 'shell shock', a pathology which foreshadows contemporary understandings of traumatic experience.[4] Exemplifying the implicitly political nature of such conditions (something that will have strong implications for the discussion of trauma in the context of 9/11), the concept of shell shock was not readily accepted, but resulted in lengthy and acrimonious negotiations over how to define apparently inexplicable reactions to the experience of modern warfare in terms that went beyond mere 'cowardice' or 'weakness'. Shell shock was not formally categorised until the 1990s, when it was subsumed under the broader umbrella of posttraumatic stress disorder (PTSD).

In 1980, PTSD was classified by the American Psychological Association (APA) to explain the psychological symptoms exhibited by veterans of the Vietnam War, before being steadily extended to other forms of victimhood linked to both private and public histories. Some ten years after the APA's classification of PTSD in 1980, literary critics at Yale University established the foundations of contemporary trauma theory – shifting attention from the specifically psychical to the more broadly cultural (and particularly literary) dimensions of the condition. The work of Geoffrey Hartman, Cathy Caruth, Shoshana Felman, and Dori Laub combined an interest in the memory of catastrophic historic experience (arising out of the study of Holocaust testimonies at the Yale Fortunoff Archive) with poststructuralist theories of representation (influenced by the work of Paul de Man, of whom Caruth and Felman were students and Hartman a colleague). Together, these critics couched the psychological dimensions of trauma as a problem of referentiality.

Caruth defines trauma as a pathology, consisting 'solely in *the structure of its experience* or reception', arising from an event that 'is not assimilated or experienced fully at the time, but only belatedly, in its repeated *possession* of the one who experiences it' (Caruth 1995, 4). The traumatic experience develops from 'the delay or incompletion in knowing, or even in seeing, an overwhelming occurrence that then remains, in its insistent return, absolutely *true* to the event' (Caruth 1995, 5). Trauma is symptomatic of 'a gap that carries the force of the event and does so precisely at the expense of simple knowledge and memory' (Caruth 1995, 7).

The traumatic event can be experienced only vicariously, in the form of flashbacks, sensory impressions, or dreams. Whilst ever-present, it carries with it a form of emptiness – a void in understanding or a refusal of linguistic embodiment. In its persistent yet intangible return, and 'its repeated imposition as both image and amnesia, the trauma thus seems to evoke the difficult truth of a history that is constituted by the very incomprehensibility of its occurrence' (Caruth 1996, 153). For Caruth, trauma is the experience of an event that elides both representation and remembrance. This experience is at once intrusive (repeated, disturbing, and involuntary) and elusive (the event itself is only available through indirect modes of cognition). The image that recurs in the experience of trauma appears to be a pure, unmediated event – an event, however, that remains void of substance. As Caruth qualifies, 'the traumatic event is not experienced as it occurs, it is fully evident only in connection with another place, and in another time' (Caruth 1995, 8). The traumatising event is incomprehensible because its belatedness and indirectness render it inaccessible. The structure of trauma is premised upon a moment of rupture – the instance at which memory and cognition fail and the subject becomes other to lived experience – following which the past will continue to intrude, unmediated, into the present.

Caruth's work draws an explicit connection between trauma and representation that is key to the exploration of the relationship between memory and literature. Suggesting that the attempt to articulate horrific experience perpetuates the symptoms of trauma, Caruth's work is essentially a discussion of historical experience as a form of referential collapse. The inability to 'know' the traumatic event manifests itself in the failure to bear witness to it. Caruth calls into question language's ability to articulate trauma without distorting or corrupting its purity, arguing that 'the transformation of the trauma into a narrative memory that allows the story to be verbalised and communicated, to be integrated into one's, and other's knowledge of the past, may lose both the precision and the forces that characterizes traumatic recall' (Caruth 1995, 153). Caruth points to a referential aporia at the heart of language as the causal factor in the failure to fully encapsulate experience. The rending of word and world becomes the origin of a structural trauma that frustrates all attempts at historical understanding. Accordingly, history itself becomes a chronicle of trauma and trauma 'a symptom of history' (Caruth 1995, 5); '[f]or history to be a history of trauma means that it is referential precisely to the extent that it is not fully perceived as it occurs; or to put it somewhat differently, that a history that can be grasped only in the very inaccessibility of its occurrence' (Caruth 1996, 18).[5]

In its aversion to articulation, Caruth's work differs from other theorists, most notably Felman and Laub, who suggest that the experience of being traumatised *demands* that witness be borne. Laub comments:

> The imperative to tell and to be heard can become itself an allconsuming life task. Yet no amount of telling seems ever to do justice to this inner compulsion. There are never enough words or the right words, there is never enough time or the right time, and never enough listening or the right listening to articulate the story that cannot be fully captured in *thought, memory,* and *speech* (Laub 1992, 63).

Whilst Caruth sees the act of articulating trauma as damaging and inherently impossible, Felman and Laub argue that it is essential. They posit 'literature and art as a precocious model of witnessing – of accessing reality – when all other modes of knowledge are precluded' (Felman and Laub 1992, xx). Felman describes this process as a form of 'life testimony', 'a point of conflation between text and life, a textual testimony which can *penetrate us like an actual life'* (Felman 1992, 2). Felman's formulation has two central implications: firstly, it suggests that reading or listening to historical testimony produces symptoms in the witness similar to the original traumatic experience, allowing the text to function as a vehicle of trauma; secondly, it grants the text autonomy from its author – assuming, in effect, a life (and agency) of its own. Whilst such thinking arguably devalues (and displaces) the historical event as an object of interest,[6] it nonetheless emphasises the unique centrality that literature holds in the understanding (and, the theorists above might argue, the construction and transmission) of trauma.

It comes as little surprise, therefore, that over the past thirty years trauma has formed an increasingly visible thematic in Western literary fiction, so much so that it has come to occupy a genre of its own. As defined by Anne Whitehead, 'trauma fiction effectively articulates several issues that contribute to the current interest in memory: the recognition that representing the past raises complex ethical problems; the challenge posed to conventional narrative frameworks and epistemologies [. . .]; the difficulty of spatially locating the past and the hitherto unrecognised cultural diversity of historical representation' (Whitehead 2004, 81). Michael Rothberg suggests that trauma fiction manifests two oppositional approaches to the problem of historical representation: a realist perspective, which generates an 'epistemological claim that [trauma] is knowable and a representational claim that this knowledge can be translated into a familiar mimetic universe' (Rothberg 2000,

3–4); and an antirealist position, which suggests that '[trauma] is not knowable or would be knowable only under radically new regimes of knowledge and that it cannot be explored in traditional representational schemata' (Rothberg 2000, 4). Seeking to problematise this binary, Rothberg examines a genre he terms 'traumatic realism'. Traumatic realism provides 'an aesthetic and cognitive solution to the conflicting demands inherent in representing and understanding genocide' (Rothberg 2000, 9). It searches 'for a form of documentation beyond direct reference and coherent narrative but do[es] not fully abandon the possibility of some kind of reference and some kind of narrative' (Rothberg 2000, 101). Challenging 'the narrative form of realism as well as its conventional indexical function' (Rothberg 2000, 104), traumatic realism posits the catastrophic event as a 'necessary absence', a 'felt lack' in the text, without attempting to 'produce an imaginary resolution' (Rothberg 2000, 104) in either narrative or experience.

Whilst many of the novels relating to 9/11 foreground the symptoms and effects of trauma, the texts analysed below eschew the suspended referentiality of traumatic realism in favour of the consolatory mode of imaginary resolution rejected by Rothberg. This drive towards narrative closure aims to overcome or negate the disorienting effects of the attacks by framing them within comforting and familiar representational forms. In contrast to their attention to essentially 'antirealist' themes and concerns, the majority of the novels analysed below as paradigmatic examples of 9/11 trauma fiction are presented as recognisable, 'realist', domestic dramas. Despite the repeated emphasis (in literary, critical, political, and media cultures) upon the unprecedented nature of 9/11, the attempt to represent the attacks has resulted in a template of 'accepted' (if unspoken) novelistic conventions. The corpus of 9/11 trauma fiction at once reinscribes the attacks as an incomprehensible rupture, and, privileging narrative's ability to 'heal' historical experience, elides confrontation with this very aporia. These novels thus refuse to accept, as Rothberg argues traumatic realism must, that 'traumatic extremity [. . .] disables realism as usual' (Rothberg 2000, 106), preferring instead to 'step backward into an epistemologically naïve past' (Rothberg 2000, 108) even whilst insisting thematically that trauma is unknowable and unrepresentable.

1.2 9/11 trauma fiction

The corpus of 9/11 trauma fiction recurrently returns to tropes of silence[7] and amnesia[8], evoking buried[9] or repressed[10] pasts, whose unavailability to recall destabilises the very coordinates that make it possible to interpret the world. In place of a probing self-reflexivity about the challenges of representing catastrophic events, 9/11 trauma fiction typically generates an acritical approach to the past that frames disaster within sentimental domestic settings, assimilating trauma into conventional narrative structures, and generating a standardised, almost homogenised, portrait of post-9/11 America. Focusing upon the themes of rupture, unreality, and incomprehensibility outlined by Poza above, this body of work evokes both the (in)famous media images replayed on and after September 11 2001, and the tropes of later critical discourses, constructing a strange continuity between immediate reactions to 9/11, theoretical commentaries written in the first two years after the attacks, and literary texts published over the course of the next ten years (with the majority of these novels emerging between 2005 and 2008).

The notion of rupture dominated early responses to 9/11. Days after the attacks, Jonathan Franzen recalled survivors 'stumbling out of the smoke into a different world' (Franzen 2001), whilst Jay McInerney saw 'my view, and everything else, forever altered' (McInerney 2001). In an article published in *Harper's* in late 2001, Don DeLillo described 9/11 as an event that 'changed the grain of the most routine moment' (DeLillo 2001). Critical coverage was also quick to locate Americans firmly in 'the light of what comes after' (DeLillo 2007, 246), to borrow DeLillo's phrase. In an essay published in 2003, academic and psychoanalyst Dori Laub argued that '[n]ormality abruptly ceased. Life as we have known it stopped' (Laub 2003, 205). As occupational therapists, Susan W. Coates, Daniel S. Schechter, and Elsa First assert, '[i]t was instant wisdom that the world had changed utterly' (Coates et al. 2003, 25). Critiquing such reactions, Susan Faludi writes that '"[e]verything has changed" was our insta-bite mantra, recited in lieu of insight' (Faludi 2008, 2).

Insightful or not, the sense of rupture has persisted in 9/11 trauma fiction, which imbues the reader with the impression that a yawning temporal void has opened before Americans, whose battle becomes the struggle to traverse the distance between 'before' and 'after' without falling into its depths. In the opening pages of *Falling Man,* DeLillo characterises the attacks as a period of interruptive time, a suspended reality during which the character of New York was irrevocably changed. Depicting the streets of Lower Manhattan shortly after the fall of the towers, he writes, '[i]t was not a street anymore but a world, a time and space of falling ash and near night' (DeLillo 2007, 3). Shirley Abbott conveys a similar sense of dread-full pause in *The Future of Love* as her protagonist, Mark, contemplates the ruined Trade Center site. Mark is 'aware only of the gray stuff falling all around, silent snow, a blizzard to put an end to

all school days, a snow day that might last forever' (Abbott 2008, 136).
Time, it seems, has stopped, and the familiar coordinates of New York's
spaces are fundamentally altered as the world dissolves into ash and
the 'staggering nature, the breathtaking scale' (Rozan 2008, 75) of these
events initiates a transformation that renders the city unknowable.
This fragmentation of urbanity and history is represented as having destroyed the continuity of existence, severing the future from the
past and, through this amputation, making the present appear only
half-formed.[11] As DeLillo's Keith Neudecker notes immediately after
the attacks, '[t]here was something critically missing from the things
around him. They were unfinished, whatever that means' (DeLillo 2007,
5). This unfinished, aporetic quality defines much of the trauma fiction
analysed over the course of this chapter. Abbott's Mark feels himself to
be entering 'a new epoch' (Abbott 2008, 137) in which '[e]veryday life
had been vaporised' (Abbott 2008, 141). Watching the burning towers from the window of her Manhattan apartment, Suzannah Falktopf,
protagonist of Helen Schulman's *A Day at the Beach*, comments that
'she crossed the bridge from that life to this life' as she contemplates
'the changed world' (Schulman 2007, 49) before her. The narrator of
Patrick McGrath's short story 'Ground Zero' refers to September 11 as 'a
date which was rapidly becoming a watershed in all our lives, a line of
demarcation, or a point in time, rather, before which the world seemed
to glow with a patina of innocence and clarity and health. And after
which everything seemed dark and tortured and incomprehensible'
(McGrath 2006, 212).

Within hours of the attacks, the tropes that would form the core
imagery of 9/11 trauma fiction had been established as the archetypes
of contemporary atrocity. Over the next ten years, literary texts would
recurrently recall the dust, the fire, the spiralling pieces of paper, the
horrendous images of the 'falling' men and women, and the final, seemingly impossible, collapse of the towers. September 11 was a disaster
whose enduring image was shaped by the imprint of instantaneity, a
crisis beamed live into millions of households. This was not an aftermath whose conditions would take time to emerge, but an event whose
(visual, if not political, economic, or historical) consequences *appeared*
immediately apparent (although such superficiality has arguably continued to impair attempts to gain a more distanced perspective). McInerney's *The Good Life* draws attention to the speed with which images
of 9/11 formed an iconographic lexicon. Witnessing a man staggering
down the street towards her on 12 September, or 'Ash Wednesday' as she
refers to it, Corrine Calloway comments:

Yesterday morning, and well into the afternoon, thousands had made this march up West Broadway, fleeing the titling plume of smoke, covered in the same gray ash, slogging through it as the cerulean sky rained paper down on them – a Black Mass version of the old ticker-tape parades of lower Broadway. It was as if this solitary figure was re-enacting the retreat of an already famous battle (McInerney 2007, 69).

Barely a day old, this image has already become an archetype, yet, as critics have recurrently noted, the possibility of such moments had long been engrained within the American imaginary. This brings us to the second of Poza's contentions: the sense of 9/11's unreality. Following Slavoj Žižek's *Welcome to the Desert of the Real*, it has become almost *de rigeur* to note that the terrorist attacks on New York and Washington bear a remarkable resemblance to scenes prefigured in American disaster movies. Žižek comments that, 'for us, corrupted by Hollywood, the landscape and the shots of the collapsing towers could not but be reminiscent of the most breathtaking scenes in big catastrophe productions' (Žižek 2002, 14). Arguing that the attacks were, therefore, not unimaginable, but thoroughly ingrained in the national imaginary, Žižek asserts that 'the unthinkable which happened was the object of fantasy [. . .] what happened on September 11 was that this fantasmatic screen apparition entered our reality' (Žižek 2002, 16).

Whilst many examples of 9/11 trauma fiction evoke this feeling of unreality, they do little to advance Žižek's original sentiments, merely replicating (and reducing) his thesis. Watching the events unfold on television, a group of elderly patients in Karen Kingsbury's novel *Remember* confuse what they are seeing for a film:

'Is this a movie, dear?' Irvel gestured toward the screen. 'Hank doesn't like me watching violent movies. Gives me nightmares.' 'No, Irvel.' Ashley turned and patted the old woman's hand. 'It's not a movie.' 'Looks like *King Kong*,' Helen barked. She pointed to the television. 'King Kong was on that building last time' (Kingsbury 2003, 179).

Similarly, Edith Mendel in Abbott's *The Future of Love* mistakes the attacks for '[a] movie. They were showing a thriller. Two very tall buildings, yes, it was the twin towers in Lower Manhattan, the World Trade Center, and in this film the towers were burning, smoke passing out from their upper floors. It was that old movie about a skyscraper fire' (Abbott 2008, 144). As Gus, the protagonist of Dina Friedman's *Playing*

Dad's Song, comments, '[n]one of it seemed real. Even after I saw it on TV. It looked more like a movie than something that was actually happening' (Friedman 2006, 108). Discussing reactions to September 11, DeLillo asserts, '[s]ome of us said it was unreal. When we say a thing is unreal, we mean it is too real, a phenomenon so unaccountable and yet so bound to the power of objective fact that we can't tilt it to the slant of our perceptions' (DeLillo 2001). Such sentiments raise the problematic issue of whether it is possible to represent events that take place at 'the limits of representation', to use Saul Friedlander's (1992) phrase. In the aftermath of the attacks, several authors publically stated their anxiety about whether these sickening and spectacular events – which seemed to have blurred the boundary between reality and fiction – could ever be depicted in novelistic form. V. S. Naipaul argued that the 'too astonishing' attacks had rendered the novel 'of no account' (Donadio 2005), contending that 'only nonfiction could capture the complexities of today's world' (Donadio 2005). Despite his later faith that 'fiction was uniquely suited to conveying certain kinds of truth and metaphoric equivalents for our recent trauma' (McInernery 2005), McInerney similarly conceded that '[f]or a while, quite a while, fiction did seem inadequate for the moment' as 'the idea of "invented characters" and alternate realities seemed trivial and frivolous and suddenly, horribly outdated' (McInerney 2005).

Such claims bring us to Poza's third, and final, claim: the sense that 9/11 was unrepresentable and, accordingly, incomprehensible. Such sentiments surfaced recurrently in critical commentary in the months following 9/11. Laub asserts that 'September 11 was an encounter with something that makes no sense' (Laub 2003, 204), 'an event without a voice' (Laub 2003, 204). Hartman similarly refuses to name September 11, or to engage in interpretation of what took place. He addresses it only through allusion: referring to 'that day', 'that event', conjuring the impression of an oblique, dateless, nameless occurrence, at once irrevocably in and entirely outside of history, that 'put its mark on time as if an epoch had passed' (Hartman 2003, 5). James Berger argues that, in the days immediately after 9/11, '[n]othing adequate, nothing corresponding in language could stand in for it. No metaphor could carry language across to it. There was nothing to call it because it had taken reality over entirely' (Berger 2003, 54). As Donna Bassin demonstrates, framing the attacks in this way serves to position them outside of discourse, placing them into a realm in which '[w]ords don't suffice because the experience taps into helplessness known before words can be uttered to represent and contain experience' (Bassin 2003, 198).

These contentions are replicated throughout the corpus of 9/11 trauma fiction. As he attempts to make sense of the post-9/11 world, DeLillo's Keith wonders 'what has happened to the meaning of things, to tree, street, stone, wind, simple words lost in the falling ash' (DeLillo 2007, 103). For DeLillo's characters, the undoing of Manhattan occurs in semantic form; linguistic collapse parallels material destruction as the fissure in New York's skyline is replicated in the fracturing of sign and signified. DeLillo thus underlines the extent to which we rely upon the ability to linguistically order our experience. Without adequate recourse to a vocabulary able to encompass (or at least approximate) the world, both the quality and the quantity of reality appear to diminish. This renting of referentiality is paralleled in other texts. Abbott's Antonia maligns her loss of belief in the stabilising power of language, as she reflects:

> Perhaps there was no ordering principle for the chaos, the irrationality of history, the malign indifference of biology, the inevitability of war. All that she could think of was what, as a young student, she had believed to be the organising principle of the world: grammar and syntax, iambic pentameter, the rhyme schemes of sonnets, the only reliably beautiful thing at one's disposal: words. Words that imposed order. Syntax that forbade ambiguity. That made things clear (Abbott 2008, 198).

Antonia's comments imply that language collapses in the face of history, suggesting that experience is too chaotic, too violent, too excessive to permit adequate linguistic embodiment.

These concerns resonate strongly with the theorisation of trauma outlined by Caruth, Felman, and Laub above. However, the way in which they are foregrounded in the post-9/11 novel does not suggest a nuanced examination of these ideas, or a serious (meta-fictional) consideration of their implications for the writing of fiction (as seen in Rothberg's discussion of traumatic realism). Rather, the extracts from DeLillo and Abbott above reveal a straightforward transcription of these theoretical tropes into literary themes. As the following section demonstrates, the effect is a peculiar pathologisation of the novel, which is reduced to little more than a register of the symptoms of trauma.

1.3 A symptomology of 9/11 trauma fiction

According to the APA's fourth edition of the *Diagnostic and Statistical Manual of Mental Disorders* (summarised by DiGrande et al.) '[s]ix criteria must be met for diagnosis [of PTSD]' (DiGrande et al. 2009, 50). These same criteria are minutely realised by DeLillo over the course of *Falling Man*. To qualify as pathologically traumatised, the APA asserts, '[a] person must be exposed to an extreme stress or traumatic event (Criteria A) to which he or she responded with fear, helplessness, or horror (Criteria B)' (DiGrande et al. 2009, 50). Keith narrowly escapes from the World Trade Center on 9/11 after witnessing his best friend, Rumsey, die. This event, which DeLillo describes as 'massive, something undreamed' (DeLillo 2007, 240), engenders such feelings of futility that Keith can react only with a kind of dazed detachment, unable to 'find himself in the things he saw and heard' (DeLillo 2007, 246).

In addition to this helplessness, the APA stress that, for an individual to be diagnosed with PTSD, '[t]hree distinct types of symptoms must also be present: the re-experiencing of the event, avoidance of reminders of the event, and hyperarousal (Criteria C, D, and E, respectively)' (DiGrande et al. 2009, 50–1). Keith experiences each of these conditions. Faced with a 'thousand heaving dreams, the trapped man, the fixed limbs, the dream of paralysis' (DeLillo 2007, 230), Keith is plagued by his unclaimed experiences (to borrow Caruth's terminology). The desire to escape his tormenting visions, to shut out the flood of unprocessed memories, takes him from New York to Las Vegas. Caught up in the distracting dramas of poker tournaments, Keith seeks an empty existence, pursuing a life in which '[t]he point was one of invalidation. Nothing else pertained' (DeLillo 2007, 230). Entering a 'zone of purged sensation' where 'there was nothing outside, no flash of history' (DeLillo 2007, 225), Keith attempts to cultivate a detachment from reality so devoid of memory or meaning that '[h]e wondered if he was becoming a self-operating mechanism, like a humanoid robot that understands two hundred voice commands, far-seeing, touch-sensitive but totally, rigidly controllable' (DeLillo 2007, 226). Such avoidance tactics are deployed to block out the hyperarousal Keith experiences in the wake of the attacks. Following 9/11, Keith is subject to enhanced sensitivity – both emotional and sensory. He finds loud noises intolerable; music loses its beauty: listening to a classical piece in the hospital he finds that '[t]he noise was unbearable' (DeLillo 2007, 19). In Keith's 'remote' (DeLillo 2007, 36) state, everything around him achieves the heightened vividness of hyperreality. He comments, '[t]hings seemed still, they seemed clearer to the eye, oddly, in ways he didn't understand' (DeLillo 2007, 65).

DeLillo's depiction of Keith's recovery is filled with mechanical images of him 'working through' his trauma. Dominick LaCapra defines working through as a process of 'gaining critical distance on [traumatic] experiences and recontextualising them in ways that permit a reengagement with ongoing concerns and future possibilities' (LaCapra 2004, 45). For Keith, this task is epitomised by a series of hand exercises designed to help him recover from the physical injuries he suffered in the attacks: 'an odd set of extensions and flexions that resembled prayer in some remote northern province, among a repressed people' (DeLillo 2007, 59). Keith finds these acts of faith 'restorative', describing them as 'the true countermeasures to the damage he'd suffered in the tower,' (DeLillo 2007, 40). This damage is, of course, more mental than physical, and, as he carries out his exercises, Keith is aware that 'it wasn't the torn cartilage that was the subject of this effort. It was the chaos, the levitation of ceilings and floors, the voices choking in smoke' (DeLillo 2007, 40). The repetitive exertions help Keith to cope with his memories, so that over time the exercises become obsolete. By the end of the novel he has processed his trauma and recovered 'the moments lost as they were happening' (DeLillo 2007, 243).

In accordance with the criteria outlined by the APA, DeLillo's novel thus manifests a highly formulaic depiction of trauma. However, other texts provide similarly textbook portraits of troubled individuals in the aftermath of the attacks. In the splintered households of the typical post-9/11 novel, it is frequently the children who form the focal point of the narrative. Their characterisation follows to the letter the diagnostic criteria for PTSD in infants laid down by the National Center for Infants, Toddlers and Families (NCITF) in 1994.[12] The NCITF's classifications give particular prominence to the way in which traumatic experiences may be encoded in displacement activities. The center proposes that traumatised children often exhibit a '[r]eexperiencing of the traumatic event as evidenced by posttraumatic play (i.e., compulsively driven play that represents a repetitive re-enactment of the trauma, recurrent recollections of the traumatic event, repeated nightmares, distress and exposure to reminders of the trauma, and episodes with features of a flashback or disassociation)' (Coates et al. 2003, 33).

In Ken Kalfus's *A Disorder Peculiar to the Country* (2006), Victor and Viola, the children of the two protagonists (Joyce and Marshall) play a game of '9/11'. They rehearse jumping from the World Trade Center, holding hands, believing it is possible to 'survive' as long as they keep hold of each other. The children performatively recreate the events of September 11, attempting to redeem them through their actions. When Viola is finally injured, spraining her wrist from a bad landing, she blames her brother for letting go, saying, '[h]e let go of my hand [. . .]. He broke the rules!' (Kalfus 2006, 114–5). The children fail to contain the newly revealed terrors of history within a set of regulated laws and conventions that promise – falsely, as Viola comes to realise – to keep the unexpected at bay. Such displacement activities also find detailed exposition in Foer's *Extremely Loud and Incredibly Close*, where nine-year-old Oskar Schell attempts to track down the lock that fits a key he discovers in his father's closet shortly after his death on September 11. This journey represents Oskar acting out his trauma. As LaCapra explains, acting out maintains 'the melancholic sentiment that, in working through the past in a manner that enables survival or reengagement in life, one is betraying those who were overwhelmed and consumed by that traumatic past' (LaCapra 2001, 22). Oskar's quest allows him to 'stay close to [his father] for a little while longer' (Foer 2006, 304), maintaining the illusion that his loss need not be absolute.

This fantasy resonates with other forms of self-deceptive behaviour that are foregrounded throughout the novel. Lying awake at night, Oskar invents fantastical gadgets to insulate himself from the death of his father. He conjures a skyscraper that moves up and down while its elevator stays in place. Consoling himself, he comments that this 'could be extremely useful, because if you're on the ninety-ninth floor, and a plane hits below you, the building could take you to the ground and everyone could be safe' (Foer 2006, 5). Sleepless and scared, Oskar relies upon his inventions to create a psychic barrier that will keep his fears at bay. As Jacqueline Rose argues, '[i]f fantasy can be the grounds for license and pleasure [. . .] it can just as well suffice as fierce blockading protectiveness, walls up all around our inner and outer psyche and historical selves' (Rose 1998, 4). However, if, as Rose suggests, fantasy manifests an attempt at self-protection, it can also portend psychical undoing. Having lost the ability to distinguish between the real and the unreal, Oskar's heightened imagination leads him to see danger everywhere. He comments:

> I still had an extremely difficult time doing certain things, like taking showers, for some reason, and getting into elevators, obviously. There was a lot of stuff that made me panicky, like suspension bridges, germs, airplanes, fireworks, Arab people on the subway (even though I'm not racist), Arab people in restaurants and coffee shops and other public places, scaffolding, sewers and subway grates, bags without owners, people with mustaches, smoke, knots, tall buildings, turbans (Foer 2006, 36).

Psychotherapists Susan Coates, Daniel Schechter, and Elsa First argue that this confusion of fantasy and reality form the chief constituent of the '9/11 traumatising effect' (Coates et al. 2003, 25). They comment that 'acts of terrorism make the commonplace unsafe' (Coates et al. 2003, 25), acutely destabilising the subject's interpretative faculties. DeLillo's Justin suffers from a similar fear of the everyday. Justin (the child of the two protagonists, Keith and Lianne) and his two friends, 'the Siblings', spend their time 'searching the skies', looking for a man named 'Bill Lawton', who 'has a long beard. He wears a long robe' (DeLillo 2007, 73–4). The children have misheard 'bin Laden' and incorporated this name into 'the myth of Bill Lawton' (DeLillo 2007, 74). Their 'twisted powers of imagination' insist that '[t]he towers did not collapse. [. . .] They were hit but they did not collapse' (DeLillo 2007, 72). Justin fears another attack, claiming 'this time the towers will fall' (DeLillo 2007, 72). As his mother, Lianne, comments, this 'time reversal, the darkness of the final thrust, how better becomes worse, these were the elements of a failed fair- ytale' (DeLillo 2007, 72). Justin's confusion of fantasy and reality leads to the gradual disintegration of his communicative faculties. Initially talk- ing only in monosyllables, he finally retreats into '[u]tter unbreakable silence' (DeLillo 2007, 101). Suggesting that this peculiar new reality is beyond articulation, Justin mimics the NCITF's identification of the '[n]umbing of responsiveness in a child or interference with develop- mental momentum, revealed by increased social withdrawal, restricted range of affect, temporary loss of previously acquired developmental skills, and a decrease or constriction in play' (Coates et al. 2003, 33).

Like Justin and Oskar, Joyce Maynard's four-year-old Louie is suffer- ing from the realisation that '[t]he usual rules just don't apply anymore' (Maynard 2003, 95). Struggling to cope with the death of his mother, Louie withdraws from his family, taking solace in drawing pictures of the burning Twin Towers. His trauma manifests itself as anger as he physi- cally attacks other children in school, displaying '[s]ymptoms, especially fears or aggression that were not present before the traumatic event' (Coates et al. 2003, 33). With normative expectations confounded, Louie finds the post-9/11 environment incomprehensible, accounting for the 'confusion about knowing and unknowing', which the NCITF identify as typical of the traumatised child (Coates et al. 2003, 39). He remains highly disturbed for some time after the attacks, as his elder sister, Wendy, reports: '[h]e had nightmares a lot. He didn't call out for his mother, but sometimes he said the building was falling down. When a plane passed overhead, he would look up and say, That's just a regular plane, right? The good kind?' (Maynard 2003, 361).

Whilst Louie continues to act out his trauma, Wendy is more success- ful at working through her grief, and the novel foregrounds her recovery.

In the first days after the attacks, Wendy's loss seems overwhelming. She comments:

> Sometimes it was a flash flood. Other times it came on like a slow-building rainstorm, the kind that gives you enough warning you might even have time to get inside before the clouds burst. Once it started, though, there was nothing to do but let the sorrow pound you like the most powerful current, the strongest waterfall (Maynard 2003, 83).

By Thanksgiving 2001, Wendy has begun to overcome her pain – she notes that '[t]he earth was taking shape again; color was returning. She wasn't any less sad. In fact maybe she was more so. But she was alive again' (Maynard 2003, 227). By the time of her mother's funeral, Wendy no longer struggles to imagine her mother's horrific last minutes or feels overwhelmed by suffocating memories. She has come to the realisation that '[t]hey would be very sad that day, and for many days after. In certain ways always. They would also never be the same as how they used to be. But they would also be happy sometimes' (Maynard 2003, 381).

Maynard's ending epitomises the typical conclusion of 9/11 trauma fiction, in which – the trauma of the attacks having been worked through – the protagonist finds hope returning. This phenomenon occurs not only in novels targeted at an adult market, but also in works written for a younger audience. Francine Prose's (2007) *Bullyville* revolves around the experiences of thirteen-year-old Bart. Following the death of his estranged father in the Twin Towers, Bart finds himself stranded in a '*major* nightmare' (Prose 2007, 8). Following 9/11, which he refers to as 'the Big Everything' (Prose 2007, 8), the world has acquired a menacing demeanour, allegorised by the aggressive bullying that Bart undergoes at his new school, Baileywell. Echoing the familiar impression of the post-9/11 world as a terrifying fiction, Bart remarks:

> Among the unwanted side effects of the Big Everything that happened was that I found myself transformed. My life, as I'd known it, was over. As if by magic, I was changed from an ordinary kid into a character in a fairytale, into plucky stupid little Jack scrambling up the beanstalk to find himself in a castle surrounded by evil giants (Prose 2007, 8–9).

The novel charts Bart's progress in reckoning with these 'evil giants' on both a personal and geopolitical level, confronting the bullies at his school as he attempts to overcome the trauma of al Qaeda's actions. By the end of the text, Bart is transferred back to the haven of his former school. With his mother remarrying and a safe environment restored, the traumatic 'dream state' in which Bart spends the immediate aftermath of the attacks seems to have been vanquished. As he asserts, 'things *did* work out' (Prose 2007, 257); '[a]fter enough time had passed, everything that happened that year did start to seem like the crack you can see in a piece of china that's been shattered and repaired, or an arm or leg that's been broken and mended' (Prose 2007, 258–9).

The representation of traumatised children in this corpus is heavily focused upon the child's investment in his or her own coping mechanisms. These are often encapsulated in non-linguistic or artistic modes of expression. For Gus, the eleven-year-old protagonist of Friedman's (2006) *Playing Dad's Song* (also aimed at a teenage readership), music provides the method for working through his father's death. Much like Wendy in Maynard's *The Usual Rules* (who resumes playing her clarinet after the attacks) and Dawn in Catherine Stine's (2005) *Refugees* (who takes comfort in her flute), Gus rediscovers his musical creativity in the wake of 9/11 when he begins to write music for his oboe teacher. This activity presents him with a means of recovering some of the agency he feels he has lost as a result of the attacks, allowing him to 'compose' his own future. At the beginning of the text, Gus asserts, 'if I could compose my own life, September 11 never would have happened. We'd skip that day and go right to September 12. Dad would still be alive, and he and Mum would still be married' (Friedman 2006, 17).[13] The changed landscape – both emotional and urban – around him seems unreal, incomplete. As Gus returns home one night, he comments:

> The sky began to fade, and the lights on the Brooklyn Bridge came on. I could see their reflections in the river. The whole thing looked like Never Never Land. Then I saw the skylines in different years engraved on the sidewalk below me. There was the Trade Center, closer to the bridge than I thought it had been. But where was Dad? (Friedman 2006, 109)

Writing music in memory of his father (the eponymous *Dad's Song*) allows Gus to close this gap a little, so that when he revisits the same place towards the end of the novel, he remarks that 'this time instead of the hole, I saw the buildings that still remained, the beautiful way their lights shimmered on the water' (Friedman 2006, 130).

The novels of Maynard, Prose, and Friedman do not assume responsibility for this healing. In picture-book representations of the attacks intended for younger children, however, the narrative acquires a therapeutic function, as demonstrated by a cursory glance at the subtitles of these texts: Rosina G. Schurr's (2002) *Terrorism* is followed by the caption 'The Only Way Is Through'; Susan L. Roth's (2001) *It's Still a Dog's New York* promises to be 'A Book of Healing'; and Andrea Patel's (2001) *On That Day* is marketed as 'a book of hope for children'. Drawing on her work as a clinical psychologist, Schurr aims to present 'a realistic portrait of a child's feelings and reactions to the tragic events of September 11, 2001' (Schurr 2002, 3). Written from the perspective of eight-year-old Mark, Schurr's text opens on 9/11, a day 'the same as any other day. Except that it would never be the same' (Schurr 2002, 4). Exploring the familiar themes of rupture and shock, Mark confronts the events of September 11 as he reaches the realisation that '[s]omething awful had happened to Mom' (Schurr 2002, 11), who has died in the attacks. Schurr locates her story in the domestic setting particular to the 9/11 corpus. Mark is surrounded by his family: his younger brother, Jamie, his uncle Steve and aunt Mary, and his father. Both Jamie and Mark exhibit typical symptoms of traumatisation: Jamie wets the bed, whilst Mark cannot stop revisiting images of the Twin Towers' destruction. The children are taken to see 'a nice lady who talked a lot about "feelings" and about "post-traumatic stress"' (Schurr 2002, 36). Mark comments, '[t]alking to the lady made me feel better about the things that I was thinking. I also began to understand those feelings in my tummy. She taught me how to take big breaths and relax' (Schurr 2002, 36). Therapy helps Mark to realise that 'the only way is through' (Schurr 2002, 49), and that, with the help of his family, he will eventually 'feel fine again' (Schurr 2002, 47).

Perhaps more explicitly than the other novels analysed above, Schurr's picture book thus suggests that literature can partake in the process of healing. This premise recalls some of the earliest work on memory and trauma, most notably Freud's faith in the 'talking cure' as a means of overcoming psychical disturbance, and Janet's opposition of traumatic and narrative memory.[14] This investment in the therapeutic properties of narrative has subsequently influenced contemporary work on trauma. LaCapra privileges narration as a mode of working through traumatic experience (although with well-placed and necessary reservations regarding the need to resist a totalising and redemptive 'closure' of historical experience). He argues:

> Trauma brings about a dissociation of affect and representation: one disorientingly feels what one cannot represent; one numbingly represents what one cannot feel. Working through trauma involves

the effort to articulate and rearticulate affect and representation in a manner that may never transcend, but may to some viable extent counteract, a re-enactment, or acting out of that disabling disassociation (LaCapra 2001, 42).

For LaCapra, the successful working through of trauma is premised upon a process of narration able to reconnect affect (and experience) with representation (and understanding). However, the texts analysed above are not effectively affective in the manner LaCapra suggests; rather, their narrative patterns and contents aim towards the premature closure of historical irresolution.

In so doing, these novels mimic the problematic forms of 'narrative fetishism' outlined by Eric Santner. For Santner, narrative fetishism describes 'the construction and deployment of a narrative consciously or unconsciously designed to expunge the traces of the trauma and loss that called that narrative into being in the first place' (Santner 1992, 144). Santner argues that this process is itself a form of fantasy, a willing away of traumatic loss via 'a strategy of undoing' (Santner 1992, 144) in which the superficial working through of trauma comprises a form of erasure that denies the very occurrence of loss in order to negate 'the burden of having to reconstitute one's self-identity under "post-traumatic" conditions' (Santner 1992, 144). Interpreted in this manner, literature becomes a mode of what Kali Tal describes as 'cultural coping' (Tal 1996, 6), in which '[t]raumatic events are written and rewritten until they become codified and narrative form gradually replaces content as the focus of attention' (Tal 1996, 6).

Tal argues that there is a hegemonic aspect to this codification of historical experience which engenders an emptying out of the troubling event in order to elide its ability to challenge the accepted terms of existence. Her work charts the convergence of cultural and political discourses in the representation of trauma, arguing that '[o]nce codified, the traumatic experience becomes a weapon in another battle, the struggle for political power' (Tal 1996, 6). Bearing these issues in mind, the remainder of this chapter moves from a consideration of the way in which 9/11 trauma fiction thematically foregrounds the *symptoms of trauma* to an examination of the ways in which these novels are, in turn, *symptomatic* of particular trends within popular and political culture following September 11. In so doing, I suggest the paradigmatic depiction of the attacks seen in American literature can be read as representative of a broader tendency to privilege claims to traumatisation in the aftermath of the attacks.

1.4 American trauma culture

Luckhurst's account of the emergence of trauma as a dominant Western episteme argues that, by the early 1990s, trauma had begun to 'escape narrow professional [and academic] discourses and diffuse into the wider culture' (Luckhurst 2008, 76). The term 'trauma culture' connotes the 'overlapping psychiatric, medical, legal, journalistic, sociological, cultural theoretical and aesthetic languages that contributed to such a pervasive sense of the organising power of the notion of trauma in the 1990s' (Luckhurst 2003, 28). The convergence of these discourses ensured that a 'new kind of articulation of subjectivity emerged in the 1990s organised around the concept of trauma' (Luckhurst 2003, 28). This subjectivity, which quickly acquired mass dimensions, was premised around an identity determined by some kind of traumatic 'gap'. According to Luckhurst, this concern with the fragmented character of individual experience assumed the dimensions of a cultural 'traumatophilia' (Luckhurst 2003, 39), which manifested itself in the growing number of cultural texts (literary narratives, films, television programmes, newspaper articles, museal exhibits, etc.) foregrounding the exploration of trauma.

Traumatophiliac trauma culture elides the distinction between the personal and the political, collapsing the boundaries between the home and the outside world, and privatising history by constructing a peculiarly introspective – almost narcissistic – frame of experience. Mark Selzter insists that such introspection is intrinsic to traumatic experience, which 'is the product, not of the event itself but of how the subject repeats or represents it to himself' (Seltzer 1997, 11). By this reading, it is not the trauma that defines the subject, but the subject (the individual, cultural or national) that defines the trauma. Accordingly, Seltzer suggests that '[t]he attribution of trauma [. . .] bends event-reference to self-reference, transferring interest from the event (real or posited) to the subject's self-representation' (Seltzer 1997, 11). Thus interpreted, trauma entails 'a fundamental shattering or *breaking-in* of the boundaries between the external and the internal' (Seltzer 1997, 10).

These introspective traits have characterised reactions to September 11 in literary, critical, media, and political discourses. The corpus of 9/11 trauma fiction positions us in an intimate terrain, contextualising the attacks within deeply personal and emotional territory. In these households, personal relationships shoulder the hope of overcoming geopolitical divides. Looking at her most intimate acquaintances at a Christmas party in the winter of 2001, Abbott's Antonia observes:

Two gay men, two women about to be married to whatever extent the law allowed, Maggie and Mark in therapy, probably for life. Toni [whose parents were killed on 9/11] and Ashley content with each other and with the day. A true American family, archetypal not in spite of but because of terminal illness, adultery, sexual nonconformity, a not-too-merry-widow, and a newly orphaned child. Would it play out in Kansas? China? Kenya? In Saudi Arabia? In Congress? The White House? Definitely not. Still, here they all were. Bush and Cheney did not always win. The Taliban did not always win (Abbott 2008, 222).

Aside from the unfortunate (and regrettably not unique) conflation of al Qaeda and the Taliban,[15] and the rather sentimentalised celebration of New York's liberalism, it is clear that Antonia is carving out the home as an alternative realm where the divisions of the wider world may be healed. This collapsing of distinctions between individual biography and geopolitical history represents the most notable trait of this corpus. In these texts, the domestic arena promises an escape from the sudden terror of the external world, whilst paradoxically replicating the dramas playing out on the geopolitical stage in an altogether more intimate setting.[16]

Schulman's *A Day at the Beach* documents the progressive erosion of the distinction between events occurring 'outside' and 'inside' the home of her protagonists, the disillusioned and emotionally distanced Falktopfs, Gerhard and Suzannah. As events unfold around their Manhattan apartment, Suzannah reflects that 'outside their window these people were diving to their deaths. On TV it was so fucking quiet. Here in Suzannah's home, sirens screamed' (Schulman 2007, 59). The atrocities are playing out in triple aspect for Suzannah: remotely outside her window, silently on her television screen, and deafeningly inside her apartment. The narrative suggests that the attacks belong more substantially within the province of her home than in either the realm of the outside world or the media. This internalisation of the events continues as Suzannah and Gerhard flee Manhattan. Suzannah questions, 'What was that smell? Plastic, paper, metal? All was burning. She was burning. The buildings were burning, the world' (Schulman 2007, 78).

Other characters interpret 9/11 in altogether more solipsistic ways. Kingsbury's Luke Baxter fears that the attacks might be a consequence of God's displeasure at his having sex outside of marriage with his girlfriend, Reagan. Having ignored a call from Reagan's father (who worked at the World Trade Center) as they had intercourse on 10 September

2001, Luke prays after hearing of the attacks: *'Please God. Get Reagan's father out. She didn't get a chance to talk to him yesterday because . . . I'm sorry, God. It was my fault. Please don't punish her for my mistake'* (Kingsbury 2003, 187, italics in original). Contemplating the unfolding devastation before her, Abbott's Antonia wonders whether 9/11 can be attributed to her affair with a married man, commenting: 'maybe it was her fault that terrorists had knocked down the World Trade Center. She was committing adultery, or at least Sam was. Or fornication. The Taliban didn't recognize the difference probably' (Abbott 2008, 171). For Sam's wife, Edith, 9/11 represents the possibility of restarting her marriage. Following the attacks, 'A wisp of satisfaction, of comfort, crept into Edith's heart. Manhattan was finished. Sam would have to come home, be content with this house, this land, her company. She had foolishly allowed Sam a long lease. This attack was an omen, or a portent. Things had to be set right' (Abbott 2008, 146–7).

Although the causalities proposed by these characters are clearly ridiculous, with the exception of Kalfus's novel,[17] the broader cultural dynamics that inform this personalisation of historical experience are handled rather uncritically in these texts. Similar tendencies have been replicated in the work of trauma theorists following 9/11. In the wake of the attacks, a new genre that I describe as *testimony-criticism* has emerged. This term does not refer to the critical analysis of testimony as elaborated in the seminal work of Felman and Laub (1992), but a form of theory that draws upon the author's own experiences as its principal frame of reference, creating a problematic identification between author and subject that leaves little room for any distanced critical perspective to emerge as self-witnessing threatens to eclipse the wider subject of enquiry. Exemplifying this discourse, E. Ann Kaplan presents her response to the attacks in explicitly personal terms. The events of September 11, she argues, 'radically altered my relationship to New York, to the United States qua nation and produced a new personal identity' (Kaplan 2005, 2). This 'new personal identity' hinged upon a constellation of the trauma of 9/11 and her earlier experiences as a child in England during the Second World War. Kaplan asserts, 'the traumatic event merged with the childhood events, so that history and memory, time and space collapsed into one present time of terror; 9/11 produced a new subjectivity' (Kaplan 2005, 4), a conflation of historical circumstances that threatens to despecify the particular sociopolitical context of September 11.

Kaplan is far from the only theorist to have framed her analysis of 9/11 in this manner. Many critics dealing with trauma begin their discussion of September 11 with a lengthy exposition of their own experience.

Some of these chronicles are relatively benign (for example, Judith Greenberg, editor of the collection *Trauma at Home after 9/11*, explains at some length how she 'spent the morning "safe" at home six miles away on the Upper West Side of Manhattan' [Greenberg 2003, 21]). Others reveal more painful encounters, such as Berger's account of the way in which the attacks engendered flashbacks to 'my two mentally retarded sisters and my failures to save them' (Berger 2003, 53). Whilst it would be unfair to negate the importance of authors' need to bear witness to their experience of the attacks, or of the psychical connections they may have forged with earlier times of trouble, it seems important to highlight the ubiquity of this tendency (in their discussions of 9/11 in Greenberg's collection, Laub, Marianne Hirsch, Suheir Hammad, Irene Kacades, and Donna Bassin all similarly foreground their own experiences of September 11, as does the introduction to Susan W. Coates and Jane L. Rosenthal's (2003) collection *September 11: Trauma and Human Bonds*).

This rather unreflexive pathologisation of history not only operates as the organising principle of both 9/11 trauma fiction and post-9/11 testimony-criticism (each of which may at least justifiably be expected to deal with the psychologies of individual subjects), it has also been extended, more problematically, to inanimate (in some cases, even immaterial) systems, objects, or discourses. In his discussion of literary responses to September 11, for example, Gray contends that post-9/11 fiction ought to foreground the notion that the novel itself was 'traumatised' by the attacks. Gray's work is shot through with the rhetoric of trauma. Whilst he offers valuable and original readings of a number of texts (and though both his critique of the domestification of the 9/11 novel and the need for an 'interstitial' perspective that positions the attacks in a global context are well made), Gray's discussion is flawed by the terms of his enquiry.[18]

Gray argues that 9/11 is 'a story that cannot yet be told yet has to be told' (Gray 2011, 49), viewing the failure of these novels to evidence (what he believes to be) requisite levels of structural traumatisation as itself a product of trauma. He resolves that, in the aftermath of atrocity, the (inevitably) traumatised writer has to achieve some kind of resolution, however fragile and fleeting, between the imperative of silence (since trauma is that for which there is no language) and the imperative of speech (since trauma is that which demands language as an alternative to emotional paralysis). The writer cannot write but must; words are no good but they are all he or she has (Gray 2011, 54).

In rather formulaic terms, Gray thus replicates the founding paradoxes of orthodox trauma theory. In so doing, he constructs a self-perpetuating cycle of trauma transferred from the traumatic event to the (uncomprehending) traumatised writer and manifested (impossibly) in the traumatised text before being transferred (in linguistic form) to the soon-to-be, if not already, traumatised reader.

Gray positions the novels of the 9/11 corpus as failed acts of testimony and traumatised witnesses to the attacks. He describes the texts he discusses as a 'symptom, in this case, the registering that *something* traumatic – perhaps too dreadful for words, unsusceptible as yet to understanding – has happened' (Gray 2011, 27). In so doing, Gray reproduces not only Caruth's depiction of trauma as a non-symbolic cognitive absence, but also the very themes that dominate the texts he criticises. Indeed, throughout his monograph, Gray's analysis fluctuates between critiquing and reinforcing the terms around which 9/11 fiction is structured. His discussion of *Falling Man* indicts DeLillo's 'symptomatically numb' prose on the grounds that 'the novel is immured in the melancholic state, offering a verbal equivalent of immobility that is symptom rather than diagnosis' (Gray 2011, 27–8); yet, whilst Gray argues that DeLillo's novel 'evades [the] trauma' of 9/11 (Gray 2011, 28) in its failure to register these effects formally, he simultaneously presents the text as an example of the very pathology it allegedly elides.

Gray's failure to separate the terms of his critique from the object of his enquiry is replicated across many critical responses to the attacks. In her analysis of media coverage, Edkins revives the well-worn assumption that the recurrent replaying of the planes hitting the towers of the World Trade Center appeared like a traumatic flashback, revealing the media's inability to assimilate the events into a recognisable narrative. She comments:

> Without words, let alone expectations for what was happening, television channels were reduced to playing over and over again the images of the aircraft hitting the building, the scenes of people fleeing, others falling from the windows, and the final unbelievable collapse. As in traumatic nightmares or flashbacks, the scenes were endlessly repeated, the incredible, unbelievable events were relived time and time again as if in an attempt to overcome the shock and surprise of what had happened (Edkins 2003, 224–5).

Whilst, empirically speaking, Edkins's analysis of this repetitive televised replay of the attacks is astute, it is also instructive in demonstrating the immediacy with which the understandable perplexity in the face of what had happened was interpreted as a sign of media traumatisation.

These same models have been used to characterise the former World Trade Center site in ruin, reconstruction, and remembrance. Firstly, Bassin describes the devastated area as at once trauma*tised* and trauma*tising*, arguing that '[b]eing inside this violated and dismembered space of ground zero evoked terror and anguish. [. . .] The rubble screams the collapse of individuality, security, and mastery that is impossible to represent' (Bassin 2003, 198). Secondly, Kaplan maintains that the troubled reconstruction process has further proven symptomatic of trauma, obscuring the political and economic interests contending over the ownership of Ground Zero in the assumption that '[t]raumatic residues of "acting out" may be seen in the tensions, conflicts, and intense debates about the site that moved to the fore as the city began to think about rebuilding' (Kaplan 2005, 136). Thirdly, the WTC Tribute Center at Ground Zero (before the opening of the National September 11 Museum in 2014, the focus of museal activity at the site) utilises the symptoms attributed to trauma by Caruth and others as a curatorial template for commemoration.

Established by the September 11th Families' Association, the centre's philosophy is grounded upon the transmittal of a 'person to person history', continuing the personalising discourses noted in both fiction and criticism. The centre's approach is highly emotive and reliant upon affectivity to achieve its pedagogical aims. Rather than explicating the events of 9/11, its goal is to generate an emotional connection to the victims, their families, and the Twin Towers, offering visitors 'guidance, friendship, and the opportunity to carry with them a significant memory for the rest of their lives' (WTC Tribute Center 2010). The main exhibit constructs a narrative from various artefacts rescued from Ground Zero, accounts from survivors and victims' family members, and the comments of selected visitors who have come to the museum. The focus here is almost exclusively testimonial. There is little exposition in evidence, with the timeline of 9/11 and scant historical detail depicted on vertical columns located in such proximity to each other that they are difficult to read in the cramped exhibition space. Instead, artefacts are expected to tell their own story, displaying a problematic faith in the transparency of such objects and their ability to 'speak' to a visitor. A partially melted cell phone, for example, creates the impression of ruination, but the actual subject of the loss encountered is difficult to locate (especially without knowing to whom the phone belonged and having no hint as to the fate of this person).

The exhibits generate a rather generalised sense of destruction attached variously to the artefacts, the museum, Ground Zero, the surrounding city, and the nation as a whole. This transference of loss is replicated in the Walking Tour of Ground Zero offered by the Tribute Center. As the website affirms, 'more than 150 volunteers, all from the 9/11 community, guide visitors around the site, each sharing his or her own unique experience' (WTC Tribute Center 2010). The autobiographical stories of the tour guides are intended to give visitors 'an unparalleled opportunity to connect with history first-hand', an approach compounded by the guides' insistence that their personal losses on 9/11 were the losses of 'us all'; that the trauma of the attacks was shared equally by everyone, everywhere (WTC Tribute Center 2010.). This *viral* history recalls Caruth's theorisation of trauma as a form of *contagion* that can be transmitted from person to person via the language community. However, as trauma bespeaks a history that is accessible only in its incomprehensibility, in Caruth's terms, the attempt to gain any knowledge about the past through testimonies such as those offered by the guides of the walking tour can herald only a failed act of witnessing that threatens 'the traumatisation of those who listen' (Caruth 1995, 10).

More explicitly, perhaps, than either the corpus of 9/11 trauma fiction, or the offerings of testimony-criticism (each of which confines traumatisation to a particular, if representative, subject), the work of Gray, Edkins, Bassin, and Kaplan, and the curation of the Tribute Center, threatens to untether trauma from any basis in individual pathology and redefine it as an uncontainable contagion, attached to (and seeping between) sites, images, individuals, and cultural technologies and discourses. This liberation of traumatic pathology from any psychological or experiential basis has been mirrored in the widespread generalisation of the trauma of 9/11, most clearly evidenced in the recurrent conceptualisation of the attacks as a national, at times, even universal trauma. Such accounts draw parallels between the loss of security felt by individuals in the aftermath of the attacks and the damage to citizens' perception of the invulnerability of the United States, suggesting a direct (and misleading) correspondence between individual identity and national(ist) narratives.

Exemplifying these tendencies, Brow and Silver assert that on 9/11 Americans 'experienced a tragedy unprecedented in its scope and impact on both individual lives and the national psyche' (Brow and Silver 2009, 37), whilst Skitka et al. argue that the 'attacks on the World Trade Center and Pentagon had both immediate and long-term effects on the American psyche' (Skitka et al. 2009, 63). Wary of such claims, Kaplan rightly contends that 'it is necessary to distinguish the different positions and contexts of encounters with trauma' (Kaplan 2005, 2). In so doing, she constructs a continuum of trauma, suggesting:

At one extreme there is the direct trauma victim while at the other we find a person geographically far away, having no personal connection to the victim. In between are a series of positions: for example, there's the relative of trauma victims or the position of workers coming in after a catastrophe, those who encounter trauma through the accounts they hear, or clinicians who may be vicariously traumatised (Kaplan 2005, 2).

However, in her valuable move to instil a more specific and reflexive reading of trauma, Kaplan paradoxically threatens to generalise the condition, opening it up as an experience with an almost inexhaustible set of manifestations.

This is most obviously the case in her discussion of 'mediatised trauma', which reveals the impossibility of maintaining the very distinctions she establishes. Kaplan claims that 'most people encounter trauma through the media' (Kaplan 2005, 2).[19] She further suggests that the fact that most people encountered 9/11 via digital technologies demonstrates 'the difficulty of fully distinguishing trauma from vicarious trauma' (Kaplan 2005, 2). Her account thus points to a number of problems in the notion of secondary traumatisation. Firstly, the concept of media witnessing deterritorialises trauma, making it possible to be traumatised by almost any occurrence, anywhere in the world, regardless of one's direct exposure to or impaction by the event. Secondly, as a cultural technology, media coverage blurs the distinction between vicarious trauma and actual pathological traumatisation,[20] rendering the very distinctions she constructs vulnerable to collapse. Thirdly, although she concedes that the 'experience of 9/11 [. . .] demonstrates the difficulties of generalising about trauma' (Kaplan 2005, 2), Kaplan, like other theorists, does not acknowledge the extent to which trauma itself has become generalised in the aftermath of September 11.

Without careful application, Kaplan's inclusive approach to trauma may threaten to result in any, and every, emotional disturbance being bracketed under the sign of trauma. Whilst she differentiates between 'classic trauma' (for example, first-hand experience of the attacks) and 'trauma to include suffering terror' (a kind of secondary or 'post'-trauma involving vicarious experience of an event) (Kaplan 2005, 1), the distinction between pathologically traumatic and intensely disturbing experience needs greater development. As LoCicero et al. have suggested, there are 'methodological weaknesses' in '[s]tudies of the psychological impact of the terrorist attacks of 9/11', which include 'the tendency of researchers to focus on PTSD' (LoCicero et al. 2009, 105). Whilst understandable, this focus on PTSD at the expense of other modes of psychical response 'unnecessarily limited the types of psychological effects examined' in the aftermath of the attacks (LoCicero et al. 2009, 100). Continuing to define traumatisation as the dominant reaction to 9/11 ignores the fact that, for the most part, the symptoms of PTSD were found to disperse in a matter of weeks.[21] Furthermore, the likely severity of the sufferer's symptoms could be determined by a distinct set of criteria. As psychiatrists, DiGrande et al. assert, '[t]he mental health consequences have been dependent on degrees of exposure coupled with demographic and socioeconomic characteristics historically shown to increase one's risk for psychopathology' (DiGrande et al. 2009, 50). This suggests that traumatic experience is likely to assume specific, rather than general, dimensions.

Radstone thus argues that by extending conditions pertaining to an individual pathology to collective dimensions, such studies make the mistake of 'hardening into literality what might better be regarded as a series of compelling metaphors – the "traumatisation" of a nation, for instance, or the "healing" of a culture' (Radstone 2005, 137). Given the organising power of trauma during the previous decade, it was perhaps inevitable that many of the discussions that have taken place (in both critical and cultural contexts) following 9/11 have been marked by a distinct lack of specificity about the parameters or particulars of traumatic experience. Whilst *The New York Times* described 9/11 as a 'trauma that rippled outward' (Haberman 2009), it seems more accurate to suggest that it was the not the trauma itself but the size of the community to whom the label was extended that was progressively expanded. Accordingly, more attention needs to be given to the important (yet often negated) specificities of particular forms of traumatic narratives and their cultural and institutional provenances. As the final section of this chapter will argue, such discourses are not always easy to separate, and their convergence in the American public sphere after 9/11 has led to the emergence (or at least, intensification) of the phenomenon I define as *hegemonic trauma culture*, a forum in which differences in the agenda and intention of memory-texts are elided, causing counter-narratives and master-narratives to appear mutually reinforcing.

1.5 Hegemonic trauma culture

Luckhurst describes trauma as a 'cusp term' (Luckhurst 2008, 209), a 'conceptual knot whose successful permeation must be understood by the impressive range of elements it ties together and which allows it to travel to such diverse places in the network of knowledge' (Luckhurst

2008, 14), including 'psychology, medicine, law, military history, literature, autobiography, confessional TV, fine art and film' (Luckhurst 2008, 209). Trauma is thus a contested concept, whose application conjoins private and public realms, bridging diverse academic disciplines, and bringing psychical, cultural, and political worlds into collision.

Prior to 2001, Lauran Berlant argued that the privileging of trauma in the US had created a culture of universal victimhood in which to be traumatised was to be valued. Discussing the attitude of the confessional media, Berlant contends that 'the public rhetoric of citizen trauma has become so pervasive and competitive in the United States that it obscures basic differences among modes of identity, hierarchy and violence. Mass national pain threatens to turn into banality, a crumbling archive of dead signs and tired plots' (Berlant 1997, 2). Thus, she alleges, 'nationality has become a zone of trauma that demands political therapy' (Berlant 1997, 7–8). As the public sphere has been personalised with the testimonies of innumerable 'traumatised' individuals, previously domestic or emotional matters have been mooted as the concern of the state.[22] Berlant suggests that this highly personalised political trauma culture is aimed towards the infantilisation of its populace. She argues that, in 'the process of collapsing the political and personal into a world of public intimacy, a nation made for adult citizens has been replaced by one imagined for fetuses and children' (Berlant 1997, 1).

The infantile citizen of this sentimentalised nation is a person who has substituted political agency for patriotic inclination, exercising 'a political subjectivity based on the suppression of critical knowledge' (Berlant 1997, 27). In the aftermath of 9/11, cultural and political discourses have portrayed such individuals as representative of the average American. In the corpus of 9/11 trauma fiction, a genre dominated by child protagonists, adult characters are frequently associated with regressive behaviour. In *Falling Man*, DeLillo repeatedly emphasises the infantile aspects of his protagonists. The language Lianne Neudecker uses to describe her husband, Keith, her mother, Nina, and her Alzheimer's patients in the aftermath of the attacks resonates with phrases that evoke their childlike nature. After he has appeared, without warning, at her door on September 11, Lianne walks Keith to the hospital, 'step by step, like walking a child' (DeLillo 2007, 9). She herself is also reduced to 'being a child' (DeLillo 2007, 48) in this newly confusing world. Abbott's Mark is similarly rendered an 'infant' (Abbott 2008, 63) in the wake of the attacks, whilst the titles of Messud's *The Emperor's Children* and Price's *The Good Priest's Son* exemplify the pervasiveness of the infant as the model for the post-9/11 citizen of the United States.[23]

Dana Heller contends that early media accounts were also eager to infantilise the American populace by assimilating the attacks into a domestic framework intended to suggest that:

> the trauma of 9/11 is in large part the trauma of having been abandoned by our fathers, who were unable to prevent the attacks from recurring. [. . .] Major television networks were quick to exploit the infantile aspects of this emotional framing of the attacks, banking on narratives of Oedipal displacement that fashioned George W. Bush as the nation's patriarchal protector (Heller 2005, 15).

Deborah O'Donnell and Jessica Powers believe that this framing of 9/11 facilitated a fundamental (if temporary) redefinition of the parameters of the American family, extending it from the domestic realm to the very borders of the nation. They assert that, 'following the terrorist attacks, our definition of "family" temporarily broadened, prompting behavior and attitude changes [. . .] motivated by a view of the victims as part of an "American family"' (O'Donnell and Powers 2009, 162).

Susan Faludi argues that such attitudes were bolstered by political rhetoric that portrayed the attacks as an assault upon the homes of Americans. Faludi recalls numerous accounts of:

> Homemakers in the suburbs held hostage by fear and little children traumatised by television footage. The threat, according to this revised script, wasn't to our commercial and governmental hubs but to our domestic hearth. 'We face an enemy determined to bring death and destruction into our homes,' George W. Bush emphasised in his speech on the fifth anniversary of September 11, as if the hijackers had aimed their planes not at office towers and government buildings but at the white picket fence of the American domicile (Faludi 2008, 5–6).

This movement inverts the localised focus seen in fiction and criticism, utilising identical tropes to *expand* the definition of the 'family' affected by 9/11 rather than *contracting* the scope of the attacks to the dimensions of the domicile. Donald Pease interprets this domestification of the nation in radical terms. Arguing that the 'foreign violation' of the Homeland that took place on 9/11 'drastically altered the national people's foundational fantasy about their relationship to the national territory, redefining it in terms of the longing of a dislocated population for their lost homeland' (Pease 2009, 158), he points towards the Bush

Administration's 'introduction of the signifier of the Homeland' as a means 'to capture this experience of trauma' (Pease 2009, 193).

The creation of the Office of Homeland Security institutionalised the conceptual slippage between the public and the private. It was authorised (under the guise of the Homeland Security and PATRIOT Acts) to implement the emergency abridgement of civil liberties on the grounds that the post-9/11 world represented an indefinite state of exception. Pease contends that the 'term Homeland was the keystone that anchored all of the other terms in the Bush Administration's new symbolic arrangement' (Pease 2009, 194), generating a definition of the domestic that 'not only links the familial household to the nation but also imagines both in opposition to everything outside the geographical and conceptual borders of the home' (Pease 2009, 168). This process ushered in a series of policies rhetorically premised on the idea of the Homeland-as-home, the United States as fatherland, and Bush as its paternalistic guardian. This construction was used to suggest that, if the protection of America's 'children' is the first priority of the nation, then parents become exemplary national figures, charged with carrying out their patriotic duty. In a time of war, this duty demands that parents surrender their children to conflict in the name of preserving the national family – accordingly, the 'mother is supposed to show her love for the nation-state by sacrificing her progeny to the state for the purpose of its reproduction' (Pease 2009, 197). Having 'enlisted the family in the service of the state's militarisation' (Pease 2009, 197), 'after the state separates her from her children, the mother is supplanted by the homosociality of the state's desire' (Pease 2009, 197).

Echoing Pease's claims, Edkins argues that the state was quick to capitalise on 9/11's incorporation into frameworks of trauma. She asserts that the attacks 'had two contradictory effects. First, they brought trauma into the heart of the safe areas of lower Manhattan, disrupting the linear narrative of security and state control. But, second, they opened up the way for the state to move quickly with its offer of revenge retaliation as a suitable and legitimate answer to that traumatic tear in the fabric of normality' (Edkins 2003, 19). Her remarks are reinforced by Richard A. Clarke, the national coordinator for security and counterterrorism under Presidents Bill Clinton and George W. Bush. Clarke concedes that the administration manipulated the psychological impact of the attacks to facilitate their political and military agendas. He labels this strategy the 'White House 9/11 trauma defense' (Clarke 2009). Such a defence, Clarke comments, suggests that '[representatives of the Bush Administration] want to be excused for the measures they authorised after the attacks on the grounds that 9/11 was traumatic' (Clarke 2009). Testifying to the validity of this claim, and contending that the need to protect America's traumatised citizens necessitated 'special measures' such as so-called 'extraordinary rendition' and the use of practices inseparable from torture, Condoleezza Rice asserts that '[u]nless you were there, in a position of responsibility after September 11, you cannot possibly imagine the dilemmas that you faced in trying to protect Americans' (Clarke 2009). As Walter A. Davis contends:

> The response of the Bush Administration to the trauma of 9/11 presents a particularly revealing, if extreme, example of the [. . .] dominant response to trauma. First, a proclamation of our innocence and victimage. Second, a massive act of projective evacuation – the war in Iraq – as the only way to restore our identity. Any chance that 9/11 might have brought about painful reflections on America and its actions in the world are thereby banished. Blowback is blown away. The trauma is 'resolved' in a way that perpetuates it (Davis 2009, 139–40).

Davis's remarks intimate a kind of duplicity in the discourse of trauma as manifested in the context of 9/11. Trauma is simultaneously conceptualised as a mode of devastating destabilisation and redemptive resolution, both eradicated and produced by the actions of the state and able at once to undermine and reinforce its legitimacy.

A number of critics suggest that the disenfranchisement of the allegedly traumatised national subject witnessed in political discourse after 9/11 is unwittingly, yet intrinsically, pre-empted in the tenets of foundational trauma theory. As Robert Eaglestone asserts, the most worrying aspect of many conceptions of trauma is their ability to strip 'any agency from the survivor, revictimising the survivor as (only) a traumatised victim' (Eaglestone 2004, 32). Leys further suggests that both psychological and literary theories of trauma have long failed to adequately nuance the relationship between trauma's genesis as an external event and its endurance as psychical experience. She contends that, whereas in the early neurological work of Charcot et al., trauma was understood as 'an experience of hypnotic imitation or identification' (Leys 2000, 8), and thus an *internal*, cognitive disorder, there existed from the start a competing approach, which regarded trauma as 'a purely external event coming to a sovereign if passive victim' (Leys 2000, 10).

As we have seen, Caruth positions trauma as an autonomous referential aporia, a textual contagion that, as Richard Crownshaw defines it, is 'culturally endogenous and un-locatable in or uncontainable by witness and event, and forever departing' (Crownshaw 2010, 8). By labelling trauma as a cognitive absence – an absence, moreover, liberated in language by failed attempts at testimony – Caruth denies the subject control over their own experience. As Crownshaw argues, 'the witness is devoid of potential interpretative agency and has become the mere carrier of trauma' (Crownshaw 2010, 6). The attempt to testify necessitates ceding interpretative control to another – a secondary witness to whom the subject surrenders their experience. In Caruth's terms, '[t]o listen to the crisis of a trauma [. . .] is not only to listen for the event, but to hear in testimony the survivor's departure from it; the challenge of the therapeutic listener, in other words, is *how to listen to departure*' (Caruth 1995, 10). In this departure, the subject is split from their trauma, which becomes a free-floating contagion, passing from uncomprehending witness to uncomprehending witness, dislocated from either historical or subjective origins – untethered to temporal or spatial coordinates.

Trauma is thus destined to be repeated without end as it spreads, virally, from subject to subject via the language community. This movement from an individual to a collective frame of reference, which Luckhurst describes as the 'transvaluation of trauma' (Luckhurst 2008, 62), is key to considering how the concept has acquired its hegemonic and ideological dimensions. As Janoff-Bulman and Usoof-Thowfeek assert, the rhetoric of trauma has very different implications depending on the setting in which it is mobilised:

> Following instances of individual trauma, survivors struggle to re-establish a sense of safety through self-regulation of emotions, cognition and behaviors. Following collective trauma, efforts to re-establish a sense of security are often accomplished through attempts at *social regulation*. Self-regulation is the domain of psychology, whereas social regulation is the province of politics (Janoff-Bulman and Usoof-Thowfeek 2009, 81–2).

However, the ubiquity of trauma as a frame of reference in the American public sphere has made it hard to identify the divergent agendas of various interest groups, especially as mental health practitioners and academics have remained insufficiently alert to trauma's instrumentalisation in political discourse.

Edkins argues that 'the status of victim of post-traumatic stress disorder serves to render the survivor more or less harmless to existing power structures. In contemporary culture victimhood offers sympathy and pity in return for the surrender of any political voice' (Edkins 2003, 9). Her remarks have particular pertinence when considered in relation to the guidelines published by the APA in the immediate aftermath of the attacks. The APA posits the state as the institution responsible for helping individuals recover from the trauma of 9/11, asserting that victims should take comfort from 'the actions our government is taking to combat terrorism and restore safety and security' (APA 2001). This statement places the narrative of trauma firmly in a political framework, disavowing individuals' responsibility for their own psychical recovery by promoting a simplistic trust in the government, elevated here to the role of protector. This refutation of the need to critique the actions of the Bush Administration is further exacerbated by the APA's assertion that those considering themselves traumatised should cede their problems to 'trained officials throughout the country', and '[l]imit exposure to media coverage' (APA 2001). The APA thus place Americans (or rather, the unlimited number of Americans considered to be suffering from trauma) in a peculiarly helpless position – negating their ability to exert agency over their recovery, and advocating the suppression of critical knowledge as a primary coping mechanism.

Edward Linenthal contends that a similar disenfranchisement of survivors was instigated after the 1995 Oklahoma bombing as a means of disarming difficult questions about what may have led an American citizen to the murder of 168 of his compatriots. In the aftermath of the atrocity, Linenthal comments, 'the "medicalisation" of grief [. . .] as a therapeutic narrative became a dominant social voice and often transformed victims of political violence into patients' (Linenthal 2001, 12). Tal describes this medicalisation of the survivor as a common means of stripping traumatised subjects of agency. In her analysis of the treatment to which Vietnam veterans have been subject in American culture, Tal identifies this process as one means by which the narratives of survivors may be discounted as the product of a 'sick' mind in need of treatment by 'positing that they suffer from an "illness" that can be "cured" within existing or slightly modified structures of institutionalised medicine and psychiatry' (Tal 1996, 6). She argues that, in situations where individual pathological trauma is metaphorically extended to collective or national dimensions (as seen after 9/11), 'the appropriation of survivor experience and its reduction to metaphor is a crucial component of the process of depoliticising the survivor and then medicalising her condition' (Tal 1996, 59).

Whilst there is no denying that those most affected by the attacks were traumatised by their impact, I cannot help but believe that some of the theorists cited may have found trauma everywhere they looked, because they simply looked for it everywhere. Part of the problem seems to stem from a subscription to pre-existing paradigms in the wake of 9/11: an immediate (and henceforth uncritiqued) assumption from cultural practitioners, psychoanalysts, and academics alike that trauma offered the most suitable mode of interpretation for the attacks and their aftermath. These claims are reinforced by Ann Cvetkovich's commentary on 9/11. She reports, '[o]n September 11, I was in the midst of finishing a book about trauma [. . .]. The events of September 11 and their aftermath have not changed what I know about trauma; they have confirmed it' (Cvetkovich 2003, 60). It is difficult not to feel that these preformed ideas were imposed upon 9/11 before their suitability had been properly assessed. As James Trimarco and Molly Hurley Depret write of media coverage in the aftermath of the attacks, 'most newspapers and television stations labeled the event a national trauma without hesitation or explanation. Much of what has been written about the attacks assumes that the attacks formed a "wound" on the collective psyche of *all* Americans, causing trauma and requiring particular sorts of healing' (Trimarco and Depret 2005, 30).

Interpreting the diverse elements of 9/11's memorial culture through the homogenising lens of trauma serves to veil the many interests at stake in the representation and remembrance of the attacks, disguising the degree to which the rhetoric of trauma has itself become an ideological vehicle. Greater attention needs to be paid to the interrelation of popular and hegemonic trauma cultures and their relation to the discipline of trauma studies. Within the academy, critics need to take care not to conflate psychological and literary templates of trauma in ways that risk universalising traumatic experience or disempowering traumatised subjects. As this chapter has endeavoured to illustrate, trauma, initially perceived as 'a fundamental disruption in our received modes of understanding' (Caruth 1995, 3) has, in the context of 9/11, become *the* received mode of understanding itself. Caruth comments that '[t]he phenomenon of trauma has seemed to become all-inclusive, but it has done so because it brings us to the limits of our understanding' (Caruth 1995, 4). However, taking us to the 'limits of our understanding', but failing to look beyond them, opens a path that seems only to lead to mystification, offering no way to better understand either the past or our present, revealing only an 'impossible history', defined by events that we 'cannot entirely possess' (Caruth 1995, 5).

2

The New American Jeremiad
after 9/11

The previous chapter examined the predominance of trauma as a frame of memory after 9/11, arguing that its centrality in the American public sphere can be at least partially explained by widespread subscription to the attacks as a moment of national unhoming. This chapter considers attempts to 'rehome' the United States by reconnecting post-9/11 American society to the founding mythologies of the nation. Whilst the narratives considered in the last chapter tended to personalise geopolitical concerns, many of the discourses analysed below evidence an oppositional tendency to nationalise private experience. Similarly, whilst my analysis of American trauma culture after September 11 exposed the ways in which existent academic and popular conceptions of trauma had been mobilised in political discourse following the attacks, here I identify a converse process through which historic ideologies of exceptionalism and triumphalism have been absorbed into official, vernacular, and commercial memorial culture in the wake of 9/11. This pattern has, once again, facilitated the development of a series of intrinsically politicised memorative regimes, perpetuated by their conscription into a dominant frame of memory: the American jeremiad. As the following analysis will argue, the jeremiad has operated as the exemplary mythic vehicle for the national imaginary from the early seventeenth century and can be seen in resurgent form in American memorial culture after 9/11.

2.1 Nation, myth, and ideology

Jean Baudrillard positions the United States as a liminal conceptual space, 'neither dream nor reality. [. . .] It is a hyperreality because it is a utopia which has behaved from the very beginning as though it were already achieved. Everything here is real and pragmatic, and yet it is all the stuff of dreams too' (Baudrillard 1988, 28). Baudrillard suggests that

America's uniqueness is comprised of its ability to coexist as ideal and reality. Richard Crockatt similarly contends that 'America has always been an idea – an invention – as much as a place or a country' (Crockatt 2003, 47), whilst Frederick M. Dolan argues that, from its earliest manifestations, imagined by the likes of John Winthrop and John Cotton in their sermons aboard the *Arbella* in 1630, 'America [was] less a territory or place than a goal, a project, a making' (Dolan 1994, 21). Dolan suggests that the fragile mutuality of ideal and reality generates an 'interpretative problematic' that 'incessantly negotiates the two poles of, on the one hand, solid foundations or grand narratives and, on the other, the ever-present threat of the collapse of absolutes' (Dolan 1994, 2–3). In order to overcome this hermeneutic instability, hegemonic cultural and political discourses attempt to create a coherent image of the United States able to unite past, present, and future in glorious accord. Critics have variously characterised this ideal as an 'American consensus' (Bercovitch 1981), the 'American ideology' (Nash Smith 1986), its 'national symbolic' (Berlant 1991), a 'state fantasy' (Rose 1998), the 'American Creed' (Hughes 2004), or a collective 'compact' between people and state (Pease 2009).[1] Most simply, perhaps, this transcendent image might be thought of as a myth.

As defined by Richard Slotkin:

> Myths are stories, drawn from history, that have acquired through usage over many generations a symbolising function central to the culture of the society that produces them, through the processes of traditionalisation historical narratives are conventionalised and abstracted, and their range of reference is extended so that they become structural metaphors containing all the essential elements of a culture's world view (Slotkin 1986, 70).

Whilst respondent to the changing demands of history, myths aim to bestow a sense of timelessness upon the present that universalises and eternalises its image. In seeking homogeneity with past origins, myth denies the very presentness of the here and now. Mythmaking 'is a reifying process, through which metaphorical descriptions of reality come to substitute for an apprehension of reality' (Slotkin 1986, 73). As a form of 'socialised metaphor' (Slotkin 1986, 72), mythology functions as an invaluable vehicle for ideology, working to formulate a collective 'consensus' that is able to determine the ideal (and, to some extent, the real) shape of the nation. It also serves to protect ideology from critical scrutiny, allowing it to naturalise its biases as the contemporary manifestation of eternal values.

Richard T. Hughes argues that 'myths have converged to preclude any meaningful sense of history in the United States' (Hughes 2004, 155), with two important consequences: firstly, this lack of historicity has generated the impression of (modern) America as a peculiarly amnesiac nation[2]; secondly, it has presented the United States as 'removed [. . .] from the power of human history with all the ambiguity that history inevitably bears. In this way, America [has] remained, as it were, as an innocent child among the nations of the world' (Hughes 2004, 155). This view of the United States as an innocent nation is one that has recurred throughout the country's past, most notably at points where its apparent isolation from history – and thus, its illusion of childlike innocence – has appeared threatened (Pearl Harbor or 9/11, for example). This impression of the nation as a bastion of virtue is deeply rooted in the nation's most fundamental, and indeed foundational, mythology – that of American exceptionalism.

Donald Pease defines American exceptionalism as 'a complex assemblage of theological and secular assumptions out of which Americans have developed a lasting belief in America as the fulfilment of the national idea to which other nations aspire' (Pease 2009, 7).[3] Exceptionalism, then, identifies both what the nation *is* (or will be) and what it *is not* (or is defined against). Pease imbues the discourse of exceptionalism with considerable hegemonic power – defining it as the dominant 'state fantasy' since the establishment of the first New England colony. Referring to the work of Jacqueline Rose (1998),[4] Pease classifies such fantasies as 'unacknowledged legislators' between the state and its people (Pease 2009, 6), arguing that the state is dependent upon 'subjects' affective investment in fantasy for its legitimation' (Pease 2009, 2).

Pease does not always successfully nuance the differences between his understandings of fantasy and myth (American exceptionalism at times seems to occupy both spheres), however, early in his analysis, he offers the following distinction, which is worth quoting at length:

Myths usually do the work of incorporating events into recognizable national narratives. But traumatic events precipitate states of emergency that become the inaugural moments in a different symbolic order and take place on a scale that exceeds the grasp of the available representations from the national mythology. Before a national myth can narrate events of this magnitude, the state fantasy that supplies the horizon of expectations orienting their significance must already have become symbolically effective (Pease 2009, 5).

Here, Pease defines fantasy as a *transitional* form of identification that bridges the mythic void generated by disaster. Fantasies might thus be seen as the interim ideological mechanism that facilitates the reassertion of state power in the aftermath of traumatic loss, clearing the way for (re)imposition of a transcendent national mythology able to reconnect the (horrific) present to the (heroic) past and reopen the prospect of a glorious future. Pease positions American exceptionalism as the master-fantasy of modern America, augmented by remediated versions of itself – emergency fantasies – in the aftermath of various historical transitions and traumas. It thus appears as though there are two levels of exceptionalism at work in the American imaginary: the first, a transient collective engagement with a specific *fantasy* of exceptionalism, which takes hold in the immediate aftermath of disaster; the second, a much more general *myth* of exceptionalism that transcends particular historical circumstances.[5]

The discourse of exceptionalism performs its most potent work in periods of sociological transition and moments of national crisis. Pease argues that since the early seventeenth century, the 'apocalyptic imagination [has] described the collision of end-time with events in US history as the quintessential sign of American exceptionalism, which represented America itself as an eschatological event' (Pease 2009, 78). By this reading, American exceptionalism embodies its own catastrophe, yet it also functions as a cultural talisman that may be mobilised to deflect calamity. Therefore, whilst exceptionalism is the ideology most invoked by the state in times of crisis, crisis itself has recurrently been utilised to affirm the very vision of America as an exceptional nation. As James Berger explores:

> In its official historical consciousness, the United States remains the City on the Hill, the New Jerusalem, a new world conceived in innocence and perfection and getting better ever since. In this fantasy, America contains no flaw (that has not been corrected), no wound (that has not healed stronger than before), no loss (that has not been redeemed many times over) (Berger 2003, 57).

In his analysis of American responses to disaster, Kevin Rozario identifies a historic 'culture of calamity' in the United States, which 'reveals a general psychological addiction to images and stories of disaster' (Rozario 2007, 2). This fascination with atrocity must partly be seen as a consequence of disaster's prevalence in the cultural realm. As Rozario asserts, and as we see plainly after 9/11, 'disasters have been, and continue to be, occasions for extraordinary cultural production' (Rozario 2007, 3). The desire for cultural products thematicising disaster presents an opportunity for both commodifying and consuming catastrophe. This market has the effect of making crisis socially meaningful. However, Rozario contends, there is 'a decisive structural or ideological component to the American dependency on disasters' (Rozario 2007, 2). The pervasiveness of calamity in the American imaginary has blurred the distinction between cultural and ideological discourse, as spectacles of disaster have 'laid the cultural groundwork for the expansion of a powerful national security apparatus' (Rozario 2007, 9). Arguing that the 'current political system depends on disasters to justify exercises of power' (Rozario 2007, 9), Rozario thus perceives the imagination of disaster as an organising factor in America's cultural, political, and economic life. He suggests that 'Americans, especially those in power, have often viewed disasters as sources of moral, political, and economic renewal' to such an extent that he comes to question 'whether dominant American ideas of progress would even be imaginable without disasters' (Rozario 2007, 3).

This vision of redemptive catastrophe has its roots in the form that Sacvan Bercovitch has described as 'America's first distinctive literary genre' (Bercovitch 1978, 7): the jeremiad. Dedicated to generating an 'apocalyptic history for America' (Bercovitch 1978, 68), the jeremiad posits the ideal narrative structure for the 'revitalisation and rededication' of American exceptionalism (Bercovitch 1978, 18). Bercovitch identifies the American jeremiad as the quintessential form in which disaster is 'qualified [. . .] in a way that turn[s] threat into celebration' (Bercovitch 1978, 8). Like both the doctrine of American exceptionalism and the culture of calamity, the jeremiad is simultaneously a transient and transcendent presence in American culture, remaining a dominant form across the centuries, but adapting its agenda to historical contingency. This is the source of what Bercovitch describes as its 'extraordinary cultural hegemony' (Bercovitch 1978, 155). The jeremiad is at once timeless and time-*full*. Emplotted in, and respondent to, the present, but denied any form of critical historicity, it seeks to cultivate consensus by translating history into myth, individuals into collectives, and politics into natural law. Bercovitch describes the jeremiad as 'a ritual designed to join social criticism to spiritual renewal, public to private identity, the shifting "sign of the times" to certain traditional metaphors, themes, and symbols' (Bercovitch 1978, xi), intended to function as a 'vehicle of cultural continuity' (Bercovitch 1978, 61) to represent the United States as 'an errand in sacred history' (Bercovitch 1978, 69).

From its origins as a political sermon in the seventeenth century, the American jeremiad has straddled the terrains of the sacred and the profane, associating transient ideologies with timeless 'divine' truths. Bercovitch charts a secularisation of the form in the eighteenth century, following victory in the War of Independence. Where once biblical typology was employed to imagine the course of the glorious American future, now the chronicle of American history became the sacred doctrine to which the jeremiad subscribed. This conjoining of providence and politics has subsequently formed a rhetorical tradition in presidential addresses. As crisis and covenant have been evoked and invoked by successive leaders, the task of the president has been to act as a national theologian, creating the historical 'truth' of exceptionalism by utilising the tropes of the jeremiad to preach what Jeffrey F. Meyer describes as the 'civil religion' of the United States (Meyer 2001, 81).

Assuming the office of president of the newly independent America in 1789, George Washington inaugurated a perennial theme in presidential addresses – underscoring the nation's covenant with God as an assurance of its exceptional historical destiny and guarantee of recovery from calamity. He commented:

> No People can be bound to acknowledge and adore the invisible hand, which conducts the Affairs of men more than the People of the United States. Every step, by which they have advanced to the character of an independent nation, seems to have been distinguished by some token of providential agency. [. . .] These reflections, arising out of the present crisis, have forced themselves too strongly on my mind to be suppressed (Washington 1789).

Such constructions have themselves become sacred references in times of crisis. Departing for the capital as president-elect in 1861, with America on the brink of civil war, Abraham Lincoln likened his situation to Washington's own. To an audience in Springfield, Illinois, he declared:

> I now leave, not knowing when, or whether ever, I may return, with a task before me greater than that which rested upon Washington. Without assistance of that Divine Being, who ever attended him, I cannot succeed. With that assistance I cannot fail (Lincoln 1861).

Eighty years later, facing not a civil but a world war, Franklin Delano Roosevelt recalled the speeches of his predecessors as proof of America's inevitable victory over fascism. In his unprecedented third inaugural address on 20 January 1941, Roosevelt declared:

> On each national day of inauguration since 1789, the people have renewed their sense of dedication to the United States. In Washington's day the task of the people was to create and weld together a nation. In Lincoln's day the task of the people was to preserve that Nation from disruption from within. In this day the task of the people is to save that Nation and its institutions from disruption from without. [. . .] The destiny of America was proclaimed in words of prophecy spoken by our first President in his first inaugural in 1789 – words almost directed, it would seem, to this year of 1941: 'The preservation of the sacred fire of liberty and the destiny of the republican model of government are justly considered . . . deeply, . . . finally, staked on the experiment intrusted to the hands of the American people.' If we lose that sacred fire – if we let it be smothered with doubt and fear – then we shall reject the destiny which Washington strove so valiantly and so triumphantly to establish. [. . .] We do not retreat. We are not content to stand still. As Americans, we go forward, in the service of our country, by the will of God (Roosevelt 1941).

It is perhaps, then, of little surprise that it was to these metaphors that Bush returned in the aftermath of 9/11. On the evening of September 11, Bush addressed the nation from the Oval Office to declare, 'America was targeted for attack because we're the brightest beacon for freedom and opportunity in the world' (Bush 2001a). He defined the crisis facing the United States as arising from its historically exceptional nature, asserting that '[t]errorist attacks can shake the foundations of our biggest buildings, but they cannot touch the foundation of America' (Bush 2001a). In so doing, he underlined America's union with 'a Power greater than any of us', affirming (as he declared three days later in a speech given at the National Episcopal Cathedral during the National Day of Prayer and Remembrance) that 'neither death nor life nor angels nor principalities, nor powers nor things present nor things to come nor height nor depth can separate us from God's love' (Bush 2001b). Amidst the chaos and carnage of the immediate aftermath, America remained 'one Nation under God' (Bush 2001c), blessed with a new 'responsibility to history', safe in the knowledge that '[g]rief and tragedy and hatred are only for a time. Goodness, remembrance and love have no end, and the Lord of life holds all who die and all who mourn' (Bush 2001b). Bush characterised the coming months and years as a 'monumental struggle of good versus evil' (Bush 2001d), a battle of biblical proportions in which America's sacred destiny would ensure that 'good will prevail' (Bush 2001d), as proven by the fact that 'history has an author who fills time and eternity with his purpose' (2001e).

These remarks highlight the way in which the tropes of the jeremiad attempt to both universalise (in a paradoxically nationalistic) fashion and eternalise historical events. Given this elision of temporal particularity, it seems, in many ways, peculiar that the jeremiad should have been mobilised as the central frame of American memory. However, official memorial culture has frequently mobilised this paradigm as a means of drafting events into the heroic narrative of the United States. As the following section will demonstrate, the National Mall in Washington, DC, has historically represented a topographical inscription of the jeremiad. Although the exceptionalism of these memorials has been problematised, to some extent, by new movements in commemorative practice in the late twentieth century, in the aftermath of 9/11, the Mall has witnessed a return to established modes of triumphalist remembrance.

2.2 The American jeremiad and official memory: 1776–2001

Astrid Erll contends that memorial texts are often *premediated* by established mythologies, citing 'the use of existent patterns and paradigms to transform contingent events into meaningful images and narratives' (Erll 2009, 114) as an organising factor in public memory discourse. Erll demonstrates that, as 'existent media which circulate in a given society provide schemata for new experience and its representation', what is known about an event 'seems to refer not so much to what one might cautiously call the "actual event", but instead to a canon of existent medial constructions, to the narratives, images and myths circulating in a memory culture' (Erll 2009, 111). In so doing, she neatly underlines the way in which existing narrative templates – or frames of memory, as I describe them – may be conscripted to structure the representation of new and unfamiliar occurrences.

As intimated above, the paradigm of the jeremiad has long served as the master-frame of official memorial culture in the United States. As defined by Robert Burgoyne:

Official memory [. . .] is a commemorative discourse about the past that offers an overarching, patriotic interpretation of past events and persons. It is most often produced by governments or other civic institutions. As Bodner says, it restates the reality of the past in 'ideal rather than in complex, ambiguous forms . . . it presents the past on an abstract basis of timelessness and sacredness'. Moreover, it seeks to neutralise competing interpretations of the past that might threaten social unity, the survival of existing institutions, and fidelity to the established order (Burgoyne 2006, 210).

Both the jeremiad (as characterised by Bercovitch) and official memory (as outlined by Burgoyne) evince a peculiar temporal structure constituted around the mutuality of timelessness and presence: each reacts to the demands of the context in which it was created, but does so with the intention of emptying out the complexities of history; even as it responds to the historical moment, the text (oratorical or monumental) denies its own historicity by connecting the present to a mythic rendering of America.

In his nuanced study of 'memory, mythology, and national identity', Duncan Bell asserts, 'nationalist sentiments and national identity are structured and reproduced through variegated and temporally extended representational structures' (Bell 2003, 69). These structures are intended to bestow the impression of historical coherency, validating the image of the present by illustrating its congruity with an essentialised national identity. An innately 'temporally extended representational structure', memory makes a central contribution to this process. As Katharine Hodgkin and Susannah Radstone argue, 'the appeal to memory articulates the narrative of the nationalist past, and enjoins its subject to recognise and own it. Memory is thus at the heart of nationalist struggles, transmitted from one generation to the next as a sacred injunction' (Hodgkin and Radstone 2006, 169). In turn, they contend, '[n]ationalist memory describes a geography of belonging, an identity forged in a specified landscape, inseparable from it' (Hodgkin and Radstone 2006, 169).

The National Mall in Washington, DC, forms America's most visible geography of belonging. Running from the Lincoln Memorial to the Capitol, the Mall houses memorials and monuments to key figures and events from the chronicle of American history. America's central memorial landscape is integral to its geographical nexus of power.[6] This two-mile stretch of parkland thus constitutes a 'national symbolic' which, in Lauren Berlant's terms, 'transforms individuals into subjects of a collectively held history. Its traditional icons, its metaphors, its heroes, its rituals, and its narratives provide an alphabet for collective consciousness or national subjectivity' (Berlant 1991, 20). The development of the Mall as a commemorative terrain was concomitant to America's rise to geopolitical prominence. As Meyer argues, in the early years of the twentieth century, Congress approved plans to transform the Mall into a monumental core 'expressive of the spatial mastery of an imperial government, [which] would gradually become the physical expression of a new nationalism' (Meyer 2001, 229). From 1910, the Mall began to assume the shape it takes today: the various institutions of the Smithsonian that line its course were constructed in the early decades of the twentieth century; the Lincoln Memorial dedicated in 1922; the Jefferson Memorial in 1943; the Vietnam Veterans Memorial in 1981; the Korean War Veterans Memorial in 1992; and the National World War II Memorial in 2004.[7]

In the latter half of the twentieth century, the exceptionalist myth previously so coherently enshrined in the monuments, memorials, and museums has been subject to contestation. The earlier monumental structures of the Mall (the memorials to Washington, Lincoln, and Jefferson) contrast dramatically in tone (both emotional and visual) to the more contained, modest sites intended to remember contentious Cold War conflicts – an acknowledgement of their ambiguous (in the case of the Korean War, one is tempted to suggest, ambivalent) position in national memory. This aesthetic divide is most visibly projected in the colour-coding that projects a rather simplistic moral symbolism: the older white marble edifices to heroic presidents reflective of 'good' histories; the newer black granite structures to more uncertain recent pasts suggesting 'bad' times in the nation's chronicle. Superficially at least, these distinctions appear to mirror the conventional delineation between monuments as celebratory edifices and memorials as sites of mourning. However, as the following analysis will demonstrate, such definitions rely on a reductive – and often highly politicised – reading of history.

Maya Lin's memorial to Vietnam comprises two granite walls cut deep into the landscape of the Mall.[8] Carved into the structure are the names of 58,256 American casualties (no acknowledgement is made of Vietnamese losses), listed chronologically from the earliest death to the final known victim. The memorial forces the visitor to react bodily and emotionally to the events it commemorates, channelling them down into the earth. The walls project the visitor's reflection, drawing them into the litany of loss, just as the carved names facilitate a tactile engagement with death. Rather than imposing a prescriptive reading of the past, the memorial aims to operate as a site of continuing engagement and negotiation. Initiating a new generation of commemorative practice that appeared to acknowledge America's vulnerability and fallibility, Lin's design become paradigmatic of an abstract movement in contemporary memorial practice. Its influence can clearly be seen in recent commemorative endeavours such as the Oklahoma City National Memorial, the 9/11 memorial at the Pentagon, and Arad and Walker's *Reflecting Absence* at Ground Zero (considered in more detail below).

On the Mall, the structure has been joined by counter-monumental texts offering a similar challenge to the exceptionalist symbolic. Completed in 1995, the Korean War Veterans Memorial acknowledges losses from all countries involved in the war, not just American casualties, allowing others to share in the space of the National Mall. This internationalist approach is replicated in the Franklin Delano Roosevelt memorial, opened in 1997, situated on the edge of the tidal basin. The FDR memorial is an expansive, and inclusive, commemorative text. Constructed across five outdoor 'rooms' (the Prologue Room and one area for each of Roosevelt's four presidential terms), the layout bears witness to the seminal events of FDR's presidency (from the Depression and the New Deal to World War II). Unlike the other structures on the Mall, it neither attempts to frame the past as a heroic national parable, nor to render it in abstract and reflexive sculpture, but to pay testament to changes in the nation over this period, positioning American history as an unfinished journey to an unknown destination.

The memorial resists the binary visual symbolism identified above and is carved instead in muted pinks and greys. It includes several montaged reliefs that pay tribute to diverse sectors of American society (from children's handprints to symbols from American Indian mythology); other communities are represented figuratively – Room Two, for example, depicts groups from an urban breadline to the rural poor. However, it is the citations that adorn the walls of each room (all of them quotations from speeches made by Roosevelt) that do most to democratise this memorial. The sentiment expressed here is more global in outlook, and more critical in perspective, than any other memorial on the Mall. Taken from a speech made by Roosevelt in 1943, one quotation urges that 'unless the peace that follows recognises that the whole world is one neighbourhood and does justice to the whole human race, the germs of another world war will remain as a constant threat for mankind'; another that 'the structure of world peace cannot be the work of one man, or one party, or one nation . . . it must be a peace that rests on the cooperative effort of the whole world'.

Such claims disrupt the introspective ideology espoused by the traditional memorial jeremiad. However, the post-9/11 period has seen a reversion to the nationalist forms of commemoration eschewed by the memorials to Vietnam, Korea, and FDR. This is most surprisingly the case in the newest addition to the Mall: the Martin Luther King Memorial, opened in 2011. Unlike the tribute to FDR (to which it stands directly parallel), the MLK memorial marks a return to monumentalism in both scale and hue. Whilst the five rooms of the FDR memorial encourage the visitor to trace a temporal journey through the events of Roosevelt's presidency, the statue of MLK has exchanged horizontality for verticality, human history for godlike awe. The structure returns to the black-and-white colour-coding of other memorials on the Mall, with the added complication that here the two are deployed in stark contrast (the white monolith, from which the incomplete bust of King protrudes celebrating his contribution to the Civil Rights movement, the black wall behind mourning his assassination), engendering a peculiar 'whitening' of King's visage. The enormous stone out of which King is carved heralds the teleological progression of American history, proclaiming: 'out of the mountain of despair a stone of hope'. This text (a quotation from King, which has been taken out of context and transformed into a redemptive mantra) recollects the tropes of the jeremiad. King is presented in the image of Washington, Lincoln, or Jefferson – a stern and sombre patriarch, a privileged establishment figure, rather than a civil rights activist striving for equality. The half-finished nature of the statue (meant to symbolise the fact that the struggle against prejudice continues) is only visible from certain aspects – a head-on contemplation of the monument gives the impression that King's work is completed. In this sense, the structure operates as a form of closure rather than an enduring critical engagement with ongoing discrimination.

This refusal of reflexivity is replicated in the most visible new addition to the Mall – the National World War Two Memorial. Even at first glance, it is possible to see this grandiose structure as a return to the monumental architecture of the late nineteenth and early twentieth centuries. Dedicated by President Bush in 2004, the World War Two Memorial reinforces a singularly heroic reading of the American past and a unilateral approach to world history. The foreign nations acknowledged in the Korean memorial have been replaced by an elaborate tribute to each state of the union. Various inscriptions from presidential and military addresses present America as an unstoppable, victorious force – brutal in strength and righteous in task. One particularly zealous example, from a speech by General George Marshall, reads 'we are determined that before the sun sets on this terrible struggle our flag will be recognised throughout the world as a symbol of freedom on the one hand and of overwhelming force on the other'.

The World War Two Memorial thus returns commemoration to the chronicle of American mythic history. Its location on the Mall symbolises this commitment. As the information leaflet for the site states:

> Placing the memorial between the Washington Monument and the Lincoln Memorial reflects the importance of World War II in preserving and internationalising the democratic ideals won under George Washington and defended under Abraham Lincoln. This memorial continues America's story of striving for freedom and individual rights (National Park Service 2010).

In its architecture and accompanying rhetoric, the memorial celebrates the exporting – one might argue, imposing – of American ideals and ideologies on other nations. Although it was commissioned prior to 9/11, it is not hard to see a correspondence between this message and the tenor of American foreign policy in the period between late 2001 and 2004 during which the memorial was constructed.[9] The World War Two Memorial appears to internationalise the tropes of the jeremiad, paradoxically universalising the national symbolic whilst insisting upon its quintessential Americanness. In so doing, it neatly reflects much of the rhetoric emanating from the White House in the weeks, months, and years following 9/11. However, as the following section will demonstrate, it also parallels (and indeed pre-empts) the predominant tone of commemorative practice in the United States in the early twenty-first century.

In the aftermath of the attacks, the most visible commemorative landscape to have been transformed by the rhetoric of the jeremiad was that of New York City. Unlike the national space of the Mall, prior to 9/11, the sites and spaces of New York constituted a diverse and (with the exception, perhaps, of the more formal memorial terrain of Battery Park) decentralised space of memory. Since September 11, however, commemorative practice in New York has undergone a marked standardisation as the tropes of the jeremiad appeared to provide an almost instinctive lexicon of remembrance in American memorial culture.

2.3 The new American jeremiad after 9/11

As critics have frequently suggested, the 'rupture' of 9/11 appeared to sever America's connection to its established mythologies. Susan Faludi states that the 'intrusions of September 11 broke the dead bolt on our protective myth' (Faludi 2008, 12–13), whilst Marita Sturken contends that 'in the attacks of 9/11, the United States experienced a kind of "image defeat" and was wounded at the level of spectacle' (Sturken 2007, 172). Accordingly, the treatment and recovery of the national image was one of the priorities of the public-political sphere. As politicians and public figures hastened to enlist the nation 'in a symbolic war at home, a war to repair and restore a national myth' (Faludi 2008, 12–13), the need to reappropriate 9/11 into a recognisably 'American' narrative generated a search for a redemptive mythology. This 'symbolic war' was undoubtedly heavily ideologically loaded. As Rozario asserts, '[t]he terrorist attacks did not so much end up disclosing reality as providing an occasion for constructing a sense of "reality" [. . .] that validated some ideologies and feelings while casting others as insignificant, inauthentic, and lacking in moral urgency' (Rozario 2007, 185). For the Bush Administration, the jeremiad was the paradigm that proved most efficacious in serving such agendas. As Bercovitch contends, the jeremiad is an inherently ideological form, reliant upon the simultaneous cultivation of cultural anxiety and a sense of national Errand. These two strategies, he argues, 'define the ritual import of the jeremiad: to sustain process by imposing control, and to justify control by presenting a certain form of process as the only road to the future kingdom' (Bercovitch 1978, 24) in 'the American city of God' (Bercovitch 1978, 9).

Established in a matter of hours, the new American jeremiad remediates the genre's historic tropes to fit the contingencies of the post-September 11 environment. It conceives of 9/11 as an attack on 'American values'. In a speech given at Barksdale Air Force Base on September 11, Bush remarked that '[f]reedom itself was attacked this morning by a faceless coward' (Bush 2001f). He continued to make similar assertions during the following days, weeks, and months: declaring on 12 September that '[f]reedom and democracy are under attack' (Bush 2001d); on 14 September that '[t]hey have attacked America because we are freedom's home and defender' (Bush 2001b); in an address to the United Nations on 10 November that 'freedom and fear are at war' (Bush 2001e); and, most forcefully arguing in his State of the Union speech on 29 January 2002, that '[w]e have known freedom's price. We have shown freedom's power. And in this great conflict, my fellow Americans, we will see freedom's victory' (Bush 2002). Having defined America as the indisputable arbiter of freedom, the jeremiad's second tenet is the evocation of American unity, founded upon the nation's heroic history. In his address of 14 September, Bush declared that 'the commitment of our Fathers is now calling our time', prevailing upon Americans to 'feel what Franklin Roosevelt called "the warm courage of national unity"' (Bush 2001b), echoing his declaration that '[t]his is a day when all Americans from every walk of life unite in our resolve for justice and peace' (Bush 2001a), and emphasising the attacks as a 'national tragedy' (Bush 2001g; 2001h). United in their cause by 'a kinship of grief and a steadfast resolve to prevail against our enemies' (Bush 2001b), the new jeremiad thirdly requires Americans to enter into the battle of good versus evil, to embrace this Errand as a charge into the wilderness, fortified by the knowledge that 'evil is real, and it must be opposed' (Bush 2001g).[10] Finally, this binary moral vision is understood as emanating from God's will, born of the awareness that '[t]his world He created is of moral design' (Bush 2001b), 'there is honor in history's call' (Bush 2001e), and thus 'even in tragedy – especially in tragedy – God is near' (Bush 2002).

This paradigm is most clearly exemplified by the address that Bush gave to Congress on 20 September 2001. This was the president's public baptism as the twenty-first century's Jeremiah, performed before a congregation that contained representatives of key figures from the post-9/11 community: American politicians; victims and their families (notably Todd Beamer's wife, Lisa)[11]; and international allies for the coming War on Terror (such as Tony Blair). It was in this speech that Bush laid out his vision for revenge and retaliation, announced the creation of the Office of Homeland Security, and uttered his notorious warning to the rest of the world: '[e]ither you are with us or you are with the terrorists' (Bush 2001g). On 20 September, Bush firmly enshrined the events of September 11 as the beginning of another sacred chapter in America's providential history, arguing that 'there are struggles ahead and dangers to face. But this country will define our times, not be defined by them' (Bush 2001g). He began by presuming a self-evident national solidarity ('in the normal course of events, presidents come to this chamber to report on the state of the union. Tonight, no such report is needed; it has already been delivered by the American people'). He then moved on to outline the new Errand of the American nation, declaring that the 'advance of human freedom, the great achievement of our time and the great hope of every time, now depends on us' (Bush 2001g). So, Bush proclaimed, '[o]ur nation, this generation, will lift the dark threat of violence from our people and our future. We will rally the world to this cause by our efforts, by our courage. We will not tire, we will not falter and we will not fail' (Bush 2001g).

Most importantly, however, Bush cast this Errand as a task of memory, firmly intertwining the duty of remembrance with his political and military vision. He continued:

> Each of us will remember what happened that day and to whom it happened. We will remember the moment the news came, where we were and what we were doing.
> Some will remember an image of a fire or story or rescue. Some will carry memories of a face and a voice gone forever.
> And I will carry this. It is a police shield of a man named George Howard who died at the World Trade Center trying to save others.
> It was given to me by his mom, Arlene, as a proud memorial to her son. It is my reminder of lives that ended and a task that does not end (Bush 2001g).

These sentiments reflect the ways in which memory has repeatedly been mobilised in political discourse in the years since 2001. Over the past decade, there has been a raft of federal legislation relating to the commemoration of 9/11. In December 2001, by order of House Resolution 71, Bush officially designated September 11 as Patriot Day, drafting the attacks into the sacred calendar of national events.[12] Four years later, the True American Heroes Act of 2005 sought to validate chosen individuals and institutions for their 'patriotic' actions on the day itself.
The intentions of the Act were:

> To award a congressional gold medal on behalf of all government workers and others who responded to the attacks on the World Trade Center and the Pentagon and perished and people aboard United Airlines Flight 93 who helped resist the hijackers and caused the plane to crash, to award a duplicate in silver of such gold medals to the personal representative of each such person, to require the Secretary of Treasury to mint coins in commemoration of the Spirit of America, recognising the tragic events of September 11, 2001, and for other purposes (HR 1057).

Whilst it was originally only meant to celebrate the actions of the passengers of flight 93, its remit was extended specifically to include government personnel. As Faludi clarifies, '[u]ltimately, all thirty-seven passengers and seven crew [of United 93] received medals – along with every officer, firefighter, emergency worker, and government employee who responded to the World Trade Center and Pentagon attacks, Mayor Giuliani, Governor

Pataki, the Port Authority Commissioners and every city fire precinct' (Faludi 2008, 61). Notably excluded were all the civilian workers who volunteered on 9/11, and afterwards at Ground Zero – several of whom have become fatally ill after imbibing the toxins at the site.[13] The state's continuing involvement in commemorative practice was exemplified by the passing of the bipartisan Fallen Heroes of 9/11 Act in November 2011. Unlike the 2005 legislation, this Act awards every victim the designation of 'hero', and also 'provide[s] for a medal of appropriate design to be awarded by the President to the memorials established at the 3 sites honoring the men and women who perished as a result of the terrorist attacks on the United States on September 11, 2001' (HR 3421).[14] The rhetoric of heroism has important implications for the framing of 9/11: firstly, it lends itself to the transformation of tragedy into triumph (victims into heroes); secondly, it provides an ideal platform for the espousal of American values (or the abstraction of individuals into heroic examples of the national character); thirdly, it presents the most obvious (certainly, most immediate) convergence of popular and political discourse, constituting the central symbolic of official, vernacular, and commercial cultures of memory.

In an address to the Senate in October 2001, Edward Kennedy asserted that '[i]f we meet the new standards of September 11th, no one will stand in our way [. . .] the heroes of that day will have left an undying legacy – a proud new chapter in the annals of American greatness' (Kennedy 2001). Kennedy's speech is included as the preface to Lenore Skomal's *Heroes*. In this collection of '50 stories of the American spirit', Skomal constructs a 'call to action' (Skomal 2002, 6), constituted upon accounts of the actions of 'heroes' on September 11. It is not entirely clear how Skomal frames the notion of heroism – her subjects include representatives of the emergency services at Ground Zero, the passengers of United 93 (whom she designates as 'God's All-Star Team' [Skomal 2002, 12]), Rudy Giuliani, workers in the Twin Towers, and, rather incongruously, schoolchildren who sent letters of comfort to the bereaved. These sketches serve as parables for the American public, aiming to 'demonstrate that each and every individual, no matter what his age or profession, is capable of rising to the occasion and serving the greater good' (Skomal 2002, 10). Skomal presents these individuals as representative of the 'collective spirit of America' (Skomal 2002, 10), eclipsing their diversity in an image of national oneness. These stories are intended not only to project, but also to construct, an affective patriotic identification between reader and victim in order to 'celebrate the good that came out of the tragedy and the goodness of Americans' (Skomal 2002, 9).[15]

The group of people most frequently heralded as heroes in the aftermath of 9/11 were the firefighters who responded to the attacks on the World Trade Center. These individuals have repeatedly been transformed into validatory symbols of the nation. As Bush declared in his address to Congress on 20 September, '[w]e have seen the state of our union in the endurance of rescuers' (Bush 2001g).[16] The disproportionate losses suffered by the FDNY,[17] and the sense that – unlike other victims – these men and women knew the danger that they were facing and consciously chose to approach it (making their deaths more viably an act of sacrifice than those of the civilians trapped in the Twin Towers), have contributed to the elevation of the firefighters into mythic figures. As Clifford Chanin writes:

> The concept of service – the duty of taking on the dangers of that day – fuses the public and private elements of the tragedy. This is what accounts for the overwhelming presence of firefighters in such a wide array of memorials. Here, they are surely individuals, but also something more. They are a unifying presence. The famous image of the firefighters raising the flag at Ground Zero – recalling the Marines' flag-raising at Iwo Jima in World War II, and later echoed in 9/11 memorials – speaks of a continuity of purpose that survives the fallen firefighters, a continuity of purpose that can only be collective (Chanin 2006, 9).

In their incorporation into memorial culture, the firefighters have been positioned at the intersection of public and private realms: they are individuals who stand as national heroes; private men with public duties; a symbol of American resolve.

The fire department's own memorial to the employees who died on 9/11 was unveiled in June 2006. The six-foot-high, 7,000-pound mural, located on the side of '10 House' (the home of Engine Company 10 and Ladder Company 10, across Liberty Street from Ground Zero) comprises 'a bold, literal and almost neo-Classical 56-foot-long bronze relief dedicated to the firefighters "who fell and to those who carry on"' (Dunlap 2006). The memorial depicts a frozen image of the burning towers, whilst 'heroic and humbled firefighters' are portrayed either side of the buildings in 'scenes of valor and camaraderie to be celebrated' (Dunlap 2006).[18] Celebrated they have been. Within hours of the Twin Towers' collapse, the media was feting Ground Zero as the domain of heroes. In a memorial service held on 16 September 2001, Archbishop Edward Egan memorably announced that the site of the former World Trade

Center had been transformed into 'Ground Hero' (Zehfuss 2003, 517–8). As the search for survivors became increasingly futile, the media's 'hero hunt' (as *The New York Times* labelled it) intensified. The language of the serious media began to reflect the hyperbole of comic books as the fluidity between the fantastic and the real became visible. As Marvel Comics' editor-in-chief, Joe Quesada, commented, '[r]ight now, the difference between Peter Parker putting on a costume to become Spider-Man and a man off the street putting on a uniform to become a fire-man is really wafer-thin' (*Today,* NBC, 4 June 2002). These sentiments are reflected at length in Marvel's extended response to the attacks. In *Heroes* (2001), many of Marvel's most famous illustrators pay homage to the rescue workers at Ground Zero.[19] The comic conjoins familiar superheroes with the heroes of 9/11 identified by Skomal: showing figures from the Marvel universe helpless before the devastation as rescuers work on; the uprising on board United 93; respondents and superheroes united in triumph; a male office worker carrying a female co-worker out of the collapsing World Trade Center[20]; a firefighter and a police officer manifested as the Twin Towers; and Giuliani making an address at Ground Zero. Collectively, they construct an exemplary jeremiad, tracing 9/11's culture of calamity from its early, traumatised manifestations ('*Words* fail to describe what we feel. *Pictures* cannot capture what we've experienced' [Quesada et al. 2001]), to the redemptive reinscription of American exceptionalism.

Early in the collection, a panel by Alan Davis, Robin Riggs, and Pat Prentice pictures the Silver Surfer (harbinger of the end of the world) watching over Manhattan to witness 'its teeming population [. . .] unite in tragedy', 'humbled by the sacrifice of [. . .] firefighters, medics, police officers and good Samaritans', but sure in the belief that '[h]istory will recall them with a single name . . . *heroes*' (Quesada et al. 2001). A later image (that recalls both a cinema poster and a wartime propaganda campaign) positions representatives from each of the heroic groups cited by Prentice et al. in front of an American flag above the legend 'Liberty carries on presents Faces of America – a more perfect union production' (Quesada et al. 2001). Over the page, a reworking of the Iwo Jima image includes a faceless firefighter, reinforcing the impression of these heroes as the American everyman. So, too, does the 'Diagram of Heroes', which attempts to anatomise the values attributed to such figures ('Lungs – breathing heavy with purpose'; the brain as the home of honour, fearlessness, and duty; the heart as the realm of compassion, bravery, and determination), imitating kitsch photo-montages in the spaces left for 'your face here', 'your heart here'.

Jim Shooter's contribution connects these universalising sentiments to the glorious American past, revealing a series of police officers and firefighters drawn around the American flag above the inscription, 'let us all thank our choice of deities – guaranteed by the founding principles of this great nation – that there are heroes among us. God bless America' (Quesada et al. 2001). Robert Weinberg completes the jeremiad by mobilising these images of heroism past and present in the service of America's new Errand, presenting the valour of servicemen and women as the catalyst for collective action. Below an image of a couple in mourning, he writes:

Now, we must join with the heroes of that day – ordinary men and women who met that attack with extraordinary courage – to demonstrate we can't be beaten, that we can't be intimidated. 'That', as Lincoln once proclaimed, 'from these honored dead we take increased devotion to that cause for which they gave the last full measure of devotion – that we highly resolve that these dead shall not have died in vain – that this nation, under God, shall have a new birth of freedom – and that government of the people, by the people, for the people, shall not perish from this earth (Quesada et al. 2001).

The unreflexive terms in which artists and authors construct their response to 9/11 leads the overall project of *Heroes* precariously close to caricature. This can perhaps be seen most clearly in Stan Lee's contribution, which imbues the familiar hyperbole of the comic book with biblical significance. Above an image of a torn American flag, held in the hand of Captain America and fluttering defiantly over Ground Zero,[21] Lee states:

A day there was of monumental villainy. A day when a great nation lost its innocence and naked evil stood revealed before a stunned and shattered world.

A day there was when a serpent struck a sleeping giant, a giant who will sleep no more. Soon shall the serpent know the wrath of the mighty, the vengeance of the just.

A day there was when Liberty lost her heart – and found the strength of her soul (Quesada et al. 2001).

Lee's commentary recalls the simplistic moral binary of Bush's rhetoric of good and evil. Against the subversive culture conventionally offered by the graphic novel, Marvel's *Heroes* provides an excellent example of the way in which an uncritical subscription to nationalist symbols presents cultural narratives as inseparable from the more general 'apocalyptic theology' (Rozario 2007, 200) that dominated the public sphere in the aftermath of the attacks.

Rozario argues that apocalyptic theology deflects critique by presenting both 'politics and morality in black-and-white terms, treating the world as a place where "innocence" is always imperilled and where retribution is demanded against violators of virtue', advocating a culture that 'privilege[s] the sentimental [. . .] over political knowledge to such an extent that complexity can begin to seem like the last refuge of fools and the corrupt' (Rozario 2007, 200). As Slotkin contends – whether explicitly or implicitly, intentionally or unwittingly – this mythic mode of discourse 'projects models of good or heroic behavior that reinforce the values of ideology, and affirm as good the distribution of authority and power that ideology rationalises' (Slotkin 1986, 84). David Simpson suggests that through such endeavours, the dead are deindividualised, abstracted to become 'heroes, sacrificial victims, icons of patriotic life, above all saturated with meaning. They connect the present to the past and the future, and enumerating and accounting for their deaths is a national commitment' (Simpson 2006, 50). This commitment has been resoundingly taken up by memorial culture, where a number of projects have sought to enumerate and account for the dead of 9/11.

Between 15 September and 31 December 2001, *The New York Times* embarked on an attempt to write an obituary for each of the victims, later published in a collected edition entitled *Portraits of Grief* (2002). This endeavour has attracted critical attention for a number of reasons. Firstly, as Simpson argues, it appears to suggest a democratisation of death, featuring tributes to 'the firefighters, window washers, janitors, and waiters whose lives and deaths would normally have gone unrecorded by the most widely circulated newspaper in the United States' (Simpson 2006, 21). Secondly, it makes the impact of the attacks clear in human terms – E. Ann Kaplan recalls, for example, collecting each of the portraits as a means of accounting for the victims (an activity which she somewhat predictably ascribes as a further symptom of trauma) (Kaplan 2005, 16). Thirdly, the portraits function as a way of giving private loss collective dimensions – as Nancy K. Miller describes, 'they are crafted to serve as the microcosm of family life, of community values, of a valiant, though wounded, America. The domestic detail of the toothbrush comes to stand for the intimacy of the home, and the home for the nation's public life: the homefront against incursions of terrorism' (Miller 2008, 27). However, critics argue that the *Portraits* exacerbate the more problematic dimensions of 9/11's memorial culture. The series presents its subjects in a particularly idealised form that has the effect of sanitising (and standardising) the obituaries, rendering the victims almost interchangeable. As Simpson contends, 'even within the expected bounds of memorial decorum, the notices seem formulaic. They seem regimented, even militarised, made to march to the beat of a single drum' (Simpson 2006, 26). This beat is neither unmediated (the notices were of course heavily edited), nor without ideological dimensions ('clearly being put to work in the cause of a patriotic momentum' [Simpson 2006, 26]).

Simon Stow asserts that, in pursuing its nationalist agenda, 'the series took on a pornographic form' (Stow 2008, 231). Stow traces a 'longstanding connection between pornography and death [that] identifies both the prurience at the heart of our contemporary modes of mourning and remembrance and its potentially negative consequences for the American democratic process' (Stow 2008, 231). In so doing, he highlights a failure to distinguish between empathy and identification that results in the occlusion of difference between victim and witness. As Dominick LaCapra has argued, in contemporary memorial culture, '[e]mpathy is too often conflated with identification, especially with the victim, and this conflation leads to an idealisation or even sacralisation of the victim as well as an often histrionic self-image as surrogate victim undergoing vicarious experience' (LaCapra 2004, 65). Whilst this overly associative process appears directed towards empathic connection, Carolyn J. Dean suggests that it engenders a form of solipsism that requires the victim to assume the identity of the witness. She designates this 'narcissistic blotting out of the other as a sociocultural problem that impedes mutual recognition and thus precludes empathy' (Dean 2003, 98).

This fetishisation of victimhood can be seen in E. L. Doctorow's tribute to September 11. Published in 2002, *Lamentation 9/11* is one of many photo books collated in the wake of the attacks. The book combines photographs of New York taken by David Finn in the days after 9/11 with a highly emotive text by Doctorow. Doctorow positions himself as a twenty-first-century Whitman, sowing unity among New York's disparate residents. He extends the much-vaunted feeling of communality cited after the attacks into an attempt to identify with the victims themselves. He writes, 'I didn't know them, the people who died there, [. . .] But I counted on them'; '[t]he rhythms of their speech were my rhythms, the figures of speech, the attitudes, the postures, the moods, were my rhythms and phrases, my attitudes and postures and moods', '[w]e naturally understood one another though we had never met' (Doctorow 2002). Doctorow thus transforms a commonality of time and space into a partnership of shared values and experience. In so doing, he threatens to negate the difference between himself and the victims, enacting a process of transference that allows him to presume unproblematic unity with the dead by casting them in his own likeness.

LaCapra contends that such forms of over-identification are integral to the ideologisation of culture, facilitating the establishment of an acritical discourse that attempts to deflect critique. He argues that 'certain forms of identification may approach a quasi-religious experience that resists ethical and political judgement' (LaCapra 2004, 130). It is, then, perhaps of little surprise that, alongside their 'disintegration of the normative frameworks of likeness' (Dean 2003, 98), both the *Portraits of Grief* and Doctorow's prose evince other features reminiscent of the new American jeremiad. In an editorial published in October 2001, *The New York Times* declared that the obituaries presented 'archetypal' pictures of Americans, constructing a 'map of loss' that revealed 'the larger story of the world': 'where Americans come from, how they get ahead, and what they expect when they do get ahead' (New York Times 2001). In so doing, the article reduces the victims to an essentialised set of symbols – a national parable of 'generosity' and 'selflessness', whose 'knowledge comes as a gift' (New York Times 2001).

Doctorow's presumptive narrative technique cancels the diversity of the victims in a similar manner. His text presumes a unity derived from the shared 'American' covenant; a 'fervent love' of freedom, guaranteed by the 'necessary humanity of the secular state'; enshrined in the certainty that '[t]his country and its institutions are a work in progress . . . Our story has just begun . . . Our raucous and corruptible political system lumbers on toward a true and universal justice' (Doctorow 2002). Doctorow underscores this national affirmation by appropriating the victims as symbols of (and for) the nation, declaring (in a direct address to the 'killer'), 'our thousands of dead were transfigured, and in their names and numbers they stand now for our Democracy. So that even as we mourn them, we know that they are our endowment' (Doctorow 2002). These texts thus attempt to absorb the victims into the national symbolic by transforming them into emblems of American values. In so doing, they bear all the hallmarks of the jeremiad, designed 'to fuse the particular [the victim], the social [the nation], and the cosmic [values such as justice, freedom, and democracy]' (Bercovitch 1978, 42).

As we have seen, this symbolic is firmly enshrined in official memorial culture; however, its tropes are also clearly visible in vernacular forms of commemoration relating to 9/11.[22] According to Burgoyne, '[v]ernacular memory can be characterised as the memories carried forward from first-hand experience in small-scale communities; it conveys the sense of what "social reality feels like" rather than what it should be like' (Burgoyne 2006, 210). Whilst this definition appears to posit vernacular memory as being more concerned with the 'real' than the 'ideal', making it diametrically opposed to the exceptionalist mythologies constructed by official commemorative culture, vernacular memory's imbrication in the public sphere serves to mediate (and to some extent minimalise) the difference between the two. Crockatt suggests that the transference of tropes between official and vernacular cultures of memory is premised on a form of 'Americanism' that is at once diverse and standardising, composed of 'certain profoundly unifying symbols, attitudes, and values' (Crockatt 2003, 50). Americanism 'is by no means only a matter of high politics or ideology. It expresses itself on a more homely level in, for example, devotion to the flag and celebrations of national events and heroes' (Crockatt 2003, 50). It may thus be seen as the preserve of the individual and the collective, the state and the domestic, blurring the boundaries between official and vernacular forms of memory, and demonstrating the localisation of the national symbolic.

As a 2006 exhibition funded by the World Trade Center Memorial Foundation (and thus co-opted into official memory culture) suggests, in the context of 9/11, localised forms of vernacular memory are strongly influenced by 'Americanist' symbols – none more so than the American flag. Featuring photographs by Jonathan Hyman, *9/11 and the American Landscape* aimed to offer a journey 'into the heartland of American grief to document the multiplicity of expressions of public art in the aftermath of 9/11', and depict 'individual landscapes of loss and regeneration' (Greenwald 2006, 4). As Alice Greenwald (Director of the National September 11 Museum) comments:

> Hyman's odyssey brings us to the point of exquisite intersection, where emblems of patriotism and identity, and reiterations of events seared into our collective imagination, coexist with the most basic and mundane elements of our lives. Surfaces of cars and houses, urban walls and rustic woods, church signs and even human skin become the canvas for a quintessentially American vernacular of longing, remembrance, defiance, and hope (Greenwald 2006, 4).

Although intended to show the diversity of responses to 9/11 across the United States, the 'quintessentially American vernacular' assembled by Hyman demonstrates the conformity of the response to the attacks in its delimitation to 'the most hallowed symbol of the American collective' (Chanin 2006, 9).

As Clifford Chanin (senior program advisor to the World Trade Center Memorial Foundation) asserts in his foreword to the exhibition catalogue, '[i]nstinctively, the tribute artists of 9/11 looked to the flag. To enshroud the fallen. To comfort their loved ones. To enfold their sacrifice within the narrative of American history. The flag offers assurance that this story continues, and that inscribed within it are the dead of 9/11' (Chanin 2006, 9). Chanin positions the flag as a symbol that translates commemorative practice from an act of mourning to an act of celebration, from the memorial to the monumental, from subjective to universal, private to public, vernacular to official, blurring the distinctions between each category. Documenting memorials to 9/11 from 'within sight of Ground Zero to the far corners of rural America' (Chanin 2006, 8), Hyman's pictures are collated to generate the impression of a unity of response, to make 9/11 '[n]ot simply New York history, but American history' (Hamil 2006, 7). By recurrently foregrounding the flag, they attempt to nationalise the tragedy by suggesting that what 'is missing from Ground Zero has been recaptured in memory and dispersed across the American landscape' (Chanin 2006, 9). The exhibition draws diverse responses to the attacks into a single image, returning the catastrophe of 9/11 to the optimistic culture of American calamity by demonstrating 'a rare and dramatic intersection of private emotion and public expression' (Hyman 2006, 41) that catalyses the creation of 'a new Americana around the attacks' (Hyman 2006, 41).

The object that most exemplifies this new Americana is perhaps the National 9/11 Flag. The flag is modelled on the precedent of the AIDS Memorial Quilt (although operating with a less countercultural remit).[23] It was initially recovered from Ground Zero where it was partially destroyed in the attacks. Since 2008, the flag has travelled across the United States 'to empower local service heroes in all 50 states with the privilege of stitching the flag back to its original 13-stripe format' (New York Says Thank You Foundation 2011). The work of sewing is seen as a therapeutic act of remembrance (both for the individual and the nation) and the flag is claimed to be 'rebuilding America one stitch at a time' (New York Says Thank You Foundation 2011).[24] The flag (which will eventually be displayed at the National September 11 Museum) thus occupies the peculiar position of being at once a 'grassroots' endeavour, administered by a charitable trust, and a 'National Treasure'. According to its founders, the flag is intended to 'to inspire 300 million Americans [. . .] in order to deepen our sense of citizenship and national pride' by symbolising 'the transformation of tragedy into triumph' (New York Says Thank You Foundation 2011).

Such sentiments are, of course, highly redemptive, however, they are also extremely marketable.[25] It is perhaps of no surprise, therefore, that the symbols examined above are replicated in the third sphere of memory identified by Burgoyne: commercial culture. Burgoyne argues that 'commercial culture engages the discourses of memory by invoking commercial products and representations as an aspect of national heritage' (Burgoyne 2006, 211). As Sturken (2007) has shown, 9/11 has been subject to a significant degree of commodification, not least in the increase in the sale of American flags in the period directly following the attacks. Sales of the stars and stripes totalled a record $51.7 million in 2001 (although, ironically, 67 per cent of these flags were made in China) (Heller 2005, 16). On 9/11 itself, Wal-Mart alone sold 116,000 flags, 110,000 more than on September 11 2000 (Scanlon 2005, 177). As Dana Heller outlines, '[i]n the weeks and months following 9/11, the market for goods representing American patriotic unity and pride expanded dramatically. American consumers both participated in, and bore witness to, a rapid transformation of the World Trade Center attacks into commodities aimed at repackaging turbulent and chaotic emotions, reducing them to a pious, quasi-religious, nationalism' (Heller 2005, 6).

Conceptualising consumption as a collective ritual, Heller considers 'the complex relations of commodification and commemoration, marketing and militarism, commercial patronage and patriotism, that took shape long before American Airlines Flight 11 struck the North Tower, but were brought to the fore and reinvested with nationalist solemnity in that tragedy's wake' (Heller 2005, 2). Discussing the mass consumption of kitsch Americana (from bumper stickers, to WTC toilet rolls, casino chips, teddy bears, fake dollar bills, and other commemorative items), and documenting the increase in sales of the flag decal after the attacks, Heller's collection vividly describes how marketers promoted 'the promise of closure through consumption' (Heller 2005, 20). The investment in items of 9/11 memorabilia thus exemplifies the ways in which commodification practices attempt to counter loss by promoting national symbols as sites of unity from which an apparently traumatised nation may draw solace. Heller argues that the designation, '9/11', 'has attained the cultural function of a trademark, one that symbolises a new kind of national identification – or national branding awareness, to adopt the jargon of advertising – alongside the almost sublime spectacle of national trauma' (Heller 2005, 3).

The travelling of these symbols across the (official, vernacular, and commercial) spheres of memorial culture creates an illusion of coherence that masks a multiplicity of motives and perspectives. As Hodgkin and Radstone assert, icons such as the flag are invested with a certain amount of hermeneutic fluidity, which cross 'boundaries between different versions of the American past, summoning up patriotism and protest, the working class and the nation state' (Hodgkin and Radstone 2006, 172). Symbols such as the flag, and frameworks such as the jeremiad, mask these contradictions by appearing to homogenise the intention, production, and reception of diverse memory texts. However, properly understood, public memory is continually in flux – shaped by divergent interests and motivated by diverse agendas, even as they appear to assume identical form. Attentive to such nuances, Burgoyne contends that the sphere of public memory thus 'serves to mediate the "competing restatements of reality" that emerge from the clash of vernacular, official, and commercial interpretations of past experiences' (Burgoyne 2006, 209). As the final section of this chapter will argue, nowhere has the relationship between the official, the vernacular, and the commercial proved more problematic after 9/11 than in the reconstruction of Ground Zero. Consequently, nowhere have the terms of the jeremiad been evoked more frequently than to mask the tensions and conflicts at work in this most emotive and politicised of spaces.

2.4 The new American jeremiad and the reconstruction of Ground Zero

Terry Smith argues that, in the aftermath of 9/11, the former World Trade Center site 'became, for a time, in the eyes of the world's media, the new century's site of ambiguity, its metaphorical ground' (Smith 2006, 169). The aim of the redevelopment programme was to rehome this 'non-place'[26] by reintegrating it into the national symbolic, thus clearing the way for its rehabilitation as both a centre of commerce and a site of memory. However, as the troubled reconstruction process has shown, it has not always been possible to serve both of these agendas adequately. Over the past thirteen years, the sixteen acres of Ground Zero have become the site of a highly charged collision between personal, local, national, and global interests, involving grieving families, Manhattan residents, representatives of regional and federal states, and multinational corporations.[27] Overseen by the Port Authority (a publically funded body possessing, by dint of its dual administration by the states of New York and New Jersey, an almost extra-legal authority), the rebuilding of Ground Zero has seen the symbolic centre of the globalised market acquire national dimensions as a site of American tragedy – a mass grave where private citizens mourn apparently collective losses.

Questions about the future of Ground Zero surfaced from the immediate aftermath of the attacks, with suggestions for memorial designs being posted on the Internet as early as 12 September 2001.[28] Ideas ranged from leaving the ruins of the Twin Towers as a haunting reminder of the catastrophe, to rebuilding the World Trade Center, restoring the historic streetscape of the area, landscaping the site as a community park or garden, or creating some form of educational and cultural centre.[29] After a controversial and convoluted competition process, in December 2003 it was announced that Studio Daniel Libeskind had been awarded the master plan for the site. The rhetoric in which the original features of the master plan – *Memory's Eternal Foundation* – were presented signifies Libeskind's deployment of the redemptive aesthetic familiar to the American culture of calamity.

Libeskind produced a modernist skyscraper that incorporated the requisite commercial space alongside heavily symbolic and commemorative elements, such as a museum located 'On the Edge of Hope', and a 'Garden of the World' suspended at 1,776 ft to depict 'Life Victorious'. This auspicious height was intended to evoke the date of the signing of the Declaration of Independence, placing the design firmly in a nationalist framework connecting the 'sacred' site to the nation's providential past. As Philip Nobel comments, 'Libeskind's assignment of patriotic and heroic meaning to otherwise mute forms was the hallmark of his plan' (Nobel 2005, 140). Among the key features of the master plan was the 'Park of Heroes'. This not only reiterated the discourse of heroism found elsewhere in memorial culture, but performed the work of connecting Ground Zero, spatially, to the streets of New York, and, symbolically, to the chronicle of America's mythic history. As Libeskind comments, 'I wanted to remember the heroes of the day, and I'd traced on a map the routes taken by rescue workers, police and firefighters to arrive at the tower. I incorporated those lines into the design, turning them into pathways shooting into the city' (Libeskind 2004, 48).

The site of the former World Trade Center is bordered to the south by Liberty Street, to the east by Liberty Plaza, and, one block down, by the Canyon of Heroes and Liberty Place. To the west of Ground Zero, in the middle of the Hudson, is Liberty Island, upon which stands the Statue of Liberty. Libeskind's design was thus integrated into a topography that is at once mythic and heavily memorial. As James Young notes:

> by dint of its location at the tip of lower Manhattan, the New World Trade Center will necessarily become part of a national memorial matrix and landscape much larger than itself. It will be within

sightlines of the Statue of Liberty, Ellis Island, the war memorials in Battery Park and the Museum of Jewish Heritage (Young 2003, 222).

Libeskind's master plan was reliant upon these associations for both its emotive affect and its (cultural, political, financial) effect, but its success was also dependent upon his faith in architecture's powers of transcendence. Libeskind contends that that architecture 'expresses, stabilises, and orients in an otherwise chaotic world' (Libeskind 2004, 288). Of buildings, he argues, '[i]f designed well and right, these seemingly hard and inert structures have the power to illuminate, and even to heal' (Libeskind 2004, 288).

For Libeskind, in striving 'for universality' (Libeskind 2004, 16), architecture assumes an almost mythic function. Throughout his architectural practice (at the Jewish Museum in Berlin, as well as at Ground Zero, and in his 9/11 memorial in Padua, Italy), Libeskind has attempted to eternalise his buildings through the use of light. As he explains in his autobiography, light's 'perfection lies beyond anything we can think of. It's almost a point of view from beyond, from God's perspective' (Libeskind 2004, 54). Whilst the Jewish Museum's Holocaust Tower deploys light to sparing effect (eschewing full transcendence and offering just a glimpse of illumination in an otherwise darkened abyss), in Libeskind's original design for Ground Zero, light became an emblem of redemption. Connecting Wall Street in the east to the Hudson in the west, and traversing the entirety of the World Trade Center site, the 'Wedge of Light' was intended to be the largest public space in Manhattan. Flooded with sunlight continuously between the period of 8:46 am and 10:28 am on every September 11, the space was designed to mark the time between the attack of the first plane and the collapse of the North Tower, elevating this interval into a period beyond history: a timeless, sacred moment.[30] Light, Libeskind comments, is capable of such transcendence because it 'is the measure of everything. It is absolute, mathematical, physical, eternal' (Libeskind 2004, 56).

By evoking the eternalising tropes of the jeremiad, Libeskind's design thus undoubtedly served to yoke Ground Zero to the mythic framework of American history. In so doing, it sought to transform Ground Zero from a site of atrocity to a sacred space of memory by reintegrating it into the 'cosmo-national' symbolic (Foote 2003). Linking the process of sanctification to a crisis in, and subsequent reaffirmation of, national narratives, Kenneth Foote contends that '[s]anctified places arise from battles, such as Gettysburg, that mark the traumas of nationhood and from events that have given shape to national identity' (Foote

2003, 10). Edward Linenthal traces this link between sacred spaces and national identity back to the early jeremiads that 'provided generations of Americans with images of the New World as sacred space' (Linenthal 1993, 1). As Sturken notes, however, in the aftermath of 9/11, the 'concept of sacred ground [. . .] has been a particularly powerful and limiting designation both at Ground Zero and in national politics' (Sturken 2007, 199).

Claims to the sacredness of the site have repeatedly been mobilised as means of masking the commercial interests that have informed, and dictated, the process of reconstruction. In the early aftermath of the attacks, the police tightly monitored the sale of commemorative objects at Ground Zero. To this end, as Trimarco and Depret demonstrate, they drew 'an invisible line down the middle of the venue, which extended and continued in a large ring around the entire disaster area, separating the vendor-free sacred space that surrounded the site from the mundane and commercial space around it' (Trimarco and Depret 2005, 48). In March 2004, state legislature passed a bill restricting the sale of objects to a very small portion of the area outside Ground Zero. Whilst this legislation undoubtedly responds to valid concerns about the appropriation and commodification of loss, it hides the extent to which '[t]he storm of controversy about commercialisation at the site conceals an underlying harmony in the current context of twenty-first century American capitalism – between trade and the construction of a national sacred space' (Trimarco and Depret 2005, 39). Such contentions are not new. As Rozario asserts, disaster has commonly been perceived as playing a 'revitalising role [. . .] for American capitalism' (Rozario 2007, 76), and those managing the redevelopment of Ground Zero ensured that 9/11 did not prove an exception to this rule.

From the outset of the redevelopment process, the project of reconstruction has been led by commercial concerns. In its first press release in November 2001, the Lower Manhattan Development Corporation (the body established to oversee the rebuilding of Ground Zero) announced that its aims were to 'work closely with the private sector to determine a proper market-driven response to the economic and infrastructure needs of Lower Manhattan, as well as with the Port Authority of New York and New Jersey to identify the appropriate redevelopment of the World Trade Center site' (LMDC 2001). No mention was made of the commemorative effort, or of the interests of community groups, survivors, or victims' families. This missive (alongside the demands of the site's leaseholder, Larry Silverstein, that the space must incorporate substantial retail, corporate, and hotel facilities) established the principles of a redevelopment process that has recurrently prioritised market-driven concerns.

Whilst it provided a suitable framework for the early design process, Libeskind's redemptive aesthetic has been increasingly marginalised over the course of the redevelopment. Libeskind's design initially presented a compromise for the LMDC: offering the requisite amount of commercial space, whilst retaining a sufficiently prominent commemorative element to satisfy both the families of victims and the general public. However, Silverstein's insistence that his preferred firm, Skidmore Owings & Merrill (SOM), be employed alongside Libeskind, and that their principal architect, David Childs, should have ultimate responsibility for the design of the Freedom Tower, has seen all traces of the jeremiad gradually expunged from the site. Although a respected architectural practice, SOM are renowned for unremarkable corporate buildings (such as their rapid post-9/11 reconstruction of World Trade Center 7), commercial structures largely devoid of any symbolic value. SOM's focus at Ground Zero has been to fulfil Silverstein's requirements that the site must provide 10 million square feet of office space, 600,000 – 1,000,000 square feet for a shopping mall, and 600,000 square feet for a hotel.[31] As Nobel comments, '[t]he need to fit all that space – under Silverstein's self-imposed seventy-story height limit [for leasable commercial units] and minus the acreage of the increasingly sacred footprints – proscribed the future of the site in a way nothing else would' (Nobel 2005, 101).

By late 2003, it was clear that the project had become architecturally and philosophically confused. Childs wanted to regulate the Freedom Tower, to make it symmetrical, cheaper to build, with even spaces that would be easy to rent. In short, he sought to make it commercially viable, discounting the commemorative elements and eschewing Libeskind's emotive rhetoric. As Paul Goldberger asserts, these decisions signalled that '[c]ommercial development was going to dominate Ground Zero' (Goldberger 2005, 211), and 'implicitly downgraded the memorial' (Goldberger 2005, 213). In 2009, the Freedom Tower was renamed One World Trade. In its explicit reference to the Twin Towers, this gesture suggests a desire to eclipse the difficult history of the past thirteen years by constructing a neat continuity with the earlier history of the site in order to reassert the forces of global capitalism. In its implicit elision of the period of 9/11 and its aftermath, this gesture places the commemorative elements of the site in a rather awkward position. If the majority of the site has been rehabilitated as a place of commerce and trade, found closure, and moved on from the events of September 11, how should an inherently retrospective memorial interact with its forward-looking surroundings?

Whilst Childs's corporatisation of the master plan undermined many of the mythic narratives attached to Ground Zero, the design of the memorial has remained dominated by the notion of sacredness – a discourse that has proven politicised and prescriptive. Campaigning for re-election in 2002, then Governor George Pataki labelled the 'footprints' of the Twin Towers 'sacred ground', demanding that these areas of the site should be preserved. This instruction was respected by the guidelines issued by the advisory committee (comprised of victims' families) established to select the jury for the memorial competition in 2003. These stipulations have imposed significant restrictions upon commemorative possibilities at the site. As Nobel argues, '[t]he designation of the footprints as holy ground had a devastating effect on the planning possibilities at Ground Zero, but the two enormous squares also made a very awkward site for the memorial they were intended to contain' (Nobel 2005, 116). Without the stabilising framework of the jeremiad (which has been undermined by the commercialisation of the master plan), it has proved difficult to accommodate these spaces alongside a strong symbolic identity for the site, and the memorial process has become aesthetically compromised.[32]

In its final form, Arad and Walker's *Reflecting Absence* is almost entirely subsumed by the footprints of the Twin Towers. These bronze-lined structures contain two pools in which water cascades to a depth of 30 feet. The pools are lined with the victims' names, ordered (after much debate) into associative groups. Whilst resonant of the abstract aesthetic that dominates much contemporary commemorative practice, the memorial is monumental, covering 7.5 acres of the 16-acre site. Even the names of victims seem uncomfortably large, not easily traceable (and thus touchable) as they are at Lin's Vietnam memorial. This confusion of scale and sentiment makes the claims of the structure hard to situate, and the completed site offers a rather peculiar visitor experience. The footprints are overshadowed by the commercial development occurring around them. The area representing the North Tower, in particular, is located uncomfortably close to One World Trade (previously the Freedom Tower),[33] and the noise from the surrounding building works, traffic, and melee of downtown Manhattan is intense. Intrusive security precautions (airport style scanners, bag checks, long queues, barriers, and the very visible presence of armed officers) underscore Ground Zero's designation as a site of exception, and signs around the memorial outline 'correct' codes of behaviour, prescribing authorised modes of commemorative engagement. Such measures restrict the opportunity for spontaneous and subjective forms of remembrance. Although it is possible to leave small tokens (flowers or ribbons) around the footprints, the official control of the site and the distraction from the surrounding city eschew the potential for reflectiveness suggested in the name of the memorial:[34] there is definitely a feeling of absence here, but, problematically, little sense of loss.[35]

LaCapra argues that too often in memorial culture, the difference between absence and loss is elided. He contends:

> When absence is converted into loss, one increases the likelihood of misplaced nostalgia or utopian politics in quest of a new totality or fully unified community. When loss is converted into (or encrypted in an indiscriminately generalised rhetoric of) absence, one faces the impasse of endless melancholy, impossible mourning, and interminable aporia in which any process of working through the past and its historical losses is foreclosed or prematurely aborted (LaCapra 2001, 46).

Whilst loss is a historical consequence of a specific event, locatable in time and space, absence refers to an ahistorical, structural lack. In translating historical *loss into absence*, Arad and Walker's memorial appears to create an open and endless wound inscribed on the landscape of New York. As LaCapra suggests, this 'impasse of endless melancholy, impossible mourning, and interminable aporia' (LaCapra 2001, 46) threatens to foreclose the process of working through the past by forever foregrounding the void at the tip of Manhattan. By contrast, the celebratory tropes of the jeremiad that inform the wider commemorative culture analysed throughout this chapter pursue the opposite end, generating a 'utopian politics in quest of a new totality or fully unified community' (LaCapra 2001, 46) by translating *absence into loss*. Yoking the events of 9/11 to the heroic history of the United States, the tropes of the jeremiad attempt to rehome the national symbolic that was destabilised in the aftermath of the attacks. However, LaCapra contends, such endeavours 'must be reductive, based on misrecognition, and even close to myth' (LaCapra 2001, 49).

Thomas Foster suggests that 'the re-emergence of debunked nationalist myths and clichés after 9/11 [are] more or less recognizably empty or inauthentic forms that are nevertheless presented as necessary and unavoidable, even moving in their very emptiness' (Foster 2005, 258). Foster contends that the attacks engendered a climate of 'cynical nationalism' that led to 'a weakening of the distinction between culture and politics' (Foster 2005, 258). Cynical nationalism is an ideology that is aware of its own hermeneutic arbitrariness. In contrast to conventional 'nationalism', 'cynical nationalism' understands the hollowness of its terms of reference, but continues to deliberately employ such reified figures in the service of its own validation. Just as the traditional jeremiad exploits 'a mode of ambiguity that denied the contradiction between history and rhetoric' (Bercovitch 1978, 17), cynical nationalism constructs the truth it wishes to see in the world, excused of the need to reconcile it with any basis in material fact. Foster thus contends that the cultural-political consensus it forges is merely 'a mask, an empty form, a rhetorical gesture' (Foster 2005, 258).

This empty consensus is forged around the universalisation of historical loss. By foregrounding the dead of 9/11 as the exemplary representatives of an idealised America, the official, vernacular, and commercial modes of memory analysed above mobilise the lost victims of September 11 as symbols of an absent (and impossible) community, constructed around the dubious contention that everyone 'is a victim, that all history is trauma, or that we all share a pathological public sphere or a "wound culture"' (LaCapra 2001, 64). The absence occluded by this vision is the lack of a genuine foundation for the shared sense of community (based as it is on mistaken claims to collective victimhood) upon which the myths of national unity are contingent. Thus, LaCapra suggests that the translation of absence into loss bespeaks a deeper structural lack (the lack of any basis in historical reality for the claims upon which collective identity, or rather, *identification*, is based). This engenders an attempt to present a version of history in which 'a putatively naïve or pure beginning – something constructed as a variant of full presence, innocence, or intactness – is lost through the ins and outs, trials and tribulations, of the middle, only to be recovered, at least on the level of higher insight, at the end' (LaCapra 2001, 52).

This transcendental vision is exactly the aim of the jeremiad. In its multifaceted conflations of loss and absence, the new American jeremiad has occasioned a hollow memorial culture, burdened under the attempt to yoke the attacks (and their violent aftermath) back into the sacred chronicle of American history. In the aftermath of 9/11, official, vernacular, and commercial discourses have underscored the jeremiad's status as an organising narrative of American memorial culture. However, the gradual abandonment of its tropes (and the marginalisation of Libeskind's master plan) during the redevelopment of Ground Zero also reveals the essential emptiness of this framework. Whilst the rhetoric of the jeremiad proved useful for symbolically rehabilitating the site in the early years after the attacks, its eternalising claims were discarded once the space had been re-established as a centre for corporate capitalism, exposing them as little more than an affective façade and rendering the memorial site symbolically ambiguous.

Bercovitch contends that, throughout its long history, the very invocation of the jeremiad has attested to the ineffectiveness of the vision it attempts to espouse. He argues that '[e]ven when they are most optimistic, jeremiads express a profound disquiet. Not infrequently, their affirmations betray an underlying desperation – a refusal to confront the present, a fear of the future, an effort to translate "America" into a vision that works in spirit because it can never be tested in fact' (Bercovitch 1978, xiv). Bercovitch suggests that the tropes of the jeremiad thus attempt to conceal their own inadequacy, masking the troubled reality of the nation beneath a consolatory and, ultimately, empty ideal. In the aftermath of 9/11, the discourses of the public sphere have elided reflexivity by evoking the myth of national exceptionalism, attempting, impossibly, to transform crisis into certainty and tragedy into triumph. However, the symbolically stranded memorial at Ground Zero destabilises this endeavour – revealing a hidden ambiguity about the meaning of the attacks that other auspices of American memorial culture have attempted to hide by retreating into the familiar framework of the jeremiad.

3
Analogical Holocaust Memory after 9/11

Building upon recent critical attempts to foreground the comparative properties of memory, this chapter examines the ways in which cultural and political discourses have sought to construct analogical frames of reference for 9/11. I focus upon the widespread recourse to the Holocaust as a point of reference for September 11, investigating the convergence of two pre-existing cultural discourses in the American public sphere: the 'Americanisation' of the Holocaust in memorial culture from the early 1990s, and the mobilisation of the Holocaust in support of US military intervention in foreign policy rhetoric in the post-Cold War period. Contrary to recent critical attempts to construct ethical paradigms of transcultural memory, in these discourses recourse to Holocaust memory paradoxically results in a renationalisation of American memorial culture and a corresponding reassertion of American exceptionalism. In the decade since September 11, the pre-eminence of the Holocaust has ensured that certain memorial constellations have been ignored and the traces of their paths erased in favour of less problematic acts of historical analogy. Accordingly, I suggest that it is not always the most visible points of connection that offer the potential for ethical modes of remembrance, but the hidden histories, the forgotten memories, whose relationship to 9/11 presents the most important claims to attention.

3.1 The transcultural turn

The most seminal development within memory studies in recent years has been 'the transcultural turn' (Bond and Rapson 2014). Following the work of Daniel Levy and Natan Sznaider (2006), Michael Rothberg (2009a), and Astrid Erll (2011b) among others, this movement sees attention shift from sites of memory towards a focus on the dynamics by which it is articulated. As Frank Schulze-Engler has argued, 'in the wake of previous concepts in cultural and literary studies such as creolisation, hybridity and synchretism, and signalling a family relationship with terms such as transnationality, translocality, and transmigration, "transcultural" terminology has unobtrusively, but powerfully, edged its way into contemporary theoretical and critical discourse' (Schulze-Engler 2009, ix). Wolfgang Welsch describes transculturality as 'the most adequate concept of culture today – for both descriptive and normative reasons' (Welsch 1999, 194). Arguing against an outmoded 'unificatory' model of national (or 'container') cultures premised upon 'social homogenisation, ethnic consolidation and intercultural delimitation' (Welsch 1999, 914), Welsch contends that contemporary life (in its local, national, and global dimensions) is 'characterised by mixes and permeations' (Welsch 1999, 196) that result in a 'multi-meshed and inclusive, not separatist and exclusive understanding of culture' (Welsch 1999, 200).

The notion of transculturalism may be used to characterise exchanges that take place *within* national, religious, or ethnic collectives and *across* different communities, as well as those that attempt to *transcend* any notion of discrete cultural entities. Recent conceptualisations of transcultural memory consider both the critical and the cultural implications of processes of remembrance that create new forms and forums of commemoration *between* and *beyond* the borders of the nation-state. Levy and Sznaider point to the emergence of *cosmopolitan* modes of memory in which local, national, and global cultures of commemoration exist in dynamic and dialogic negotiation. They argue that 'national and ethnic memories are transformed in the age of globalisation rather than erased. [. . .] They begin to develop in accordance with common rhythms and periodisations. But in each case, the common elements combine with pre-existing elements to form something new' (Levy and Sznaider 2006, 3). Maintaining this attention to the dialectical aspects of remembrance, Rothberg suggests that we consider 'the public sphere as a malleable, discursive space in which groups do not simply articulate established positions but actually come into being through their dialogical interactions with others' (Rothberg 2009a, 3.). In so doing, he positions 'memory as *multidirectional*: as subject to ongoing negotiation, cross-referencing, and borrowing; as productive and not privative' (Rothberg 2009a, 3). A similar contention informs Erll's work on *travelling* memory, which analyses 'the incessant wandering of carriers, media, contents, forms, and practices of memory, their continual "travels" and ongoing transformations through time and space, across social, linguistic and political borders' (Erll 2011b, 11).

Despite the undoubted ethical potential of such ideas, exponents of transculturalism have not always been sufficiently alert to the important differences between the 'ideal' and the 'real' attributes of memory (that is, between the optimistic paradigms of memory outlined in scholarly criticism, and the more problematic dynamics of material memorial culture). In the aftermath of 9/11, a number of theorists and practitioners have demonstrated a worrying lack of regard to the way in which transcultural frames of memory have become imbricated with the phenomenon Terri Tomsky (2011) describes as the 'trauma economy'. Noting trauma's use 'as transcultural capital and commodity' (Tomsky 2011, 53), Tomsky defines the trauma economy as 'a circuit of movement and exchange where traumatic memories "travel" and are valued and revalued along the way' (Tomsky 2011, 49), mediated by 'economic, cultural, discursive and political structures that guide, enable and ultimately institutionalise the representation, travel and attention to certain traumas' (Tomsky 2011, 53). These traumas include the Holocaust and, increasingly, (as Tomsky herself makes explicit) 9/11 – atrocities that have acquired hegemonic capital through their cultural visibility, political impact, and social, ideological, or even economic, weighting.

A. Dirk Moses describes such discourses as assuming a 'phallic' relation to traumatic loss, arguing:

> [i]n the wake of the so-called 'war on terror' after September 11 2001 in particular, the debate about empire, colony, and genocide is marked by a phallic logic. Commentators shout, 'my trauma is bigger than yours' in order to defend or attack the theodicy that the brutal extermination and disappearance of peoples is redeemed by human progress in the form of the Western dominated global system of nation-states (Moses 2008, 6).

Moses maintains, (for better or for worse) that '[t]raumatic memory is necessarily analogical: we did not just suffer; we suffered like this or that, or we suffered more than or differently from them. Even claims to unique suffering are implicitly comparative, that is, transcultural' (Moses and Rothberg 2014, 29). He continues, '[w]ithout analogues, it is difficult to successfully bid for recognition, because the common sense of a public sphere will ascribe significance to certain types of suffering and not to others' (Moses and Rothberg 2014, 29). Thus, Moses highlights the more problematic aspects of comparative memory. In so doing, he raises a series of questions that will prove central to the discussion that follows: if we accept that traumatic memory is *necessarily* analogical, does this mean that *all* forms of transcultural memory are analogical or, conversely, that every mode of analogy is inherently transcultural? If so, how do we prevent the ethical visions of transculturalism outlined above from collapsing back into the highly politicised, 'zero-sum' model of memory (to use Rothberg's terminology) identified by Tomsky and Moses? Aligning the process of analogisation with the theodicy of progress described by Moses, Jay Bergman suggests that analogical frames generate inherently hegemonic representations of the past, commenting:

> the misuse of historical analogy, at least in the West, may be an unfortunate consequence of the tendency of Western Civilisation, traceable ultimately to its origins in Judaism and Christianity, to consider history a linear and meaningful process in which historical events are thought to be appropriate for analogies with others by virtue of their all being part of a larger and unifying development or design (Bergman 1987, 98).

Bergman implies that, through its articulation in analogical frameworks, memory is oriented in a teleological direction that assumes a futural and eternalising aspect. In this sense, the temporality adopted by analogy may be read as peculiarly ahistorical, equating rather than differentiating discrete occurrences. As Elliot Zashin and Phillip C. Chapman contend:

> What analogies do, essentially, is offer those to whom they are proposed a ready-made conceptual organisation for something unfamiliar or problematic. They do this by suggesting that the object of concern is 'isometric' or parallel with or similar in relevant respects to something else which is familiar, well-understood and uncontroversial (Zashin and Chapman 1974, 312).

A form oriented towards generating 'abstract categories and relationships' (Zashin and Chapman 1974, 299), analogy aims towards the occlusion of difference; it is dedicated to the production (or at least pretence) of sameness. As analogical frames of memory are generally oriented towards constructing similarities between diverse experiences and events, this can lead to the negation of the important specificities that render such occurrences part of a homogenised (national) past rather than constitutive elements of a heterogeneous transcultural narrative.

Bergman suggests that 'historical analogies, especially inappropriate ones, can often obscure more than they clarify, particularly when the object of one's analysis [. . .] proves to be far more rooted in a nation's history and culture than any transnational comparison or analogy might suggest' (Bergman 1987, 73). Thus, just as all examples of transcultural memory do not necessarily assume analogical form, so all examples of analogical memory are not ultimately (perhaps despite superficial appearances) transcultural in perspective.[1] Although Erll (following Welsch) argues that transculturalism should manifest a turn towards the other, I contend that, in some instances, this apparent outwardness can in fact mask a turn *against* the other (or at least, a turn *away* from the other). This understanding pre-empts a crucial aspect of the deployment of analogy in American memorial culture after 9/11: a commemorative environment in which transcultural reference often serves as a mask for resurgent nationalism.

3.2 The analogical impulse after 9/11

It may seem surprising that an event that has been as enduringly exceptionalised as 9/11 should have been widely positioned within comparative frames of memory, yet, over the past thirteen years, practitioners and theorists have recurrently sought analogical equivalents for the attacks. In the immediate aftermath of September 11, the apparent inability to situate 9/11 within any readily available interpretative framework (analysed in Chapter 1) seems to have triggered an instinctive recourse to historical reference. As David W. Blight records, 'we searched desperately for analogies, for moments of recognition from our past. [. . .] Where could we find markers in our historical memory to help this make sense?' (Blight 2011, 93). Writing shortly after the event, Richard Powers recalls:

> when the first, stunted descriptions came, they came in a flood of simile. The shock of the attack was like Pearl Harbor. The gutted financial district was like Nagasaki. Lower Manhattan was like a city after an earthquake. The gray people streaming northward up the island covered in an inch of ash were like the buried at Pompeii (Powers 2001).

Powers implies that such analogies were seized upon because of their availability in the absence of any more suitable mode of representation. He concedes that the resulting 'failed similes' were at once consolatory and 'anemic' [sic] (Powers 2001), substituting a pre-digested past for the unexplained present. However, the speed with which such analogies could be conjured, and the recurrence of certain points of reference (Pearl Harbor, Hiroshima, Nagasaki, the Holocaust), suggests that some events have become metonyms of atrocity: understood as universal symbols for disaster rather than complex historical occurrences, utilised to stabilise – and to some extent standardise – the narrative of 9/11.

Such associative dynamics are familiar characteristics of contemporary memorial practice. Over the past half-century, the recurrence of certain rituals and devices has contributed to the emergence of a distinct lexicon of commemoration – behaviours that are transferred from event to event, constructing a recognisable (though of course, far from exhaustive) chronicle of responses to atrocity. Memorial museums in particular tend to draw heavily upon analogical frames of memory, illustrating the potency of their subject through reference to other atrocities. In the move away from linear, narrative-based exposition towards more affective styles of curation, the haptic dynamics of such spaces (of which the Oklahoma City National Museum, the National September 11 Museum, and the United States Holocaust Memorial Museum are prominent American examples) are replicated across institutions. Accordingly, Paul Williams concludes, '[s]ome standardisation in the symbolisation of atrocity has emerged' (Williams 2007, 94–5). Museums not only rely upon similar curatorial devices ('reality effects' such as 'architectural styles that pointedly show the authenticity of the space [. . .], glass walls that display archaeological finds, stage-set like scenes, and the use of personal testimony' [Williams 2007, 97]), but frequently frame their histories within identical series of tropes.

Such techniques are exemplified by the curatorial strategies of the Center for Empowered Living and Learning in Denver, Colorado. Located in Denver's downtown museum quarter (opposite the extension to the Denver Art Museum designed by Studio Daniel Libeskind), the centre's institutional base is known as the CELL (the Counterterrorism Education Learning Lab). Formulated around a permanent exhibition entitled 'Anyone, Anytime, Anywhere – Understanding the Threat of Terrorism', the CELL contends that '[t]errorism knows no boundaries' (CELL 2011). Rather than positioning acts of terrorism as historical events with particular causes and consequences (some of which – like 9/11, 7/7, the Madrid bombings, and other atrocities committed by the diverse divisions of al Qaeda before and after 2001 – are, of course, related), the museum renders it an omnipresent, cellular force that moves unpredictably from target to target. A sign in the entrance lobby outlines its mission to 'remember all those who have been affected by terrorist attacks across the world, and pay tribute to their lives by educating others about the devastating impact of terrorism'. This remit has two important effects: firstly, it positions 'terrorism' as an undifferentiated pan-global phenomenon; secondly, it suggests that the centre's intent is not to educate the public about the contexts of different terrorist atrocities, but about the emotional impact of their aftermath. In other words, CELL's emphasis is upon the traumatic – rather than the historical – dimensions of terrorism. The centre's curation is correspondingly affective and makes consistent use of emotively deployed music and other audio-visual effects. In the entrance hall, visitors are met by 'Faces of Terror': portraits of victims, accompanied by a scrolling list of names and haunting music. In the lobby, more names are depicted around a cracked screen, which states, '[t]errorism shatters . . . friendships, marriages, families, hopes, dreams. Terrorism shatters lives'.[2] These two displays provide an introduction to a decontextualised approach to the phenomenon of terrorism, in which the specificity of victimhood is effaced as historicity is replaced by reliance upon special effects designed to generate instinctual emotional responses. An introductory video, accompanied by threatening music and sirens, provides a montage of (principally domestic) 'terrorism' from the religious wars of the seventeenth century to the Ku Klux Klan, anti-Vietnam protests, Lockerbie, the Oklahoma City bombing, and al Qaeda's twenty-first-century attacks on New York, Madrid, and London. Whilst the attempt to contextualise 9/11 within a broader span of terroristic activities is welcome, the brevity with which these events are attended to, and the speed with which different images are presented, replicates the universalisation of terrorism inherent in the exhibit's slogan.

This perspective is reinforced by the following display, an interactive encounter that places the visitor in the position of vicarious witness or victim. Enclosed in a small capsule, the visitor is surrounded by a 360-degree projection of a video entitled '[i]t was just an ordinary day'. The footage situates the visitor in the museum plaza outside the CELL. Everything is idyllic; it is a sunny day, people are laughing, and birds are singing. Suddenly, there is a loud explosion and the room goes dark. Following the 'explosion', the disoriented visitor is bombarded with pictures from the aftermaths of various terrorist atrocities. Whilst it is possible to identify some of the more recognisable events (most notably 9/11), the repetition of certain features (screaming, sirens, police cars, bloodied pavements, dust, dazed witnesses, covered corpses) means that the occurrences are largely interchangeable.

This associative technique deterritorialises the historical events depicted on the video, even as they are relocalised in an imagined future in which the city of Denver finds itself besieged by the invisible terroristic forces apparently circulating in the contemporary world. It is unclear what pedagogical function such exhibits are intended to serve – beyond a generalised affective response that engenders a sense of paranoia.[3] The CELL ends with an exhibit entitled 'What Can You Do? What Will You Do?' in which an address from the mayor of Denver reminds visitors to look out for the 'eight signs of terrorism'. Whilst the attempt to encourage 'vigilance' may appear reasonable, the symptoms identified are too general to be of any practical assistance. Visitors are told to do their duty as citizens, follow their 'gut instinct', and report anything that seems out of place, on the understanding that 'all threats are local' and 'there is a great risk around us'. Although the mayor insists that we need to understand 'who [terrorists] are and what they are trying to do', the vagueness of these suggestions makes this almost impossible. Terrorism is no more explicable for the work of the museum; it is rather presented as a generalised phenomenon that recurs, virally, throughout history (presenting a rather ironic conceptual analogy with the contagious reading of trauma analysed in Chapter 1, through which both terrorism and trauma are rendered ahistorical phenomena with no specific causation).

In a study of museum exhibits relating to 9/11, Jeffrey D. Feldman contends that such forms of contextual collapse make it 'difficult to distinguish between the synergy of commemorating one tragedy in reference to another, and the hegemony of one set of representational practices over another' (Feldman 2003, 843), arguing, in particular, that 'museum representations of September 11 have exhibited a "tyranny of usage" [. . .] at work in the commemoration of tragedy wherein the content of a specific tragedy has been expressed through structures and principles of expression emergent from previous memorial concerns' (Feldman 2003, 839). Feldman analyses three exhibitions curated on the first anniversary of 9/11 by American memorial museums: the Oklahoma City National Museum (OCNM); the Museum of Jewish Heritage in New York; and the United States Holocaust Memorial Museum in Washington, DC (USHMM).

The OCNM exhibition, entitled *A Shared Experience: 04.19.95 – 09.11.01*, draws similarities between the Oklahoma City bombing of 1995 and the events of 9/11. This is not an especially difficult task given their relative proximity in time and location, the character of the two events, and the similarity in cultural and media responses to these atrocities. In its depiction of the Oklahoma bombing, the OCNM evokes the tropes that dominated the American public sphere in the aftermath of

9/11, emphasising: *rupture* (a stopped clock details the moment of the bombing, a recording of the explosion shocks the visitor in a darkened room. The museum guide documents how '[w]atches and clocks lose their pulse. Time stops. Chaos begins.' [Clark 2006]); *incomprehensibility* (a 'day like any other' gives way to 'confusion' to 'chaos'); *heroism* (the bravery of rescuers, images of firefighters and fire trucks draped in the American flag); *unity* (the spirit of volunteerism – described as 'the Oklahoma standard' [Clark 2006]); and *redemption* (the guidebook claims, 'a healing tide soon rolled over the wounds. Emotional cuts were stitched with threads of t-shirts left by visitors throughout the nation, salved with the lineament of compassion and bandaged in the serenity of the three-acre tribute [the memorial adjacent to the museum]' [Clark 2006]).[4]

Synthesising the frames of memory outlined in the previous chapters, the OCNM seeks to conscript both atrocities into the pre-existing culture of American calamity by transforming trauma into triumph. As 'shared experience' the two attacks are drawn into a familiar parable of Americanism. Feldman expands:

> the exhibition seeks to define September 11 through a common language and symbolism of American suffering caused by attacks on mainland soil, as well as the heroism of the rescue and recovery following these attacks. Looking at different objects while seeing similar wounds is the key to finding moral and spiritual lessons in the resilience of the American people (Feldman 2003, 841).

The OCNM exhibition thus manifests an attempt to *reterritorialise* September 11 and the Oklahoma City bombing as national parables. This process simultaneously *delocalises* the events, co-opting them into a single, analogous entity, and eclipses the important differences between them in its insistent Americanisation (there is, for instance, little acknowledgement that, whilst the actions of Timothy McVeigh had a predominantly domestic impact, al Qaeda's attacks on Washington and New York induced significant geopolitical consequences).

Together, the practices of the CELL and the OCNM reveal two problematic effects of associative modes of memory in contemporary museum practice: firstly, in the case of the CELL, the tendency to dehistoricise (even universalise) the events under discussion, negating important specificities in their causes, consequences, and character; secondly, in the example of the OCNM, the impulse to nationalise the events portrayed in American memorial culture, marginalising their local and global implications. However, the commemoration of 9/11 has revealed a third, and potentially more worrying, upshot of analogisation that has defined, and perhaps impelled, the pervasive mobilisation of comparative memory in political rhetoric over the past thirteen years. In the aftermath of the attacks, analogical paradigms have been used to structure highly polarised debates about inclusion and exclusion. Seeking to delimit those with the right to access the nation's sacred spaces, these discourses have been neither inclusive nor empathic, attempting to close down, rather than open up, participation in the life of the nation.

Such trends are exemplified by the controversy that has surrounded Park 51, an Islamic cultural centre close to Ground Zero whose development has now stalled indefinitely. Provision for a prayer space within this fifteen-storey complex has contributed to it being widely – at times, undoubtedly, deliberately – misrepresented as a mosque. Whilst a small activist group, Stop Islamization of America, initially led the protests surrounding the development of Park 51, they acquired a heightened political dimension when they received support from prominent Republicans including Newton Gingrich, Sarah Palin, and Rudolph Giuliani. The debate has centred upon the centre's proximity to the 'hallowed' territory of Ground Zero. Charles Krauthammer frames his discussion of Park 51 by positioning Ground Zero in a global topography of sacred landscapes including Lourdes, Gettysburg, and Auschwitz: disparate parallels that he invokes to justify his opposition to the centre. Both Krauthammer and Gingrich construct their arguments with reference to the Holocaust, suggesting a misleading equivalence between the Islamic faith and the Nazi party. Krauthammer argues that 'despite contemporary Germany's innocence, no German of goodwill would even think about proposing a German cultural center at, say, Treblinka' (Krauthammer 2010); whilst Gingrich alleges that approving the cultural centre 'would be like putting a Nazi sign next to the Holocaust museum' (Wyatt 2010).

The analogies deployed by Krauthammer and Gingrich reflect a pre-existing conception of the Holocaust as the '"gold standard" in the Western memory regime' (Rothberg and Moses 2014, 29). Given the centrality of the Holocaust to critical and cultural attempts to think about remembrance, it is perhaps unsurprising that theorists should foreground the ethical potential of the genocide as a cornerstone of transcultural memory. Levy and Sznaider contend that the Holocaust offers 'the foundations for a new cosmopolitan memory [. . .] that harbours the possibility of transcending ethnic and national boundaries' (Levy and Sznaider 2006, 4), providing 'the cultural foundation for global human-rights dynamics' (Levy and Sznaider 2006, 4). Rothberg similarly asserts that 'the emergence of Holocaust memory on a global scale has contributed to the articulation of other histories' (Rothberg 2009a, 6). However, the comparisons made between the post-9/11 cultural landscape and the memorialisation of the Holocaust in the context of Park 51 cannot be thought of in Rothberg's terms, as 'producing new objects and new lines of sight – and not simply as reproducing already given entities that either are or are not "like" other already given entities' (Rothberg 2009a, 18–19). Whilst Rothberg rightly argues that '[t]oo often comparison is understood as "equation"' (Rothberg 2009a, 18) in relation to associative frames of memory, I suggest that in the context of 9/11, certain analogous narratives deliberately *equate* the attacks with the Holocaust, negating differences in scale, cause, or consequence. This at once reproduces September 11 as an 'already given entity' (by casting it in the likeness of earlier events) and facilitates its designation as exceptional.

Such constructions reveal that there is clearly political capital to be gained from perpetuating what Richard Cohen describes as the 'false analogy contests' surrounding 9/11 (Cohen 2010). Cohen argues that such 'specious' comparisons 'pollute this debate', indicting the 'hunt for the perfect analogy' on the grounds that it has a tendency to 'go from the particular to the general – to blame a people for the acts of a few' (Cohen 2010). Such tendencies derive from an unreflexive deployment of analogical frames of memory that attempts to mask the negation of historical difference, the sacralising or nationalising properties of such paradigms, and the exclusionary or polarising intent of these models.

3.3 American Holocaust memory after 9/11

Allen Meek argues (after Moshe Zuckerman) that, in contemporary memorial practice, the 'actual memory of the Holocaust has been replaced by a cultural code – continually reinforced by images, rituals, monuments, which effectively represses historical reality from conscious understandings' (Meek 2010, 178). Viewed positively, the 'Holocaust code' establishes a memorial syntax that enables individuals and collectives to encounter unfamiliar events through pre-absorbed frames of memory. However, as intimated above, such practices can mask a dehistoricising epistemology that empties events of all particularity, facilitating the appropriation of the Holocaust as a floating signifier that can be mobilised to serve multiple agendas. As the following section will suggest, in the United States, the Holocaust code has most frequently been deployed to serve (implicitly or explicitly) nationalising agendas. Against Levy and Sznaider's interpretation of the Holocaust as a 'decontextualised event oriented toward nation-transcending symbols and meaning systems' (Levy and Sznaider 2006, 5), Efraim Sicher argues that, in the United States, 'the Holocaust [has] entered popular culture as an American experience' (Sicher 2000, 56).

An established critical literature draws attention to the 'Americanisation' of the Holocaust over the past twenty years. This movement can be loosely traced to the convergence of several developments that heightened the profile of the genocide in US culture from 1993 onwards: the opening of the United States Holocaust Memorial Museum (USHMM); the release of Stephen Spielberg's *Schindler's List*; the media coverage of the war in Bosnia; renewed efforts to position the Holocaust as the touchstone of Jewish American identity; and rising critical interest in the atrocity.[5] The process of 'Americanisation' is heavily reliant upon the two discourses critiqued in Chapters 1 and 2: firstly, the overextension of trauma into a generalised culture of victimhood that encourages unproblematic identification between witnesses and victims; secondly, the conscription of this trauma culture into the nationalistic culture of calamity.

Both of these tendencies can be seen in the curatorial strategies of the USHMM, which critics have long positioned as a quintessential example of Americanised Holocaust memory.[6] Philip Gourevitch argues that the USHMM reinforces the 'centrality of victimology in contemporary American identity politics' (Gourevitch 1993, 62). Critiquing 'identification mechanisms' (Caplan 2000, 161) such as the allocation of identity cards from Holocaust victims to each visitor and the universalising themes inherent in the displays, many theorists suggest that the museum encourages visitors to 'experience themselves as Holocaust victims' (Kugelmass 1996, 202), reinforcing both the 'culture of victimisation' (Novick 1999, 189) analysed in Chapter 1 and the 'pornographic' approach to grief critiqued in Chapter 2.[7] Accordingly, Carolyn J. Dean argues, 'the sacrosanct status of the Holocaust in American life' (Dean 2003, 106) has facilitated the development of uncritical practices that 'violate the dignity of memory by decontextualising the historical event' (Dean 2003, 102). However, other commentators contend that the USHMM offers not so much a decontextualisation of the Holocaust, but a *re*contextualisation of its history on American soil.

The museum's location on Washington's official memory terrain underscores the Americanisation of its subject, positioning the Holocaust in comparative relation to the other events commemorated (or more importantly, not represented) on the National Mall.[8] In so doing, it implicitly, and somewhat paradoxically, encourages both an analogical and a competitive approach to memory. James Young draws attention to the way in which its inscription into national memorial culture has established the Holocaust as the exceptional example of historical atrocity. He asserts, 'putting the memorial museum on the Mall has not only Americanised the Holocaust but has also set a new national standard for suffering. After seeing the Holocaust memorialised on the Mall, visitors may begin to view it less as an actual historical event and more as an idea of catastrophe against which all other past and future destructions might be measured' (Young 1999, 74). Young argues that the USHMM 'enshrines, by dint of its placement, not just the history of the Holocaust but American democratic and egalitarian ideals as they counterpoint the Holocaust [. . .], it encourages Americans to recall their nation's own idealised reason for being' (Young 1999, 72). As Rothberg asserts, the exhibits of the USHMM attempt to 'shift the terrain of the Holocaust into an American imaginative space/time peopled by victims/survivors and heroes/liberators' (Rothberg 2000, 184).

The mobilisation of the Holocaust in American memorial culture after 9/11 typifies both of the trends outlined above: facilitating dehistoricising modes of identification that encourage Americans to equate themselves with Holocaust victims; and appropriating the narrative of the Holocaust as a means of reinforcing the myth of national exceptionalism. At times these discourses have appeared mutually reinforcing, engendering a strange dialectic of trauma and triumphalism. Whilst the Holocaust has long been assimilated into the hegemonic memorial culture of the United States, its ubiquity as a point of analogy for the attacks testifies to the extent to which some practitioners continue to deny its ideological loading (even as others capitalise upon it). The events of September 11 have engendered widespread comparisons with the Holocaust across cultural and critical discourses, demonstrating the genocide's position as contemporary master-trauma and the extent to which its tropes present a readily recognisable lexicon of atrocity.

In an analysis of comments left in the visitors' book of the USHMM after September 11, Michael Bernard-Donals notes that, for many visitors, it seemed 'as if the images in the museum were mnemonics for the images of the destruction of New York and Washington' (Bernard-Donals 2005, 84). He suggests that this dehistoricisation was enabled by the USHMM's ongoing attempt to reterritorialise the Holocaust as an American event, a consequence of a curatorial process that '[i]ntends visitors to understand the Holocaust (a difficult event to experience even for second-hand visitors) in terms of other events more clearly understood in distinctly American terms' (Bernard-Donals 2005, 78). As Bernard-Donals remarks, the decontextualisation involved in the analogisation of the Holocaust and 9/11 denies the historicity of both events. Accordingly:

> what happened at the Holocaust Museum after 9/11 [. . .] emptied each of them of their historical particularity, and inside of each lay an empty shell. The museum visitors filled that void with an immediate (or perhaps a future) memory: a collective memory of atrocity unconnected to a place and a name (Bernard-Donals 2005, 79).

Feldman identifies a similar mode of historical conflation in the USHMM's Day of Reflection and Remembrance, which took place on the first anniversary of the attacks. This ceremony brought Holocaust survivors together to read the names of the victims killed on September 11 in the museum's Hall of Witness. In taking the decision to have Holocaust survivors (rather than 9/11 survivors) speak the victims' names, the USHMM forged a complex connection between the two events: firstly, commemorating the dead in a ritual specifically associated with the Holocaust; secondly, reinscribing this practice within the canon of responses to American tragedy; and thirdly, framing the memory of 9/11 within the explicit discourses of survivor and victim utilised by the USHMM. Although undoubtedly planned with empathic intentions, the Day of Reflection and Remembrance simultaneously attempted to illuminate 9/11 by reference to the Holocaust (problematically cancelling out distinctions between the two) and to invoke 9/11 in the process of redesignating the Holocaust as an American tragedy. As Feldman argues, 'by associating the victims of September 11 with the testimony of Holocaust survivors, the victims of the more recent tragedy enter into the moral economy of global tragedy as defined by the museum. September 11 and the Holocaust, whilst numerically dissonant, are culturally classified as tragedies of similar order' (Feldman 2003, 842).

Literary narratives have utilised such comparisons to emphasise the horror of 9/11: Shirley Abbott's protagonist describes the attacks as 'the Holocaust', 'an end to order' (Abbott 2008, 154); in Helen Schulman's *A Day at the Beach*, Gerhard Falktopf recoils from 'this catastrophe, this holocaust' (Schulman 2007, 93–4). Some texts make more specific comparisons: an elderly Polish character in Dina Friedman's *Playing Dad's Song* compares the disruption evidenced after the attacks to his life in a Jewish ghetto under the Nazis (Friedman 2006, 69); in *Bullyville,*

Francine Prose's protagonist likens the communality of post-9/11 New Yorkers to the illusory comfort displayed for Red Cross inspectors in the Nazi ghetto of Theresienstadt (Prose 2007, 55). This recourse to the Jewish victimhood as a precursor to American experience is widely seen across the corpus of 9/11 trauma fiction analysed in Chapter 1. The texts of Abbott, Eisenberg, Friedman, Prose, and Nissenson feature characters of Jewish or European extraction marked by the events of the Nazi genocide (Schulman's Suzannah Falktopf, a Polish Jew from the Bronx, goes so far as to describe herself as 'a Yiddische maideleh with her very own stormtrooper' [Schulman 2007, 66]). Populating the post-9/11 landscape with figures inherited from the Holocaust in this manner risks effacing the particularity of the very events and experiences that these novels seek to invoke, emptying both the past and present of specificity.

This tendency is perhaps most evident in Hugh Nissenson's novel *the days of awe* – a text set in New York's Upper West Side where, Nissenson intimates, Jewish identity is defined by a sense of victimhood (as one character remarks, '"I'm a Jew because of the Holocaust and Israel"' [Nissenson 2005, 79]). In the aftermath of 9/11, images traditionally associated with the Holocaust come to define the urban environment. Partaking of the communal ablutions traditional before the Jewish festival of Rosh Hashanah, the Rabbi Klugman comments: '[a] bunch of bearded Jews taking showers together creeps me out. Can't help thinking: gas chamber' (Nissenson 2005, 189). During the ceremony, Nissenson's protagonist, Artie, watches a girl with 'sad Jewish eyes and her mother's small chin. The kid looked something like Anne Frank' (Nissenson 2005, 192). The novel constructs a continuum of private and public loss as the global histories of the Holocaust, the Gaza strip, and 9/11 overlap with cancer, heart attacks, and Alzheimer's. The narrative jumps abruptly between examples of suffering, often without a sentence of transition. Little distinction is made between traumas: bombings in Israel are compared to Auschwitz (Nissenson 2005, 48); cancer patients likened to Holocaust victims (Nissenson 2005, 28); both the city of Jerusalem and cemeteries in Queens (NY) linked to Odin's Land of the Dead (Nissenson 2005, 57, 108).

Nissenson portrays 9/11 as a catalyst that dislocates certain memories from the communities in which they have hitherto been contained; ghosts crowd the city, cloaking New York in the guise of earlier events. The travelling of these memories is enabled by the fragmented, free-flowing nature of the prose. It is often impossible to attribute the narrative to any one character, leading to the sense that everyone is filled with grief, everybody traumatised by the totality of a history of destruction they may or may not have experienced. Nissenson thus constructs history-*as*-trauma along the lines suggested by Cathy Caruth (outlined in Chapter 1). His characters struggle to confront 'the destructive force that the violence of history imposes on the human psyche, the formation of history as the endless repetition of previous violence' (Caruth 1996, 63). History has become a chronicle of crisis, inexplicable to those 'dropping for a while from eternity into time' (Nissenson 2005, 268). This violent history is dominated by the figure of the Holocaust, which is at once the symbol and the nadir of the myriad sufferings depicted throughout the text.

Nissenson portrays the Holocaust as the axis around which all memory revolves – coming back again and again to its image, transforming the genocide into the originary event to which Jewish identity defaults. Whilst his characters appear to address the genocide explicitly, they tend to engage with it obliquely – by allusion, through habit, without engaging with its reality. Accordingly, Nissenson reflects Caruth's contention that 'Jewish historical memory [. . .] is always a matter of distortion, a filtering of the original event through the fictions of traumatic repression, which makes the event available at best indirectly' (Caruth 1996, 15–16). Caruth connects the individual experience of trauma to 'the collective, transgenerational, and religious history' (Caruth 1996, 67) of the Jewish people. Following Freud, she argues that the history of the Jews 'can be explained through the occurrence of a traumatic event, the murder of Moses during his return of the Hebrews from Egypt to Canaan' (Caruth 1996, 67). The trauma arose from the failure of the Jewish people to fully claim this history as their own, and thus to a rupture in the passing on of the monotheistic tradition as Judaism survived – almost despite itself – following the murder of the original Moses. Attributing this survival to God's choice of the Jewish people as his followers, Caruth suggests that 'Jewish monotheism, as the sense of chosenness, thus defines Jewish history around the link between survival and a traumatic history that exceeds their grasp' (Caruth 1996, 67). Caruth links this sense of chosenness directly to the discourse of trauma, arguing that 'the structure of monotheism – the emergence, after the return of the repressed murder of Moses of the sense of being incomprehensibly chosen by God to survive – is very similar in certain respects to the curious nature of the survival of trauma' (Caruth 1996, 68). Thus, she contends, if '[t]he history of chosenness, as the history of survival, [. . .] takes the form of an unending confrontation with the returning violence of the past' (Caruth 1996, 69), this history raises the important question '[w]*hat does it mean to be chosen?*' (Caruth 1996, 68).

This question reverberates throughout Nissenson's text, and lies at the heart of his coupling of Jewish history and American culture, the Holocaust and 9/11. In an interview included at the end of the novel, Nissenson comments that America 'continues to be deeply influenced by the Jewish Bible and its messianic message. Americans from the very beginning have seen themselves as the Chosen People' (Nissenson 2005, 298). Here, Nissenson explicitly links the Jewish history of chosenness and trauma to the discourse of American exceptionalism. He describes his writing as 'haunted by the Holocaust, about Jewish experience in Europe, Israel, and the United States' (Nissenson 2005, 300), but also the work of an 'American patriot, in love with our country's history' (Nissenson 2005, 298). Both Caruth and Nissenson thus *build exceptionalism into the very structure of trauma*, even as they – paradoxically – generalise the pathology. However, there are important differences between Caruth's narrative of Jewish chosenness and the discourse of American exceptionalism.

Caruth conceptualises chosenness as the structure of Jewish historical experience, yet argues that this history becomes traumatic because 'the sense of being chosen is precisely *what cannot be grasped* in the Jewish past, the way in which its past has imposed itself upon it *as* a history that it survives but does not fully understand' (Caruth 1996, 68). Conversely, as the previous chapter aimed to illustrate, the rhetoric of American exceptionalism has traditionally been relied upon to frame historical experience and make it comprehensible. Unlike Jewish chosenness, therefore, American exceptionalism is a matter of conscious historical will. Whilst the chosenness of the Jewish people strips them of historical agency, American exceptionalism presents history as a narrative of man's making, there for the nation's taking. In so doing, it elides the traumatic structure of experience that Caruth assigns to the Jewish people.

Against a Jewish history defined by unbridgeable rupture, there is, ostensibly, no need for a belated reckoning with an American mythology that facilitates the continual assimilation of experience into a teleological historical narrative. However, as we have seen, the events of 9/11 appeared to pose a challenge to the nation's ability to control its own destiny. This challenge has been represented by many authors (Nissenson among them) as temporarily projecting Americans into the helpless position historically (or at least, symbolically) occupied by a Jewish people allegedly unable to master their own history. In turn, rather paradoxically, references to the Holocaust appear to have provided a means of rehoming the chronicle of American history. This rehabilitation has involved a bipartite process: firstly, the projection of Americans *as* Jews (the exemplary historical victim); secondly, the transformation of incomprehensible chosenness into national exceptionalism. As the Holocaust has been mobilised within the American culture of calamity, the convergence of the discourse of trauma explored in Chapter 1 with the triumphalist narratives explored in Chapter 2 has therefore seen the structure of Jewish historical experience outlined by Caruth approximate the form of the new American jeremiad.

Conscription into the chronicle of American history has engendered a remediation of the dominant frameworks in which the Holocaust has been represented. Whilst Holocaust remembrance has conventionally been stringently antiredemptive in thrust, much of its mobilisation after 9/11 has been determinedly affirmative.[9] The characters of Joyce Maynard's post-9/11 novel, *The Usual Rules*, transform Holocaust testimonies into redemptive narratives, describing Anne Frank as a 'tremendously hopeful, optimistic spirit' (Maynard 2003, 76), a 'comfort and inspiration for the heartbreaking times we're living in today', and lauding Elie Wiesel's *Night* (1982) for finding 'something hopeful and good' in 'the most unspeakable horror' (Maynard 2003, 359). In so doing, they convert the specific experiences of these individuals into parables for the American nation, distorting and negating this suffering even as they appear to bear witness to it. Such practices at once depersonalise and over-personalise memory, taking the specifics of one story as a blueprint for general experiences of suffering.

These tendencies can also be seen in the curatorial practices of the Ground Zero Museum Workshop in New York, which attempts to translate the memory of Anne Frank into a healing experience for post-9/11 America.[10] The museum is located in the former photographic studio of its director, Gary Suson, who claims that he was inspired to create this space after visiting the Anne Frank Museum (AFM) in Amsterdam in 2004. Suson remarks that, on his visit to Amsterdam:

> Anne and her story put a face on all the Holocaust victims within a very short period of time. I suddenly realised that as owner of the Ground Zero Recovery Collection [the photographs that Suson had taken at Ground Zero], I had a moral duty to erect a similar museum in New York City that would help people remember the fallen of September 11 (GZMW 2011).

There are a number of dubious elements to Suson's comparisons between the two museums. He equates the institutions on the basis of their intimate scale. However, unlike the AFM, the workshop possesses no site-specific properties and thus no claims to authenticity. Even more tenuously, in the recorded interpretation that accompanies the tour of the GZMW, Suson equates artefacts from Ground Zero with Anne Frank's diary. Comparing a fragment of American Airlines flight 11 (which hit the North Tower and is now part of the museum's display) with the original journal on the grounds that both are objects of trauma, he argues that 'the impact that Anne Frank's diary had on me is equal to the impact that this plane had on me. Both artifacts made everything very real for me in only a matter of seconds' (transcribed on visit to GZMW, April 2011).

There is, of course, little similarity between the testimony of a Holocaust victim and a piece of twenty-first-century technology brutally transformed into a horrific weapon, and Suson's commercialisation of the parallels to the AFM in marketing materials and pamphlets renders the GZMW a rather distasteful example of comparative memory practice (Dobnik 2005). His vision for the museum is reliant on the despecifying properties of analogical memory which, when appropriated, sentimentalised, and emptied of all specificity can be mobilised to transform a personal tragedy into a paradigm of collective redemption. Accordingly, the GZMW manifests an attempt to reterritorialise the memory of Anne Frank as a positive American experience. As Suson remarked in a 2005 interview, 'I felt, if I could create something that would have an effect on people similar to the one the Anne Frank museum had on me, it could help people connect more to 9/11. If you can't connect, you can't heal' (Dobnik 2005).[11]

A similarly redemptive intent can be seen in Libeskind's original master plan for Ground Zero.[12] A child of Holocaust survivors, who emigrated to America as a teenager, Libeskind directly attributes his design for Ground Zero to his background. Contrasting 'free' America to a corrupted and fallen Europe, Libeskind traces the inspiration for his master plan to his 'first sighting of the city skyline as the boat I was on steamed into New York Harbor in 1959' (Libeskind 2004, 16). This memory forms the centrepiece of his vision, both structurally and symbolically. Considering how to approach the redevelopment project, Libeskind remarks, 'I envisioned five towers – tall but not too tall – arranged by increasing height, so that they rose in a spiral with the same shape as the flame in Lady Liberty's torch. And the tallest, I had decided, should rise to 1,776 feet, to commemorate the Declaration of Independence, which brought democracy to the world' (Libeskind 2004, 48).

These allusions to the Statue of Liberty and the Declaration of Independence align Libeskind's design with the triumphalist national symbolic, facilitating the appropriation of the reconstruction of Ground Zero (and, by extension, 9/11) into the service of the wider political debates circulating in the aftermath of the attacks. As Philip Nobel argues, with the help of Libeskind's master plan, 'the site could be made to sing the same hymns of freedom that had been emanating from the White House since September 11' (Nobel 2005, 18). Such hymns were particularly useful in the spring of 2003 (when the result of the design competition was announced), ensuring that 'at the very moment White House rhetoric was so effectively eliding Saddam Hussein with the events of September 11, Libeskind served up a graphic talking point: a tower said to mean freedom, at the site where freedom was said to be attacked, on the eve of an invasion said to be freedom's defense' (Nobel 2005, 139–40).[13]

Together, the literary, museal, and architectural practices analysed above demonstrate how the uncritical use of analogical parallels may disguise crucial differences in the intention, transmission, and reception of commemorative media. Whilst the exhibits of the USHMM seek to generate empathic parallels between the Holocaust and the attacks (however uncritically and ahistorically), Nissenson's novel translates these connections into a parable of chosenness and exceptionalism. In turn, Suson's mobilisation of the story of Anne Frank as a template for the curation of the GZMW exemplifies the means by which the tenets of Americanised Holocaust memory may be appropriated into sentimental, and commercialised, parables of healing, whilst the nationalisation of these models inherent in Libeskind's master plan for Ground Zero, and the subsequent politicisation of his design, underscore the manner in which unreflexive commemorative processes can be exploited by the discourses of the public-political sphere in support of agendas they were not originally intended to affirm. However, as the final case study from the post-9/11 landscape of New York demonstrates, the practices of memorial institutions are, themselves, often informed by intrinsically ideological interests.

Located between Grand Central Station and the UN building on Manhattan's East Side, the stated mission of the Museum of Tolerance New York (MOTNY) is to 'challenge visitors to confront bigotry, and to understand the Holocaust in both historic and contemporary contexts' (MOTNY 2014). Owned by the Simon Wiesenthal Foundation, the MOTNY exists in partnership with the Museum of Tolerance in Los Angeles (opened in 1993, the same year as the USHMM) and the Jerusalem Museum of Tolerance (currently under construction). Unlike the Californian museum, the MOTNY is not principally a public institution, marketing itself as 'a professional development multi-media training facility targeting educators, law enforcement officials, and state/local government practitioners' (MOTNY 2014). As Wendy Brown contends, the MOTNY places the virtue of tolerance into the service of 'the construction and legitimation of a certain political positioning' that results from a 'preoccupation with the Holocaust and an investment in the unqualified defense of Israel' (Brown 2006, 108), coupled with an unfaltering interpretation of post-9/11 America as a bastion of freedom and democracy.

The displays in the museum rely upon the visitor's engagement with interactive exhibits, films, and quizzes, which positions 9/11 and the Holocaust as archetypal, and exceptional, moments of intolerance. This agenda is closely developed throughout the various exhibits, constructing a tightly controlled narrative that absolves the visitor of the need to pursue their own interpretation of either the past or the present.[14] Displays such as 'The Power of Words' replicate the binary logic of good and evil, contrasting faces of 'tolerance' (largely American – Martin Luther King, John F. Kennedy, Franklin Roosevelt) with figures of 'intolerance' (principally anti-Semitic or Islamic – Le Pen, bin Laden, Hitler). The exhibit constructs a scale of hate, which ends, as its most extreme examples, with 9/11 and the Holocaust. This strategy is repeated throughout the museum, which recurrently yokes these two atrocities together without explanation or nuance. Interactive displays such as 'Globalhate. com' chronicles hate groups around the world, privileging those whose agendas are explicitly anti-Semitic or anti-American. Videos such as 'In Our Time' offer an overview of intolerance since the Second World War, bookended by September 11 and the Holocaust. The video further links the histories of the two nations with the claim that Americans saved the world from 'racism, anti-Semitism and fascism', 'victors in a great moral crusade', which paved the way for the establishment of the promised state of Israel. The implicit message is that other events (Cambodia, Rwanda, Darfur) represent tangential examples of an intolerance whose main focus is Israel and the United States.

These dynamics are exemplified most clearly, and most problematically, by the 'Millennium Machine'. Presenting films on a series of key issues confronting the twenty-first century (terrorism, the exploitation of women and children, refugees, and political prisoners), this exhibit opens with a highly simplistic message that underscores the philosophy of the MOTNY, commenting, 'throughout time, people have had a choice between good and evil, knowledge or ignorance, tolerance or hatred, compassion or indifference'. The feature on terrorism begins with 9/11. The discussion then proceeds to connect the attacks to a series of other terroristic events in Israel, Britain, and elsewhere. The video does not draw any distinctions between these atrocities, but collapses them together as disparate examples of threats to tolerance.[15] Two examples escape this homogenisation: the first is 9/11, which is presented as the archetypal sign of terror, a moment of rupture that transformed daily life in the United States forever; the second is Israel, which, we are told, 'suffers more from terrorism and suicide bombing than any other nation' (Brown 2006, 123). As Brown contends, this claim is 'aimed at drawing post-9/11 American suffering and fear into identification and solidarity with Israel' (Brown 2006, 123) by positioning the former as the victim of the most spectacular and horrifying example of terrorism in the modern age, and the latter as the perpetual victim of ongoing and everyday terrorism.

At no point in the museum is there any acknowledgement of the fact that Israel's treatment of the Palestinian people may, in itself, be regarded as a form of aggression, injustice, or intolerance. Nor is there any discussion of the more problematic aspects of the War on Terror, or moments of American-perpetrated injustice – Abu Ghraib, Guantánamo, rendition – since 9/11. Instead, the MOTNY whitewashes these histories by framing them as battles against Islamic, anti-Semitic, anti-American intolerance. Such techniques clearly serve the interests of the Wiesenthal Center. The centre utilises the rhetoric of tolerance as a device to naturalise its political agendas. The MOTNY (and its partner institutions) present the centre as 'straightforwardly standing for justice against injustice, right against wrong, good against evil, tolerance and civility against terrorism, and not as a partisan player in a range of political conflicts, policy developments, and even wars' (Brown 2006, 124). Since 9/11, the Wiesenthal Center's politics have revolved around a bipartite agenda, which strongly resonates with the curatorial strategies of the MOTNY. Firstly, the centre is strongly pro-Israel, as its website states, 'The Simon Wiesenthal Center is a global Jewish human rights organisation that confronts anti-Semitism, hate and terrorism, promotes human rights and dignity, stands with Israel, defends the safety of Jews worldwide' (Simon Wiesenthal Center 2014).[16] Secondly, the centre has repeatedly backed the US invasions of Afghanistan and Iraq as a means of protecting Israel's interests in the Middle East.

In a 2001 press release, Rabbi Marvin Hier, dean and founder of the centre, praised George W. Bush's efforts in the War on Terror, arguing:

> This is a rare opportunity for America, and if President Bush does the right thing it will save tens of thousands of lives around the world.

But the fight against terrorism cannot be selective. We cannot distinguish between terrorists in Afghanistan and terrorists in the Middle East. There is no difference in the atrocities committed by Osama bin Laden and those committed by Hamas, Islamic Jihad, and Hezbollah (Hier 2001).

In recent years, these tenets have informed the centre's imbrication in contentious debates that belie its apparently tolerant principles. In 2010, Hier contributed to the discussion over Park 51 to declare his opposition for the Islamic community centre on the grounds that it would desecrate the memory of those who died on September 11, commenting:

> For 3000 families, the 9/11 site is . . . the site of one of the greatest atrocities ever committed in the United States, and it's a cemetery. And the opinion of the families should be paramount as to what should go near that site. Now having a fifteen-story mosque within 1600 feet of the site is at the very least insensitive (Zimmerman 2010).

Whilst Hier's remarks are notable for the way in which they connect the idea of a cemetery to the notion of sacred ground (analysed in Chapter 2), during the construction of the Museum of Tolerance in Jerusalem, designed by Frank Gehry, representatives of the centre displayed a markedly less sensitive attitude to preserving the memory of the dead.

The museum is being built on top of the Manila Cemetery, an historic Muslim burial ground that dates from the twelfth century. Despite widespread protests, thousands of gravestones have been destroyed in the construction. The centre's response to opposition has been somewhat dismissive. In a 2006 interview with NPR, its spokesman, Charles Levine, asserted:

> Jerusalem is not Pittsburgh. It's not San Diego. It is a 3,000-year-old city. And because of that almost any place that one begins building or excavating in the center of the city, one encounters archeological remains, artifacts, human remains, or whatever. And that's just the way it is (Gradstein 2006).

Such remarks, of course, contrast sharply with Hier's comments concerning the sanctity of Ground Zero. The disparity in the centre's attitude to these two sites suggests that the politics of memory are strongly inflected by what Judith Butler describes as the 'hierarchies of life' that dominate global affairs. Butler contends that, whilst 'certain lives will be highly protected, and the abrogation of their claims to sanctity will be sufficient to mobilise the forces of war. Other lives will not find such fast and furious support and will not even qualify as "grievable"' (Butler 2004, 32). Whilst the curation of the MOTNY implicitly demonstrates these ideas by elevating some examples of intolerance above others, the actions and agendas of the Simon Wiesenthal Center explicitly underscores the divergence between the value of Jewish and American lives (as manifested in the memory of the victims of the Holocaust and 9/11, and their ongoing support for Israel and the United States) and those of international Muslim communities (as evidenced by their opposition to Park 51, their failure to respect the sanctity of the Manila burial ground, and their refusal to acknowledge Palestinian suffering).

Thus, despite the apparent cosmopolitanism of the MOTNY, which claims to attend to global instances of intolerance and injustice, the hierarchies of life instilled by the museum and the centre explicitly work against the ethical priorities outlined by exponents of the transcultural turn, serving particular national interests, even as both the museum and the centre declare their commitment to greater international solidarity and tolerance. Such considerations highlight the fact that neither the Holocaust nor 9/11 are neutral signifiers in American memorial culture. As Peter Novick suggests, '[i]ndividuals from every point on the political compass can find the lessons they wish in the Holocaust; it has become a moral and ideological Rorschach test' (Novick 1999, 12). Whilst the MOTNY and the Simon Wiesenthal Center demonstrate the ways in which Holocaust memory might be appropriated to construct and maintain aggressive hierarchies of life, the next section argues that, as it has been deployed in political rhetoric after 9/11, the genocide has been instrumentalised in support of active violence in the American-led invasions of Iraq and Afghanistan.

3.4 The Holocaust analogy in American foreign policy

The aftermath of 9/11 is not the first time the events of the Holocaust have been mobilised as a justification for state violence. In his study of the 'use and abuse of the Holocaust analogy' in American foreign policy since World War II, Michael C. Desch argues that '[t]he Holocaust has become an important part of the everyday discourse in American life. Indeed, it has become one of the central historical analogies for thinking about US foreign policy in the post-Cold War world' (Desch 2010, 107). Desch attributes this centrality to the Allies' failure to prevent the Holocaust or accept significant numbers of Jewish refugees during the

Second World War. He contends that the lingering memory of historical guilt has two predominant implications for US foreign policy: the 'Holocaust analogy's twin never again obligations' mandate 'that the United States unreservedly supports the state of Israel and intervenes whenever genocide or other forms of mass killing occur' (Desch 2010, 138). However, Desch rightly cautions that these impulses 'have not always produced effective policies or served America's national interest' (Desch 2010, 138). Deployed in political rhetoric, analogical frames of memory serve an indispensible ideological purpose, providing 'compelling rationales for advocates of particular policies to sway public opinion in their favor' (Desch 2010, 109).

Desch notes that 'the pattern of US interventions in the face of the five major episodes of genocide since the Second World War – Cambodia, Iraq, Bosnia, Rwanda and Kosovo – largely tracks with the increasing frequency of the Holocaust analogy' (Desch 2010, 115). The invocation of the Holocaust as a precedent to prevent other genocide is, of course, not inherently problematic. It would be hard to object to its (considered) deployment in opposition to Serbian attempts at 'ethnic cleansing' or action against other forms of persecution, displacement, or injury. On the contrary, such mobilisations of the Holocaust seem potentially to evoke the ideal approaches to memory outlined by the discourses of the transcultural turn. However, following 9/11, the Holocaust's conversion into an analogue for the justification of unilateral American military intervention manifests a more troubling deployment of its memory that can best be understood through a brief exploration of its established place in foreign policy rhetoric.

In 1992, the American Jewish Committee, the American Jewish Congress, and the Anti-Defamation League ran a joint publicity campaign explicitly comparing the Serb camps of Omarska and Brcko to the Nazi regimes at Auschwitz and Treblinka. The advert, entitled 'Stop the Death Camps: An Open Letter to World Leaders', asked: '[i]s it possible that 50 years after the Holocaust, the nations of the world, including our own, will stand by and do nothing, pretending we are helpless?' (Cohen 1993). Cohen suggests that these sentiments were echoed across the public-political sphere in the early years of the 1990s, as journalists, politicians, and lobbyists urged intervention in Yugoslavia to prevent a second Holocaust.[17] Whilst Cohen critiques this approach – arguing that '[i]f the United States and the West are going to intervene [in Bosnia], the decision has to be based on a realistic appraisal of the situation and what is best for the Bosnian Muslims – not a pathetically tardy response to Nazism' (Cohen 1993) – many reinforced it. At a 1993 event in New

York to commemorate the fiftieth anniversary of the Warsaw Ghetto uprising, for example, Clinton's vice president, Al Gore, declared that the 'story of the Warsaw Ghetto is sacred text for our time', mobilising its memory as a parable for 'the tragedy of Bosnia and Herzegovina' (Steinberg 1993).

Ultimately, the US and its Western allies substituted decisive intervention in Bosnia for a war crimes tribunal – itself established by appeal to the historical precedent of Nuremberg (see Chapter 4). Having had to face the 'moral rebuke' of 'having missed the story the second time round' (Cohen 1993), politicians saw the chance to make amends in Kosovo, a conflict shadowed in America by the failure to address either the Holocaust or the Bosnian war in time to prevent the onset of mass suffering. Cohen labelled NATO intervention in Kosovo as a war fought 'almost as an act of remembrance of the Holocaust - a kind of "never again" cry from most of NATO's leaders' (Cohen 1999). Similarly, Bill Clinton argued in more cautious terms that, '[t]hough ethnic cleansing is not the same as the ethnic extermination of the Holocaust, the two are related – both vicious, premeditated, systematic oppression fuelled by religious and ethnic hatred' (Lewis 1999).

Given its longstanding prevalence as an analogy in American foreign policy, it is perhaps unsurprising that the Bush Administration returned repeatedly to the Holocaust to justify military action after 9/11, particularly in the build-up to war in Iraq. In his seminal jeremiad of 20 September 2001, Bush declared:

> We have seen [al Qaeda's] kind before. They're the heirs of all the murderous ideologies of the 20th century [. . .] they follow in the path of fascism, Nazism, and totalitarianism. And they will follow that path all the way to where it ends in history's unmarked grave of discarded lies (Bush 2001g).

This analogy immediately preceded both the announcement of the so-called 'Bush Doctrine' – which inaugurated the policies of military unilateralism and pre-emptive action – and Bush's infamous declaration to the nations of the world: '[e]ither you are with us or you are with the terrorists' (Bush 2001g).[18] In framing his dictum in this manner, Bush appeared to capitalise on the Holocaust's purported moral universalism to facilitate the construction of a binary universe of 'good' and 'evil' able to serve his ideological and militaristic agendas.

The president returned to this analogy two years later, launching the Bush Doctrine in Iraq. Discussing the possibility of Iraqi weapons of mass destruction (the report of which was initially cited in justification of the invasion), Bush commented:

> In the 20th century, some chose to appease murderous dictators, whose threats were allowed to grow into genocide and global war. In this century, when evil men plot chemical, biological and nuclear terror, a policy of appeasement could bring destruction of a kind never before seen on earth (Bush 2003).

Bush's remarks were echoed in a 2004 speech made by Richard Perle, chairman of the Defense Policy Board. Perle claimed that the War on Terror was premised on a choice between 'victory or holocaust' (Frum and Perle 2004, vii). He had drawn a similar analogy two years earlier when he compared the US's pre-9/11 attitude to al Qaeda to the policy of appeasement adopted towards Nazi Germany prior to World War II, commenting:

> The decision to use force is most difficult when democratic societies are challenged to act preemptively. That is why the Continental powers waited until Hitler invaded Poland in 1939 and America waited until after September 11 to go after Osama bin Laden. Hitler's self-declared ambitions and military build-up, like bin Laden's demented agenda, were under constant scrutiny long before the acts of aggression to which a response became unavoidable. Both could have been stopped by a relatively modest well-timed pre-emption (Perle 2002).

In an interview given to Fox News in 2002, Secretary of Defense Donald Rumsfeld justified America's action in Iraq in an identical manner:

> Think of the prelude to World War II. Think of all the countries that said, well, we don't have enough evidence. I mean, 'Mein Kampf' had been written. Hitler had indicated what he intended to do. Maybe he won't attack us. Maybe he won't do this or that. Well, there were millions of people dead because of the miscalculations. Had he been stopped early, as he might have been done at minimal cost, minimal cost in lives (Borger and Norton-Taylor 2002).

Other members of the administration advanced this discourse in more personal terms, drawing intimate connections with the Holocaust to justify their support for war in Iraq. Douglas Feith, under-secretary of defense, was one of many to 'look at Iraq' through what Desch refers to as 'Holocaust-tinted glasses' (Desch 2010, 119). Discussing the US's rejection of a second UN resolution on military action, Feith commented:

> I took all these nice sounding ideas and compared it to my own little personal 'cogito, ergo sum,' which was that my family got wiped out by Hitler, and all this stuff about working things out – well, talking to Hitler to resolve the problem didn't make any sense to me. The kind of people who put bumper stickers on their car that declare that 'war is not the answer,' are they making a serious comment? What's the answer to Pearl Harbor? What's the answer to the Holocaust? The surprising thing is not that there are so many Jews who are neocons but that there are so many who are not (Goldberg 2005).

Highlighting the loss of his extended family in Poland under the Nazis, Paul Wolfowitz, a Jewish 'neocon' close to the heart of the administration, similarly commented that Hussein was 'in a class with very few others – Stalin, Hitler, Kim Jong Il' (Ricks 2003). Mindful that 'the failure to confront Hitler was largely from fear of what the consequences would be, and that lead to greater consequences' (Ricks 2003), Wolfowitz underlined his unequivocal support for the war in Iraq on the grounds of comparison with Nazism.

As Cohen notes:

> once the labels of 'genocide' or 'holocaust' are attached to a government policy, once detention camps of some kind are likened to the Nazi death camps of Auschwitz and Treblinka, then human beings with an ounce of morality have an obligation to intercede – no matter what the consequences. 'Never again' is not a mere slogan. It is a solemn obligation (Cohen 1993).

Such obligations prove particularly potent when reinforced by those considered guardians of the collective conscience. In his seminal account of the build-up to the war in Iraq, Bob Woodward reports Elie Wiesel meeting privately with Bush at the White House to urge him to take military action. Woodward records Bush commenting that the meeting was 'a meaningful moment because it was a confirming moment. I said to myself, Gosh, if Elie Wiesel feels that way, who knows the pain and suffering and agony of tyranny, then others feel that way too. And so I am not alone' (Woodward 2004, 320–21). Thus, whilst their reasoning is understandable, it is somewhat concerning to see Holocaust survivors such as Wiesel and Wiesenthal so closely echoing the rhetoric of the officials quoted above in the aftermath of September 11. Wiesel commented, '[h]ad Europe's great powers intervened against Adolf Hitler's aggressive ambitions in 1938 instead of appeasing him in Munich, humanity would have been spared the unprecedented horrors of World War II' (Wiesel 2002). Wiesenthal argued, 'you cannot wait indefinitely on dictators. Adolf Hitler came to power in 1933, but for six years the world did not act' (Finkelstein 2003, 254).

The mobilisation of the Holocaust as a point of analogy for military action after 9/11 thus underscores Desch's assertion that 'a very substantial constituency for the Holocaust analogy and its never again obligation has come together through a combination of skilful manipulation of the analogy by policy advocates and very receptive Jewish and Gentile audiences' (Desch 2010, 144). Although it is important not to conflate the mobilisation of Holocaust memory in the political rhetoric analysed above with its function in the cultural narratives considered earlier, as Sicher contends, taken together, these trends suggest that the Holocaust has indeed become 'a confused myth within conflicting discourses' (Sicher 2000, 57). Whilst it may have seemed logical to turn to the most available point of analogy for historical trauma in the wake of the attacks, cultural practitioners have been inattentive to the ways in which 'interpretative analogies of a repeated past might be ineffective or counterproductive in their subordination to metanarratives and ideologies' (Sicher 2000, 79).

These dynamics demonstrate the way in which memories slip between different discourses, weaving a complex web of signification around particular historical events. What appears to happen in the aftermath of 9/11 is the conjoining of two pre-existing frames of Holocaust memory: firstly, the translation of the genocide into an inherently 'American' experience in the institutions of memorial culture (most notably, perhaps, the USHMM); secondly, the use of the Holocaust in American foreign policy as a justification for applying military force overseas. The first of these discourses transformed the attacks themselves into an event comparable to the Holocaust. In so doing, cultural (literary and museal) narratives reinforced pre-existing tendencies to universalise Jewish suffering, encouraging an uncritical (one might also argue, exceptionalising) over-identification with Holocaust victims. Such representations framed the two events in a series of identical tropes, reclaiming the Holocaust as an American occurrence even as 9/11 assumed the form of the earlier trauma, decontextualising both atrocities and making it harder to draw nuances between them. The second discursive movement did not explicitly equate either 9/11 or the American nation to the Holocaust, but instead framed the events of the War on Terror in the model of the Second World War, comparing both bin Laden and Hussein to Hitler, justifying the invasions of Iraq and Afghanistan on the pretext of preventing a second Shoah.

Both of these trends are premised on the idea of American innocence, although in notably different ways. Cultural narratives have presented the attacks as America's traumatic reawakening to history: the end of its period of innocence; its privileged isolation from geopolitical turmoil. Conversely, political discourse emphasises 9/11 as a *reclamation* of American innocence: positioning the nation as the innocent victim of (totalitarian) foreign aggression; depicting bin Laden and Hussein as fascistic enemies to be opposed at all costs; and negating America's own role as aggressor in the War on Terror. We see here two distinct notions of 'innocence': the first a Blakean concern with innocence-as-naivety, innocence-against-experience; the second, a definition of innocence as morally pure, free from culpability. Not only do comparisons to the Holocaust reinforce this impression of innocence by casting Americans in the role of the exceptional victim (the Holocaust victim), they also have the related effect of deploying America's enemies in the guise of history's most exemplary evil – Hitler and the Nazi regime.

As it is deployed across both cultural and political discourses, therefore, the notion of innocence functions as a screen, hiding complex historical dynamics from view as the representation of the Holocaust allows Americans to engage with atrocity from the comfortable perspective of aghast (and deferred) witness, reaffirming their own inherent morality and deflecting the need for critical analysis of the national past. Accordingly, Linenthal comments, there is a possibility that 'official Holocaust memory may also function as a "comfortable horrible" memory, allowing Americans to reassure themselves that they are engaging with profound events, all the while ignoring more indigestible events that threaten Americans' sense of themselves more than the Holocaust' (Linenthal 1995, 267). Similarly, Andreas Huyssen argues that the 'universalised "never again" command and with it the instrumentalisation of memory for political purposes have become a veil covering ongoing atrocities in our present. The Holocaust has become a screen memory' (Huyssen 2003, 19).[19]

3.5   The Holocaust analogy in memory and trauma studies after 9/11

Given the hegemonic dimensions of American Holocaust memory, and its widespread mobilisation in cultural and political discourse after 9/11, it seems important that theorists working within memory and trauma studies should remain alert to, and able to resist, analogical frames of memory that dehistoricise the events to which they bear witness. How-ever, the repeated use of such paradigms in scholarly criticism after September 11 suggests that many theorists have concluded, however reluctantly, with Geoffrey Hartman that '[h]istorical analogies are risky, but they are what we have to go on' (Hartman 2003, 9).

In the aftermath of the attacks, a number of the leading figures from within American memory and trauma studies have sought to expli-cate the allegedly incomprehensible events of September 11 through reference to the master-trauma of the Holocaust. Recalling the 'living' Holocaust memorials comprised by the planting of trees in the Judean Hills between Jerusalem and Tel Aviv and at Yad Vashem, James Young suggests that such tributes should not serve as 'explicit models for our own memorial downtown [at Ground Zero]', but as 'possible conceptual foundations and backdrops for our memorial thinking' (Young 2003, 219). Other theorists have been less successful in maintaining the dis-tinction between similarities encountered in the *framing* of these experi-ences (i.e., the representational paradigms into which they are drafted) and alleged likenesses between the atrocities themselves (i.e., the nature of the historical events).

Whilst E. Ann Kaplan remarks, 'I do not intend to equate 9/11 and the Holocaust – far from it', she goes on to comment that:

> The crashing into the Twin Towers using a plane full of people as the weapon parallels in terms of the thought of the perpetrators the deliberate and immediate annihilation of innocent humans by fire. And the production of a crematorium of huge dimensions, such as the Nazis daily produced over years (Kaplan 2005, 156 – 7fn17).

By drawing the Holocaust and 9/11 into parallel structures of represen-tation without noting the distinctions between the scale, duration, and nature of the two atrocities, Kaplan's comments threaten to elide crucial differences between these events, despite her avowed intentions. Several critics have, in turn, drafted the analogical frames of Holocaust memory into the paradigms of testimony-criticism identified in Kaplan's work in Chapter 1. As evidenced by the contributions of Dori Laub and Elizabeth Baer to Judith Greenberg's (2003) collection *Trauma at Home After 9/11*, such discourses draw upon the author's own experiences as their princi-pal frame of reference. However, as will become clear, these two theorists do so to very different ends.

Citing 'parallels between September 11 and the terrorism of Nazism and Fascism' (Laub 2003, 204), Laub argues that 'there is a resemblance between the attacks of September 11 and something equally unimaginable that happened in the Holocaust' (Laub 2003, 207). Adopting an intrinsically autobiographical stance, he adopts:

> the mode of an analyst, or therapist, because that's what I know best. I am also a Holocaust survivor. My life's work is listening to those who are seeking psychic healing. [. . . .] On September 11 we were all, doctor, and patient alike, witness to, and victims of, a kind of terror that was, until that morning, unknown to us as Americans (Laub 2003, 205).

Laub thus positions himself as the fulcrum that links 9/11 and the Holocaust. By gesturing towards a national culture of victimhood and witnessing, he also appears to assert a connection between the experience of all Americans after September 11 and his own status as a Holocaust survivor. He continues to make such comparisons throughout his article, switching between the particular and the general, conflating the specific experience of Holocaust survivors with a wider cultural response to the attacks.

Drawing upon his encounters with his patients, Laub remarks, after 9/11, 'Holocaust survivors living in New York City began to re-experience their terrors and their nightmares [. . .]. It all goes on, they felt; it never stops, and no place is safe' (Laub 2003, 206). This comparison between the Holocaust and the attacks is premised upon their mutual status as allegedly incomprehensible and unrepresentable collective traumas. As Laub comments:

> During the Holocaust, and for many years after it was over, nobody was willing to hear and to know what was truly happening, in spite of overwhelming evidence. It took decades for a dialogue of testimony to emerge. Yet there is this similarly: the absence of narrative. No one can really tell the story of the Twin Towers disaster, and no one is really ready to hear it. [. . .] This generalised amorphousness, bewilderment, and, most of all, numbness seems to me a hallmark of collective, massive trauma (Laub 2003, 207–8).

There are a number of issues with these claims: firstly, the slow emergence of Holocaust memory seems at odds with the instantaneous culture of commemoration, the glut of words, images, and memorials, that erupted after 9/11.[20] Secondly, Laub's uncritical subscription to the notion of a generalised national trauma is incompatible with his attention, elsewhere during the article, to the individual suffering of his patients (and, indeed, to his own psychical response to the attacks).

Thirdly, Laub's remarks exhibit the familiar tendency to collapse all of history under the sign of trauma (he claims '[h]istory is continuous. Trauma survivors' responses to September 11 bear witness to this' [Laub 2003, 206]), undermining his later contention that 'there can be no equating [9/11 and the Holocaust]. The scale is too disproportionate' (Laub 2003, 207). Several contradictions thus inform Laub's work. His argument is premised upon the ability to draw associative relations between the events of 9/11 and the Holocaust, yet his comments reveal an uncertainty about the reach, character, and sustainability of these comparisons. Rather than addressing such concerns, or reflecting on them in more detail, Laub reinscribes this confusion, collapsing disparate frames of reference into a series of opaque analogies, exacerbating the conflation of the particular and the universal, the individual and the nation examined throughout this chapter (and, indeed, the book as a whole). Perhaps more problematic, however, is the way in which his analysis moves between explicitly personalised and implicitly politicised lenses, without acknowledging the differences between these perspectives – or reflecting upon the implications of both psychologising geopolitics and politicising private life.

Laub begins by referencing the correspondences drawn between Nazism and Islamism in Bush's seminal jeremiad of 20 September 2001 (analysed in Chapter 2). He does not comment upon the highly politicised nature of these remarks (which were, after all, being mobilised to justify the onset of the War on Terror), but uses them to buttress his comparison between the twentieth-century *terror* of Nazism and the twenty-first-century *terrorism* of al Qaeda. Laub then proceeds to weave this very simplistic parallel between the character of the two events into a personalised chronicle of traumatic experience that relates specifically to his and his patients' reactions to 9/11. This discussion foregrounds Laub's visit to Israel in the immediate aftermath of the attacks. He notes that this trip served both a psychological and a professional purpose, releasing him from the apparently traumatising grip of post-9/11 American culture, and allowing him to develop his work on Holocaust testimony. Laub comments:

> In the days following September 11, I myself felt impelled to break the grip of silence, to be released from the hypnotic fascination of the endlessly repeated television images, the continual repetition of

the already well-known bits of information, fragments that did not cohere. I did so by going ahead with a planned trip to Israel on September 16. Specifically, I went to help plan a video testimony project about Holocaust survivors who themselves had never broken the seal of their silence (Laub 2003, 210).

Laub positions Israel as a place of security and safety, asserting 'Israel was, for me, a return to normalcy. [. . .] The place was only about five kilometres from Kalkilia in the West Bank. Yet it felt safer, more normal [than the United States], despite being so much closer to danger' (Laub 2003, 210). Together, these extracts demonstrate the way in which Laub slips between personal, professional, and political frames of reference. In the first of the above statements, Laub implicitly connects his status as an American after September 11 to the experiences of Holocaust survivors and his work with them as a psychoanalyst. In the second citation, he positions Israel as a place of sanctuary and recovery (recalling, as he does so, the Zionist discourses of homeland that surrounded the establishment of the nation-state following World War II).

The conflation of these perspectives is facilitated by the slippery rhetoric of trauma, which (as noted in Chapter 1) is a cusp term that operates across discursive fields. Throughout his article, Laub uses trauma to link his discussion of contemporary geopolitics to the experience of, and escape from, historical anti-Semitism. The events of 9/11 are interpreted through the frame of Holocaust memory as part of the ongoing (and inherently traumatic) chronicle of Jewish persecution. Laub comments:

> The multitude of diverse voices, public and private, that we are hearing about September 11 testifies to the absence of a coherent narrative voice for the event itself. We are faced with versions of the event's meaning that continue and coexist, some driven by a wish to know, to bear witness, and some driven by an equally powerful need to not know, to deny, to suppress the truth of witnessing (Laub 2003, 211).

He continues, in the aftermath of September 11, '[t]he latter met with too little moral rebuttal. The Egyptian press, as well as newspapers in other Arab countries, claimed from the very beginning that the Israeli central intelligence agency, the Mossad, was behind the acts of terror against the United States on September 11' (Laub 2003, 211). Laub thus instrumentalises his discussion of 9/11 as an opportunity to critique anti-Israeli factions in the Middle East. He concludes his article by mobilising the memory of the attacks as a justification for greater American support of Israel. He argues, '[n]ow that we have had our own experience of suicide bombers, it is harder for us to distance ourselves from the terror that Israelis are feeling and from the international threat that terrorist bombers pose for us all' (Laub 2003, 215).

It is here that the rhetoric of trauma gives way, for the first and last time, to an explicit statement about the politics that underlie this article. However, throughout the rest of the piece, Laub is remarkably – perhaps determinedly – acritical about the relationship between his personal experiences as a Holocaust survivor, his work as a psychoanalyst, and his perspective on the politics of the post-9/11 world. Laub's convergence of the narratives of 9/11, the Holocaust, and contemporary Israel involves a series of displacements: firstly, he conflates the particular experiences of Holocaust survivors with generalised American responses to 9/11; secondly, he evacuates both 9/11 and the Holocaust of specificity by collapsing them into the perpetual narrative of historical trauma; thirdly, he decentralises the actual victims of 9/11 (those who died on September 11) by focusing his anger on erroneous reports of Israeli involvement in the attacks, and transforming the story of the attacks into a symptom of resurgent anti-Semitism; and, finally, he collapses the events of 9/11 into the history of the state of Israel (reading America's attack by al Qaeda as inseparable from the actions of Palestinian suicide bombers), yoking the two nations together as victims of Islamic fundamentalism and eliding the important distinctions between the causes, characters, and consequences of these events.[21]

There is a strange circularity in this movement between different frames of memory that works to occlude complexity. As we saw in the discussion of the use of the Holocaust analogy in American political culture above, in the United States, the Holocaust often operates as a screen memory that can be mobilised to preclude recognition of America's historical shortcomings. Reading the Israeli-Palestinian conflict through the events of 9/11, Laub disavows the ethical and political complexity of the situation in the Middle East, masking Israel's own status as aggressor by equating the nation with the – newly victimised – United States (whose history is also sanitised). Such simplistic constructions are problematised in Baer's response to September 11. Like Laub, Baer utilises a highly personal perspective to frame the connections she draws between 9/11 and the Holocaust. However, whilst Laub interprets the events of September 11 under the sign of anti-Semitism, Baer conscripts them into the nuclear imaginary.

Baer links the 'schizophrenic' nature of a Cold War childhood lived under the threat of nuclear annihilation to both her work as 'an

academic and Holocaust scholar' (Baer 2003, 160) and her reactions to
9/11, arguing that the first of these experiences impelled her choice of
occupation which, in turn, inflected her reaction to the attacks. As with
Laub's work, these connections are construed under the sign of trauma.
Baer's article is punctuated by extracts from a 1960 brochure entitled
'The Fallout Question' (as she comments, the pamphlet exemplifies 'the
rhetoric of my nuclear childhood' [Baer 2003, 167]), which irrupt, as
if symptoms of trauma, without warning into her discussion of both
9/11 and the Holocaust. However, in contrast to Laub, for whom the
Holocaust manifests the ultimate symbol of the incomprehensible and
unrepresentable, for Baer (perhaps because of her literal and experiential
distance from these events) the genocide operates as a clarifying lens
that renders the past legible at both a personal and a political level,
allowing her to understand and decode the terror she faced during her
nuclear childhood and position herself ethically in the present.

Baer describes an 'epiphany' she experienced when visiting Dachau in
1990, commenting that, upon leaving the camp, 'all the important questions about war, evil, and human nature coalesced for me in the study of
the Shoah' (Baer 2003, 163). She examines the way in which these questions acquired renewed urgency for both herself and her students in the
aftermath of 9/11, recalling a journal entry she made on 19 September
2001, which considered the many 'sad stories, [with] so many eerie parallels to the Holocaust in terms of the consequences of hatred, racism,
and religious fanaticism' (Baer 2003, 164). Baer's article is deliberately
associative, and she is highly conscious of the convergence of her personal and professional frames of reference. She comments, '[t]he uneasy
sense during my childhood that danger lurked close by; [. . .] a decade
of devotion to studying the Holocaust; and September 11 – the device of
autobiography allows me to draw connections and parallels that objective scholarship would not' (Baer 2003, 165).

Baer thus foregrounds, rather than naturalises the transference of different frames of memory, representation, and experience that inform
her methodology. Her article is written in a fragmentary, almost aporetic
style that brings different events and interpretations together into constellation, without conflating them, drawing loose connections between
the '[f]allout of various kinds. Literal, figurative, atomic' (Baer 2003, 165)
that results from historical catastrophe. Whilst there are moments when
Baer's comments lose a little of their reflexivity (for instance in her discussion of the similarities between the posters for the missing that covered New York in the aftermath of the attacks, and the manner in which
Holocaust survivors searched for their lost relatives in displaced persons

camps after World War II), for the most part she retains an important sense of historical specificity.

Baer's chapter builds upon the political currency of Holocaust memory; however, she is both more explicit, and less polemic, in her aims than Laub. Baer comments, '[w]hile the study of the Holocaust has forced me to confront the capacity for evil in all human beings, I have also learned the dangers of singling out any group as the Other. Such a tactic so easily escalates into violence, which results in the fallout of retaliation, and so the cycle continues' (Baer 2003, 166). Like Laub, Baer constructs history as an ongoing cycle of violence, but she allows for the political and social dynamics of this pattern to emerge. Thus, whilst Laub's article mobilises Holocaust memory as a means to reassert entrenched binaries of victimhood and perpetration that emphasise the unequivocal innocence of the United States and Israel, Baer allows for a more nuanced reading of both the past and the present. Ultimately, she argues:

[t]he combination of factors that launched the war against the Jews [. . .] are lessons we need to learn. And we need to learn them not for what they teach us about another country or another time but for what they teach us about ourselves, now, and the arrogance, the racial hatred, the social injustice, the genocide of which we are all capable (Baer 2003, 167).

Despite their apparent similarities, therefore, (their personalisation of history, their comparison of 9/11 and the Holocaust, their recourse to the rhetoric of trauma), the work of Laub and Baer constructs oppositional models of comparative memory. Whilst Baer argues for the pedagogical properties of associative discourses that place disparate pasts side by side, in a necessarily self-reflexive manner, to highlight the complex dynamics of historical agency and responsibility, Laub's article construes a simplified – and sanitised – account of the recent past that collapses diverse events and experiences into undifferentiated equation, and is reluctant to question, or admit to, its own biases. Together, these accounts exemplify the slippery semantics of the Holocaust code, underscoring the way in which certain modes of analogical memory empty historical signifiers of specificity, transforming them into transferrable paradigms that may be mobilised in support of contrasting, even contradictory, interpretations and agendas.

Attentive to such dynamics, Flanzbaum contends that '[i]f the Holocaust, as image and symbol, seems to have sprung loose from its origins', its 'pervasive presence' in American culture, politics, and criticism 'demands responsible evaluation and interpretation' (Flanzbaum 1999, 8). However, the exponents of the transcultural turn (outlined above) have not always remained sufficiently alert to the ease with which Holocaust memory may be dehistoricised, appropriated, or ideologised. Furthermore, although both Levy and Sznaider's model of 'cosmopolitan memory' and Rothberg's notion of 'multidirectionality' utilise the Holocaust as the foundation for an ethical template of transculturalism, neither of these accounts gives detailed attention to the politics of the Holocaust in the post-9/11 world (indeed, neither work offers a sustained discussion of the way in which the historical issues they discuss relate to the immediate geopolitical context in which their works were written).

Uncritically deployed, Levy and Sznaider's construction of the Holocaust as a paradigm for global human rights discourse threatens to transform the genocide into an abstract parable that implicitly derealises the suffering of its victims even as their losses are made moral and symbolic absolutes. Their repeated assertion that '[t]he Holocaust is becoming a global code that no longer needs to be connected to history' (Levy and Sznaider 2006, 150) renders it difficult to distinguish at times between their *description* of processes of the abstraction and universalisation of Holocaust memory, and their *normative valuing* of such dynamics. Although Levy and Sznaider seek to generate a fluid model in which the local, national, and global interact to form new paradigms of remembrance, their deployment of the Holocaust arguably risks reifying its memory. They argue that the Holocaust's division into allegedly unproblematic categories of victimhood and perpetration allows its memory to become 'a measure for humanist and universal identifications' (Levy and Sznaider 2006, 5), which ensure that the remembrance of the Holocaust in many contexts has less to do with the event itself than with what this history can be used to represent.

There are several potential problems with this situation. Firstly, any division of the Holocaust into a narrative of 'good' and 'bad' characters is inevitably over-simplistic.[22] In its moral binarism, such an approach leaves itself open to conscription into precisely the kind of reductive parables constructed by elements of the public-political sphere in the aftermath of 9/11. Secondly, whilst Levy and Sznaider contend that the Holocaust provides a seminal example of a historical event that is able to 'provide the foundations for a new cosmopolitan memory [. . .] a memory that harbours the possibility of transcending ethnic and national boundaries' (Levy and Sznaider 2006, 4), they occlude the possible consequences of so thoroughly dehistoricising memory in their eagerness to embrace the Holocaust as 'the cultural foundation for global human-rights dynamics' (Levy and Sznaider 2006, 4), disavowing the fact that the Holocaust not only functions as a moral touchstone, but a rhetorical one as well. Invoking its horrors appears to position the speaker with right on their side, naturalising their politics as a moral imperative.

Although Rothberg is certainly alert to the dangers of universalising the Holocaust, his text is self-consciously written 'under the sign of optimism' (Rothberg 2009a, 19). This idealism at times leads him to translate attention to the political aspects of memory into a renewed advocation of his more ethical model of multidirectionality, which 'allows for the perception of the power differentials that tend to cluster around memory competition but it also locates that competition with a larger spiral of memory discourse in which even hostile invocations of memory can provide vehicles for further, countervailing commemorative acts' (Rothberg 2009a, 11). In many ways, such a positive approach is laudable, yet it becomes problematic when it allows unreflexive, even unethical, commemorative practices to continue uncritiqued. Therefore, whilst Rothberg is right to note that, uncritically deployed, the contemporary fascination with transculturalism will facilitate the 'too-easy collapse of the transnational, the global, and the comparative into the universal' (Rothberg 2009a, 264), theories of comparative memory often do not provide a clear means of distinguishing between the problematic modes of analogical Holocaust memory analysed throughout this chapter and the more reflexive and ethical approach they attempt to advocate.

There may well be productive implications for the application of Holocaust memory in the context of 9/11 – Rothberg makes an interesting point when he asserts that 'the Iraq War and the "war on terror" [. . .] with their liberal use of torture and indefinite detention have produced uncomfortable echoes of the Holocaust' (Rothberg 2009a, 28) – however, these accounts have yet to form a convincing counter-narrative in public memorial culture.[23] Bernard-Donals contends that analogical Holocaust memory has become such a normative reflexive in American memorial culture that it elides crucial differences between events and experiences, obscuring the complexities of historical responsibility, to ensure that '[w]hatever it is in front of us – 9/11, the occupation of the Palestinian territories, the War in Afghanistan or Iraq – becomes "the Holocaust"' (Bernard-Donals 2005, 97). As Mitchum Huehls asserts, analogy 'tend[s] to reduce, hypostatise, and impose meaning on constantly moving reality' (Huehls 2008, 45), transforming tenuous similarities between events and experiences into a synchronic, homotopic narrative in which the image of one overlays (one might argue, masks) the form of the other. It is thus, perhaps, not the ideal vehicle for nuanced accounts of comparative memory.

Given all of the above, it seems somewhat ironic that 9/11 has now acquired a certain memorative hegemony as an analogy for crises in the early twenty-first century. Events from Hurricane Katrina, to the BP oil spill, the global recession, to the Occupy Wall Street movement have been likened to the attacks: presented as environmental and economic '9/11s'. In 2005, Bush evoked the 'spirit of 9/11' to counter the traumatic aftermath of Hurricane Katrina, calling upon New Orleans's dispossessed residents to feel the 'resolve of nation . . . defend freedom . . . rebuild [the] wounded city . . . care for our neighbours' (Schama 2005, ellipses in original). Following the oil spill in the Gulf of Mexico in June 2010, President Obama announced, '[i]n the same way that our view of our vulnerabilities and our foreign policy was shaped profoundly by 9/11, I think this disaster is going to shape how we think about the environment and energy for many years to come' (Percival 2010). Describing the community of protesters that formed around Wall Street in autumn 2011, Rebecca Solnit pointed to the site's proximity to Ground Zero, arguing that, in terms of the collective solidarity in evidence, 'much about Occupy Wall Street resonates with what came in that brief moment a decade before and then was shut down for years' (Solnit 2011).

The different political, public, and cultural resonances of these examples underscores the way in which analogical frames of memory transform complex historical events into empty signifiers that can be deployed to serve highly divergent agendas and interpretations. The changing significance of the attacks in the above analogies implies that '9/11' is not a stable referent, suggesting that attempts to concretise the meaning of disasters is fundamentally flawed. Nowhere is this more clear than in the peculiar appropriation of the moniker 'Ground Zero' as a signifier for the ruined Trade Center site in the aftermath of 9/11. This term (coined in response to the American bombings of Hiroshima and Nagasaki) evokes the epicentre of a nuclear blast. As Richard Stamelman suggests, '"ground zero" as applied to the World Trade Center is reinvested with new analogical power; it becomes the metaphor for that earlier event to whose priority and precedence as the archetype of atrocity it cannot help but refer' (Stamelman 2003, 13). The transference of this term between events distanced by time and space brings associative images of destruction to bear on the site of the World Trade Center, coupling the attacks to a pre-existing chronicle of atrocity. Yet there is something surprising about the invocation of an atrocity perpetuated by the United States as the referent for its contemporary victimhood.

It is unclear if this nominative reclamation is intended to facilitate the screening of America's role as aggressor by naming the nation as victim through the appropriation of this term, or whether the renewed visibility of 'Ground Zero' has the opposite effect of bringing these earlier atrocities back into view, forcing a confrontation with troubling moments from the nation's past.

The invocation of Hiroshima as historical precedent complicates the narrative of 9/11 in problematic – and potentially productive – ways, blurring the boundaries between perpetrator and victim to problematise the overly simplistic construction of the contemporary world as a binary universe of 'good' and 'evil'. Thus, whilst memory's fluidity facilitates the discursive leakage that contributes to the emergence of dominant narrative frameworks across cultural, political, and critical discourses, it also potentially (and paradoxically) manifests the means of resisting such hegemonic constructions of the past. These claims underscore the potential of the ethical modes of transcultural memory outlined by Levy and Sznaider and Rothberg. However, as this chapter has aimed to show, when treated uncritically and collapsed into undifferentiated analogy, comparative frames of memory can produce problematic, and easily appropriated, renditions of history that serve to sanitise both the past and the present. Thus, practitioners and theorists need to adopt a more reflexive attitude to the frames in which they situate their work, pursuing comparative rather than competitive, associative instead of equative, models of memory.

4
Memory, Law, and Justice after 9/11

This book has argued that representations of 9/11 have recurrently been mediated by certain frames of memory (the psychoanalytic rhetoric of trauma, the triumphalist tropes of the jeremiad, and the analogical templates of Americanised Holocaust memory) in the American public sphere over the past thirteen years. These paradigms, all of which were culturally prominent prior to the attacks, have shaped the articulation of September 11 across diverse cultural, critical, and political forums. Whilst the media upon which this analysis is based are not, of course, representative of the sum of 9/11's memorial culture, they point to a number of issues that require further exploration. Firstly, they underline the absolute impression of American innocence (and exceptionalism), eliding more difficult elements of US history. Secondly, they suggest a convergence of public and private spheres, evidencing both an over-personalisation of political discourse (as in the mobilisation of trauma post-9/11 examined in Chapter 1) and an abstraction of private loss (as in the transformation of victims into national symbols analysed in Chapters 2 and 3), leading to an appropriation of personal experience. Thirdly, these frames project a contradictory relationship to otherness. On the one hand, their standardising bent appears antithetical to alterity, yet, on the other, the continual reinforcement of a national culture of memory, and the affirmation of its particularly *American* attributes, enacts an imaginary ring-fencing that symbolically separates the United States from the rest of the world. Put slightly differently, whilst these discourses appear reluctant to admit difference *within* the nation, they reinforce the impression of absolute Otherness *outside* of it. Finally (and relatedly), these frameworks conscript both the local and the global into the service of the national. This at once universalises (as the protector of the dominant world order) and particularises (as the historically exceptional nation) the United States, making it difficult for alternative viewpoints to emerge.

This final chapter considers how these dynamics have inflected the pursuit of justice for 9/11 in the American juridico-political sphere. I contend that, as judicial rulings relating to the attacks have entered (in the case of the military commissions now in process at Guantánamo Bay, have yet to enter) somewhat belatedly into the public sphere, the institutions of the legal system have struggled to impose a stable frame of memory upon the attacks. Over the past thirteen years, the master-narratives that have dominated the commemoration of September 11 have intersected in complicated ways in juridical discourses, affecting the pursuit of both restitution (which has largely taken place in civil proceedings overseen by the federal court) and retribution (which has yoked extra-legal processes – such as torture, extraordinary rendition, and the indefinite detention of terror suspects – to the judicial processes of the military commissions at Guantánamo Bay). As the case studies examined below demonstrate, each of the frames of memory analysed throughout this book have been instrumentalised by the individuals and institutions of the juridico-political sphere to construe an unequivocal impression of American innocence in the wake of 9/11 – negating the responsibility of US airlines and security firms for failing to antici-pate or prevent the attacks, and eschewing governmental accountability for the subsequent torture and abuse of detainees in the custody of the United States. However, these familiar paradigms have been destabilised in their deployment by the law, rendering an incoherent narrative of legal memory.

4.1 Framing legal memory

Over the past fifteen years, a growing body of criticism has analysed the legal afterlife of atrocities from the Holocaust to Apartheid, the Argen-tine Junta to the brutal wars that accompanied the dissolution of the former Yugoslavia.[1] This interdisciplinary corpus underscores the his-torical and cultural contingency of juridical proceedings, demonstrating how such processes evolve in relation to the precise (political, ethical, and social) demands of the context in and for which they are estab-lished, and emphasising the partial and provisional nature of all modes of redress. As these studies suggest, even in normative conditions, the nexus of memory, law, and justice is fluid, fragile, and contradictory. Theorists have recurrently positioned each of these concepts as limit terms, whose definitions are relative and contested. Andreas Huyssen remarks that memory 'is one of those elusive topics we all think we have a handle on. But as soon as we try to define it, it starts slipping and sliding, eluding attempts to grasp it either culturally, sociologically, or scientifically' (Huyssen 2003, 3). Austin Sarat and Nasser Hussain argue that '[t]he concept of [. . .] law is a difficult one, made up of multiple and sometimes even conflicting norms and values' (Sarat and Hussain 2010, 13). For Jacques Derrida, meanwhile, justice is an 'aporia' that requires us to 'calculate with the incalculable' (Derrida 1990, 947). Defining the dynamics of this triumvirate becomes even more important, and perhaps ever more impossible, in the aftermath of historical catastrophe.

In orthodox terms, legal processes are commonly understood to provide a means of framing, containing, and explaining historical experience. Shoshana Felman argues that, in its 'pragmatic role as guardian of society against irregularity, derangement, disorganisation, unpredictability, or any form of irrational or uncontrollable disorder, the law, indeed, has no choice but to guard against equivocations, ambiguities, obscurities, confusions, and loose ends' (Felman 2002, 95). These stabilising capacities become more crucial (and more compromised) in the chaotic aftermath of atrocity. As Austin Sarat, Lawrence Douglas, and Martha Merrill Umphrey contend, 'the spectre of catastrophe plays a crucial role in law's justificatory logic', for, whilst it may be true that the 'law is constituted in the effort to escape catastrophe', it is also important to recognise that 'catastrophe is both juris generative – it is the ever-present threat of chaos that creates the need for law – and the very antithesis and negation of law – it is the uncontrollable force that threatens to extirpate law's ordering effect on social life' (Sarat, Douglas, and Umphrey 2007, 4).

Legal discourses manifest a complex temporality in the wake of catastrophe. Whilst atrocity impels the law to innovate, providing new frameworks for the stabilisation of present experience, institutionalised legal memory plays a strongly constitutive role in shaping future cases. As Robert Ferguson remarks, juridical practice privileges the principle of '[s]tare decisis et non quieta movere, [. . . which] conveys more than the rule of precedent. The full phrase means "to adhere to precedent and not unsettle things that are established"' (Ferguson 2007, 11). Juridical processes are thus both *framed by*, and *frames of*, memory; memorative and legal discourses exist in a recursive relation. Joachim Savelsberg and Ryan King assert that legislative bodies 'crystallize collective memory as they mold it into institutional structures' (Savelsberg and King 2011, 584), whilst 'structures of collective memory are institutionalised in laws and law enforcement' (Savelsberg and King 2010, 581). Superficially, at least, the discourses of law and memory share a number of features: each straddles the threshold of the public and the private, mediating the relationship between individuals and collectives; each is concerned with negotiating contesting interpretations of the past; in so doing, each problematises, even as its practitioners venerate, the idea of historical truth; and each claims an intimate relationship to justice. As Daniel Levy and Natan Sznaider contend, through its incarnation in the law, '[j]ustice itself becomes a form of remembrance' (Levy and Sznaider 2010, 19).

Normative definitions of justice tend to frame the concept in *structural* terms, focusing upon the (in)equitable distribution of resources and the cultural, political, and legal recognition of groups and individuals.[2] As Nancy Fraser contends, 'the most general meaning of justice is a parity of participation. According to this radical-democratic interpretation of the principle of equal moral worth, justice requires social arrangements that permit all to function as peers in social life' (Fraser 2008, 16). Rudi G. Teitel describes this understanding as an 'idealist' position, informed by a liberal, universalist stance. By contrast, Teitel's focus is upon the construction of *historical* justice: the diverse procedures of redress necessitated when structural injustice is exacerbated by sudden, often violent, means.

Such processes also presage complicated temporal relations. In periods of social upheaval, the very idea of justice is placed in a 'threshold dilemma', 'caught between the past and the future, between backward-looking and forward-looking, between retrospective and prospective, between the individual and the collective' (Teitel 2000, 6–7). Teitel suggests that such situations impel 'realist' approaches to justice, tailored to the political, economic, and cultural specificities of the situation. Justice therefore becomes an empirical process rather than an abstract ideal, 'a compromise' (Teitel 2000, 8), involving heterogeneous forms of (political, administrative, economic, and legal) reckoning that seek to restore a sense of historical continuity. W. James Booth asserts that these proceedings predominantly adhere to three key paradigms, respondent, respectively, to presentist, memorative, and futural concerns: 'trial and punishment (criminal charges); illumination and acknowledgement (truth commissions); and forgetting for the sake of a future in common (amnesty)' (Booth 2001, 778). He continues, '[v]aried (and overlapping) imperatives drive these phenomena: to fulfill a debt to the dead by punishing the perpetrators; to preserve justice; to save victims from the second death of forgetting; to put present and future goods over our ties to the past' (Booth 2001, 788).

Booth suggests that the public courtroom functions as 'a venue for seeking the victory of the memory of justice over the will to forget, for seeking, in a sense, the rule of law' (Booth 2001, 779). High-profile trials aim to generate a consensual account of disaster in order to stabilise public understandings of an event and determine its subsequent representation in the historical record. The court thus functions simultaneously as the architect of *legal memory* (the judicially sanctioned judgement of the past) and the arbiter of *memory-justice* (the act of redress – restitutive or retributive – that follows the final ruling). Ideally, these two mandates operate in harmony as the construction of legal memory compels an act of memory-justice that is widely accepted as proportionate and fair. However, the mutuality of these imperatives depends upon a consensual agreement concerning the integrity and authority of the court: when juridical processes are discredited, it is likely that both the legal memory they decree and the memory-justice they impose will be contested.

Over the course of this chapter, I suggest that juridical attempts to reckon with the events of 9/11 and their aftermath have revealed an inherent tension between the construction of legal memory and the execution of memory-justice. The frames of memory critiqued throughout this book have failed to function as stabilising paradigms for juridical discourse, as the institutions of the American juridico-political sphere have struggled to reconcile fidelity to the historical record with the protocols of the law and the claims of restitution and retribution.

4.2 The trauma trial and restitutive justice after 9/11

Conceptions of the law as an architect of memory have their historical origins in the aftermath of World War II. As Felman notes:

> Trials have always been contextualised in – and affected by – a general relation between history and justice. But they have not always been judicially concerned with this relationship. Until the middle of the twentieth century, a radical division between history and justice was in principle maintained. [. . .] The courts sometimes acknowledged that they were part of history, but they did not judge history as such (Felman 2002, 11).

The proceedings that followed World War II (from the international military tribunals of Nuremberg and Tokyo to the US camp trials at Dachau, and Israel's later prosecution of Adolf Eichmann in the Jerusalem District Court) helped to establish a juridical paradigm that emphasised the memorative capacities of the court alongside its punitive capability. Two central frames of (Western) legal memory emerged from these proceedings.

The first underscored the pedagogic role of the trial – exemplifying this position, Robert M. W. Kemper, a junior prosecutor at Nuremberg, described the tribunals as 'the greatest history seminar ever held in the history of the world' (Douglas 2001, 2). The second constructed a therapeutic model of justice, centred upon witness testimony and the figure of the victim, building upon precedents established by the Eichmann trial.

Felman argues that '[t]rial and trauma have become [. . .] *conceptually articulated*' (Felman 2002, 1) in juridical practice over the past half-century.[3] Privileging victims' testimony as evidentiary material, and emphasising the memorative and therapeutic faculties of the court, the *trauma trial* has become a pre-eminent mode of contemporary jurisprudence. This model has proven particularly influential in US jurisprudence – as Ferguson acknowledges, in recent years, '[m]ovement everywhere in American law has been toward further recognition of the victim' (Ferguson 2007, 63). Given the ubiquitous rhetoric of trauma in the American public sphere after September 11, and the sacrilisation of victims and survivors that has informed the commemoration of 9/11 across multiple discursive spheres, it might seem reasonable to expect that such paradigms would have provided a ready frame of legal memory for the attacks. However, US district courts have appeared reluctant to admit the testimony of survivors or victims' families into the courtroom.

Parties seeking damages for losses sustained on 9/11 have done so by waiving their rights to claim from the September 11 Victims Compensation Fund, established by Congress on 21 September 2001.[4] Whilst the fund released more than $7 billion in compensation,[5] claimants accepted the money on the condition that they would not litigate any American body (government or corporate) in relation to the attacks. This stipulation offers the first indications of a juridico-political sphere eager to contain the ambiguous shades of accountability by limiting any intimation of American responsibility for the attacks or the less salutary elements of their aftermath. Resistant to such restrictions, many of those who pursued civil trials framed their cases as explicitly memorative endeavours, hoping to amend the historical record by holding airlines and security firms accountable for failing to anticipate and prevent the attacks, testify to the pain they had suffered as a result of this perceived negligence, and find a public forum in which to speak of their lost relatives.

Restitutive lawsuits in American civil courts have since taken three principle forms: cases brought against airlines and security firms by individuals and corporations seeking financial reparation for injury, property damage, or loss of a loved one; rescue workers claiming compensation for health problems acquired during the clearance of Ground Zero; and victims' families hoping to hold foreign individuals, corporations, and governments responsible for aiding and abetting terrorism. With the exception of a single case adjudicated by Judge George B. Daniels (following the death of Judge Richard Conway Casey in 2007),[6] the vast majority of these hearings have fallen under the domain of Judge Alvin K. Hellerstein. Since 2002, Hellerstein has ruled on more than 10,000 claims brought by rescue workers (to whom he collectively awarded a $680 million settlement in September 2011)[7] and 96 suits filed by those who suffered injury or loss on 9/11 (whose individual settlements have totalled more than $500 million).[8] All of these cases have been settled out of court; not a single one has gone to trial.

Hellerstein has repeatedly resisted any attempt by victims' families to use the courtroom as the setting for a therapeutic encounter. In preparation for a planned court hearing brought by the family of Paul Wesley Ambrose in 2007, Hellerstein limited the amount of testimony that could be offered by the litigants on the grounds that it was 'speculative' (Hartocollis 2007). In 2011, during the last of the ninety-six cases he adjudicated, Hellerstein made the unprecedented decision that the family of Mark Bavis could take their case to trial as long as the hearings would last no more than a month and equal time on the stand would be given to the prosecution and the defence, again restricting the testimonial opportunities available to the claimants.[9] Following this decision, the Bavis family released a statement to the press, arguing that:

> Judge Hellerstein very cleverly changed this lawsuit. The lawsuit was about wrongful death, gross negligence and a complete lack of appreciation for the value of human life. [. . .] We fought this long for two reasons, because we valued Mark's life in the time spent together, the shared experiences and the expectation of what life would continue to be. Secondly, the truth as to why this happened so easily should be important (Bavis 2011).

These remarks underscore the memorative drive of these lawsuits. However, frustrated by the dynamics of the trials they had been offered, like the ninety-four other claimants whose cases were entertained by Hellerstein, the Ambrose and Bavis families ultimately settled out of court.[10]

Hellerstein's judgements (or, conversely, Hellerstein's refusal to pass judgement) in these cases seem unusual in two respects: firstly, because, in their recourse to private settlements, they undermine the central role that the court has historically played in American public life[11]; secondly, they invert the principles of the trauma trial that have dominated US jurisprudence since the late twentieth century. Such developments are not necessarily without merit; as Ferguson contends, 'therapy is not an assigned function of the law even in a therapeutic age. [. . .] To think otherwise is to adjust the meaning of impersonal and personal as values in a process dedicated to categorical decision making over individual investments' (Ferguson 2007, 64). A number of critics have argued that the law's conscription into wider trauma culture is highly problematic. Noting that the '[h]eightened concern for the role of the victim in trial performance says as much about the culture as it does about the practice of the law, because [. . .] it has been forced on the law by outside interests' (Ferguson 2007, 62), Ferguson suggests that the punitive, therapeutic, and memorative aspects of the trauma trial manifest 'competing conceptions of the law' (Ferguson 2007, 260), which are ultimately incompatible. As Levy and Sznaider remark, a growing critical consensus suggests that, as '[p]olitical and legal theory have taken a decisive Freudian turn', '[m]emory has become the key organizer that has enabled trauma and its recovery to supersede justice and its administration' (Levy and Sznaider 2010, 119). Lyndsey Stonebridge argues that '[a]s much as historical and juridical comprehension can be transformed by trauma [. . .] it can also be thwarted or blocked by the effect to contain it' (Stonebridge 2011, 5), whilst Douglas contends that '[t]he danger of turning a trial into a pedagogical spectacle is that it becomes a legal farce' as 'the judicial process inevitably fails to grasp the most disturbing and fundamental issues raised by traumatic testimony, issues more satisfactorily explored through literature, history, or psychoanalysis' (Douglas 2001, 2-4).[12]

Read in the light of such concerns, Hellerstein's reluctance to utilise his courtroom as a therapeutic forum might well be regarded sympathetically. However, the peculiarity of his rulings lies in the fact that the judge continues to employ psychoanalytic rhetoric, even as he disavows the tenets of the trauma trial. Defending his preference for financial settlements over a courtroom encounter, Hellerstein comments, '[m]oney is the universal lubricant [. . .]. Each of us has a choice: Either to never forget that pain and have it ever present in our lives, or to fashion a life beyond the pain. [. . .] Somehow, we need to get past Sept. 11, 2001, as a country and individually' (Edelman 2007). These remarks imply that a public trial would frustrate rather than facilitate historical (and, presumably, psychical or emotional) resolution by revisiting memories of the attacks. Hellerstein also identifies a dissonance between the claims of victims and the needs of the collective, suggesting that personal grievances should remain unheard for the national good. He thus positions the trial as a *traumatising*, rather than therapeutic, medium, intimating that – in this particular context – the law's duty should be to forgetting rather than remembrance. As financial settlements require no public admission of liability, such practices constitute a rather amnesiac form of 'closure'.

Across his 9/11 cases, Hellerstein's rulings have recurrently marginalised the memorative and pedagogic capabilities of the court, privileging a decontextualised model of resolution above the interests of the historical record. In December 2013, the judge oversaw a $135 million settlement between American Airlines (whose flight 175 was flown into the South Tower of the World Trade Center) and Cantor Fitzgerald (the financial services firm that lost nearly two-thirds of its New York employees in the attacks), averting a trial that had been scheduled for early 2014. Hellerstein acknowledged that, without a court case, 'there [would] be no airing of such questions as how terrorists got through security, the best way to stop terrorists, whether there was really wrongdoing and negligence and how best to preserve liberties amid such threat' (Cheong 2013). However, he commented, whilst '[a]ll this will remain a mystery' (Cheong 2013), '[p]erhaps that is proper. [. . .] There's been no final accounting. . . . Hopefully, what is achieved is a measure of justice, a measure of reparation and closure to what for many people was a terrible tragedy' (Ax 2013).

Whilst it is difficult to comment upon the motives that have informed Hellerstein's decisions, one consequence of his rulings is that no American individual or corporation has been held publically responsible for losses sustained during the attacks in the cases under his adjudication. Although there is no reason to suspect that Hellerstein's judgements were (explicitly) informed by any ideological or political agenda, his rulings replicate a pattern that has dominated the legal afterlife of the attacks. As the remainder of this chapter will demonstrate, the discourses of the juridico-political sphere have struggled to elide the thorny issue of American accountability in diverse matters relating to 9/11 and its aftermath. The following section considers the ways in which Presidents Bush and Obama have attempted to deploy the heroic tropes of the jeremiad as a means of naturalising extra-legal forms of retribution, whilst the final case study considers the use of the Nuremberg analogy as a way of legitimising the troubled military commissions at Guantánamo Bay.

4.3 The new American jeremiad and retributive justice after 9/11

The rhetoric of the law has framed the narrative of American exceptionalism from the origins of the nation. Ferguson argues that '[s]eventeenth-century legal thought furnished a context for understanding history and acting upon it. That of the eighteenth-century created a comprehensive, secular vision of country for [. . .] Americans to define themselves within' (Ferguson 1984, 14). This vision has endured throughout succeeding centuries: Sarat and Hussain comment that '[t]oday, as in the past, Americans pride themselves on their commitment to the rule of law. This commitment is deeply rooted in America's history [. . .]. Invocations of the rule of law as a constitutive boundary separating the country from the rest of the world are pervasive' (Hussain and Sarat 2010, 1–2).

Premising the 'national values' of democracy, freedom, and justice upon the integrity of the country's juridico-political institutions, such 'commitments' were routinely evoked by American officials to differentiate the United States from its adversaries in the aftermath of 9/11. In his quintessential jeremiad of 20 September 2001,[13] Bush (2001g) firmly allied the United States with the causes of 'freedom' and 'justice', against an enemy motivated by 'fear' and 'cruelty'. In 2004, Jonathan Lippman, chief administrative judge of the State of New York similarly contended '[t]he rule of law is what separates us from those who seek to defeat our democratic institutions and way of life through violence and terror' (Lippman 2004, 9). However, as Stonebridge remarks, this affirmation of America's commitment to legal principles was in fact 'the prelude to a breathtaking contempt of the law' that has arguably rendered the 'promised civilised exercise' of justice 'meaningless' (Stonebridge 2011, 16).

From the immediate aftermath of the attacks, it was clear that certain political challenges would surround the juridical process of retribution. These related not merely to the problems of identifying an elusive, and to some extent, unknown enemy, but also to the fact that the most immediate perpetrators (the nineteen hijackers of the airplanes that crashed in New York, Washington, and Shanksville) were dead. As Anne McClintock argues:

> [t]he suicide attackers [. . .] instantly obliterated themselves in the fiery cataclysm, removing their bodies from the realm of visible retribution and thereby removing all means for the Bush Administration to be seen to recuperate its wounded potency. The state was faced with an immediate dilemma: how to *embody* the invisible enemy and *be visibly seen* to punish it? (McClintock 2011, 95).

McClintock suggests that, in answer to these questions, the Bush Administration constructed a tripartite strategy for a *visible* and *spectacular* mode of retaliation that was intended to reclaim its authority at home and abroad. These policies represent widely divergent forms of retribution, presenting disparate targets of wildly different scales:

> First, the enemy was individualised as a recognizable *face* – the epic male archenemy Bin Laden [. . . .]. Second, the dispersed forces of al Qaeda [. . .] were *nationalised,* equated with two nation-states [Afghanistan and Iraq] [. . .]. The third solution was to produce the enemy *as bodies* under U.S. supervision, subjecting them to dreadful revenge in the labyrinths of torture (McClintock 2011, 95).

These rationally, morally, and legally indeterminate policies have set the stage for an ongoing politicisation of justice that has seen legal and extra-legal modes of reckoning tethered tightly together. Focusing upon three speeches – given by Bush on 6 September 2006, and Obama on 21 May 2009 and 23 May 2013 – the following discussion considers the way in which both presidents have attempted to legitimise their retributive endeavours by framing them in the tropes of the jeremiad (see Chapter 2). Although delivered in markedly different circumstances (Bush's 2006 address and Obama's 2009 speech took place before the assassination of Osama bin Laden, the tumultuous events of the Arab Spring and their bloody legacies in Syria, Egypt, and Libya, and the withdrawal of American troops from Iraq, which are referenced in Obama's 2013 remarks), immediately prior to each of these jeremiads, both presidents had experienced significant challenges to the legality and ethicality of their retributive policies.[14] These speeches were thus required to (re)assert the authority of the president and to defend the integrity of their policies.

Despite the ideological differences between the Bush and Obama regimes, the divergent contexts in which the talks were delivered, and the disparate principles and practices for which they are arguing, the three jeremiads share remarkable similarities. Each speech references 9/11 as a historical watershed that demanded a recalibration of judicial principles; each, in turn, emphasises the legality and moral integrity of the president's current foreign policy; each ties these practices to America's historic fidelity to the law; and each is positioned as the beginning of a new era of transparency and accountability. However, as will become clear, whilst the 2006 and 2009 addresses of Bush and Obama project an unequivocal confidence in their ability to stabilise the narrative of retribution, in Obama's 2013 proceedings, the troubling legacy of the extra-legal processes deployed during the pursuit of justice for 9/11 threatens to disrupt the mythic tropes of the jeremiad.

Bush's speech of 6 September 2006 represents the first time the president publically acknowledged the existence of black site prisons (which he rather euphemistically describes as 'a separate program operated by the Central Intelligence Agency') and the authorisation of torture (referred to as 'sensitive questioning'). Bush attempts to legitimise these practices by asserting that 'America is a nation of law' (Bush 2006), a term he mentions nineteen times, emphasising the 'lawful methods' of his foreign policies, which, he claims, follows 'established legal standards' and is subject to 'multiple legal reviews' (Bush 2006). He also claims that information obtained from rendition and torture has prevented further attacks on America (something challenged by the 2014 Senate report into CIA activities in the aftermath of 9/11). He pledges:

> I'm going to share with you some of the examples provided by our intelligence community of how this program has saved lives, why it remains vital to the security of the United States and our friends and allies, and why it deserves the support of the United States Congress and the American people (Bush 2006).

Despite this gesture towards openness and transparency, Bush's speech frequently lapses into concealment. On the subject of the black site prisons, he comments, '[m]any specifics of this program, including where these detainees have been held and the details of their confinement, cannot be divulged' (Bush 2006). Discussing the interrogation of prisoners in American captivity, he acknowledges:

> the CIA used an alternative set of procedures [. . .]. I cannot describe the specific methods used. I think you understand why. If I did, it would help the terrorists learn how to resist questioning and to keep information from us that we need to prevent new attacks on our country (Bush 2006).

Under the guise of full disclosure, Bush retreats into secrecy in order to conceal the worst abuses of power after 9/11. In so doing, he exploits the ambiguity of political rhetoric. His discussion deploys a number of slippery phrases ('alternative procedures', 'authorised methods', 'rigorous process', 'sensitive questioning') to mask the reality of torture (indeed, Bush rather duplicitously takes pains to assure his audience, '[t]he United States does not torture. It's against our laws, and it's against our values. I have not authorised it, and I will not authorise it' [Bush 2006]). Judith

Butler describes such rhetoric as 'a form of "state speech"' (Butler 2004, 80) – an opaque idiom intended to deflect scrutiny by masking its own unreadability. For Butler, the linguistic basis of sovereign power is 'bound up with the extra-legal status of these official acts of speech. These acts become the means by which sovereign power extends itself; the more it can produce equivocation, the more effectively it can augment its power in the apparent service of justice' (Butler 2004, 80). This logic is premised upon a 'hegemonic grammar' which aims to produce 'a consensus on what certain terms will mean, how they can be used, and what lines of solidarity are implicitly drawn through this use' (Butler 2004, 3), by precluding 'certain kinds of questions, certain kinds of historical inquiries' in order 'to function as a moral justification for retaliation' (Butler 2004, 4).

Butler suggests that such constructions rely upon a 'sovereign temporality', which manifests a means of delimiting the historical reach of an event in order to divest it of any compromising complexity. After 9/11, she argues, 'in order to sustain the affective structure in which [Americans] are, on the one hand, victimised and, on the other, engaged in a righteous cause of rooting out terror, we have to begin the story with the experience of the violence we suffered' (Butler 2004, 4). It is, therefore, unsurprising that Bush opens his speech with a reference to the morning of September 11, stating:

> On the morning of September the 11th, 2001, our nation awoke to a nightmare attack. Nineteen men armed with box cutters took control of airplanes and turned them into missiles. They used them to kill nearly 3,000 innocent people.
>
> We watched the twin towers collapse before our eyes, and it became instantly clear that we'd entered a new world and a dangerous new war (Bush 2006).

Throughout his speech, Bush continues to mobilise September 11 as an organising framework for twenty-first century experience. However, it is not the actuality of the attacks that preoccupies the president, but the imaginary recurrence of a similar atrocity in a near, but unspecified, future.

Bush comments, '[w]e had to find the terrorists hiding in America and across the world before they were able to strike our country again'; 'our government's senior national security officials [had] to do everything in their power [. . .] to prevent another attack' (Bush 2006). The attacks are thus repeatedly transformed into a floating signifier, a symbol of unrealised threat that impels the government to take exceptional decisions and extraordinary actions. Interpreting the past and the future exclusively under the sign of terror, Bush renders each devoid of specificity: transforming the 'memory' of 9/11 into an extended metaphor for historical experience; portraying the future as an unknowable entity, defined only by the promise of further attacks. By contrast, he positions the present as a moment of utmost consequence: it is in the present that firm action must be taken to prevent future terror; in the present that the potential for heroism and redemption lies. Bush thus combines the slippery semantics of state speech with a highly presentist sovereign temporality. By framing his remarks in the familiar tropes of the jeremiad, he attempts to mask both the hermeneutic emptiness of his rhetoric and the temporal poverty of his interpretation of history.

Obama's 2009 address deploys similar rhetorical tropes to undermine many of the certainties established by Bush in 2006, highlighting the legal and ethical dubiety of his predecessor's policies and attempting to distance himself from their problematic legacy. On 22 January 2009, one day after he entered office, Obama signed an executive order mandating the cessation of enhanced interrogation techniques, the closure of black site prisons, and the dismantling of Guantánamo Bay, 'consistent with the national security and foreign policy interests of the United States and the interests of justice' (Obama 2009a). These principles strongly inform the jeremiad that he delivered at the National Archives in Washington, DC, on 21 May 2009. In his opening remarks, Obama underscores the juridical foundations of America's exceptionalism:

> The documents that we hold in this very hall – the Declaration of Independence, the Constitution, the Bill of Rights – are not simply words written into aging parchment. They are the foundation of liberty and justice in this country, and a light that shines for all who seek freedom, fairness, equality and dignity in the world (Obama 2009b).

Positioning himself as the rightful inheritor of these values, Obama's speech references the law twenty-four times, legal traditions twenty-one times, and the rule of law eight times. His rejection of the 'ad hoc legal approaches' of the Bush Administration is made on the grounds that policies such as torture transgress the judicial principles of the United States, creating a 'framework that failed to rely on our legal traditions and time-tested institutions; that failed to use our values as a compass' (Obama 2009b).

Obama's break with Bush is signalled by his adoption of a futural perspective. Rather than speaking to his current moment, Obama's speech looks towards a time in which the excesses of the War on Terror will be a distant memory. Rejecting the presentist policies of his predecessor on the grounds that they were made 'based upon fear rather than foresight' (Obama 2009b), Obama makes frequent references to 'going forward', 'focus[ing] on the future', to 'leave behind a legacy that outlasts my Administration, and that endures for the next President and the President after that; a legacy that protects the American people, and enjoys broad legitimacy at home and abroad' (Obama 2009b). The speech thus projects his confidence in the ability of the new government to transcend the problems of the past and restore the integrity of the present in order to move towards a glorious future in which the American nation is once more proclaimed as the purveyor of justice and the protector of the law. However, Obama's jeremiad of May 2013 demonstrates that it has not always proven easy to maintain this future-oriented gaze.

Delivered nearly four years to the day after his speech at the National Archives, the 2013 address makes an interesting comparison to its predecessors. Superficially, at least, the talk bears strong similarities to both Bush's speech of 2006 and Obama's remarks of 2009. The president begins by evoking the memory of 9/11 as the moment when Americans 'were shaken out of complacency' (Obama 2013). He moves on to affirm the changed nature of the world, which demands 'a different kind of war [. . .] – hardening targets, tightening transportation security, and giving law enforcement new tools to prevent terrorism' (Obama 2013). Obama continues to emphasise the nation's fidelity to the rule of law (mentioned twenty-two times, in line with both his own speech from 2009 and Bush's address of 2006), and the historic nature of this commitment, claiming:

> For over two centuries, the United States has been bound together by founding documents that defined who we are as Americans, and served as our compass through every type of change. [. . .] From the Civil War, to our struggle against fascism, and through the long, twilight struggle of the Cold War, [. . .] our commitment to Constitutional principles has weathered every war (Obama 2013).

Commensurate with the vision of his 2009 address, Obama projects these historical foundations forward to imagine a global future premised upon the ideals of American liberal democracy. He contends:

> long after the current messengers of hate have faded from the world's memory, alongside the brutal despots, and deranged madmen, and ruthless demagogues who litter history – the flag of the United States will still wave from small-town cemeteries to national monuments,

to distant outposts abroad. And that flag will still stand for freedom (Obama 2013).

As the references to cemeteries and monuments suggest, this future imaginary is founded upon the memory of a revered past (forged, presumably, in the present for which Obama is staking his claim). However, at moments throughout his speech, Obama admits an alternative reading of American history that is altogether more ambiguous.

In his opening statement, Obama remarks, 'Americans are deeply ambivalent about war, but having fought for our independence, we know that a price must be paid for freedom' (Obama 2013). He goes on to acknowledge that this liberty often comes at substantial human and moral cost, noting:

> our efforts must also be measured against the history of putting American troops in distant lands among hostile populations. In Vietnam, hundreds of thousands of civilians died in a war where the boundaries of battle were blurred. In Iraq and Afghanistan, despite the courage and discipline of our troops, thousands of civilians have been killed. So neither conventional military action, nor waiting for attacks to occur, offers moral safe-harbor (Obama 2013).

Whilst these allusions to the more problematic aspects of the American past undoubtedly represent a notable shift from the heroic view of American history conventionally established by the jeremiad, the memory that Obama struggles hardest to contain is the immediate legacy of the Bush Administration. Throughout the speech, Obama signals his awareness that the torture of Guantánamo detainees, and their ongoing detention without trial, threatens his vision of a harmonious future. These practices, he contends, have 'become a symbol around the world for an America that flouts the rule of law. [. . . H]istory will cast a harsh judgement on this aspect of our fight against terrorism, and those of us who fail to end it' (Obama 2013).

Obama thus casts the present as a site of moral urgency, in which both the American future and the future memory of the American past are placed radically in doubt. He asserts:

> America is at a crossroads. We must define the nature and scope of this struggle, or else it will define us. [. . . .] Imagine a future – ten years from now, or twenty years from now – when the United States of America is still holding people who have been charged with no

crime on a piece of land that is not a part of our country. Look at the current situation, where we are force-feeding detainees who are holding a hunger strike. Is that who we are? Is that something that our Founders foresaw? Is that the America we want to leave to our children? (Obama 2013)

Unlike either Bush's confident jeremiad of 2006 or his own, idealistic, speech of 2009, Obama is forced to concede that certain aspects of his own policies may themselves lead, not to the perfect future projected by the mythic history of the United States, but to the future imperfect imagined above. He comments:

> this is the moment to ask ourselves hard questions – about the nature of today's threats and how we should confront them. [. . .] From our use of drones to the detention of terrorist suspects, the decisions that we are making now will define the type of nation – and world – that we leave to our children (Obama 2013).

Whilst he attempts to offer a defence of these policies (which replicates, almost exactly, Bush's 2006 arguments for the use of torture and black site prisons),[15] Obama's speech slips back into a more circumspect register. He acknowledges that drone strikes raise 'profound questions – about who is targeted, and why; about civilian casualties, and the risk of creating new enemies; about the legality of such strikes under U.S. and international law; about accountability and morality' (Obama 2013).[16] Although such comments are undoubtedly mobilised as a rhetorical device (by demonstrating his anxiety over his actions, Obama affirms himself as a responsible and transparent president with a strong moral conscience), the need to continually foreground these concerns (rather than confidently asserting, as Bush did in 2006 and he himself did in 2009, that the president has right on his side) arguably demonstrates an anxiety about his ability to maintain interpretive control of history.[17]

Together, the three speeches analysed throughout this section demonstrate successive attempts to mobilise the framework of the jeremiad to legitimise the controversial foreign policies deployed during the pursuit of retributive justice after 9/11. As the 2006 and 2009 addresses of Bush and Obama demonstrate, the jeremiad provides a relatively efficacious framework for such ambitions when it operates around a presentist or futural temporality, able to elide the ethical and legal complexity of past practices and occlude their moral and political consequences. However, as Obama's 2013 speech demonstrates, when a memorative perspective is adopted, the jeremiad is destabilised by the interruptive legacy of events that threaten to undermine the heroic vision of American history. Whilst Obama continues to read the distant past (the heroic record of American history) and the far future (when American flags proclaim the triumph of freedom and democracy across the globe) under the sign of American exceptionalism, his address renders the recent past (the immediate post-9/11 period), the present, and the near future (the imperfect vision of an America ten or twenty years from now, where Guantánamo Bay remains open) sites of moral ambiguity, destabilised by the extra-legal practices of his predecessor and his own contentious policies. Building upon such claims, the following section examines the ways in which the disruptive memory of torture has intruded upon the military commissions at Guantánamo Bay, challenging the court's ability to construct either a coherent legal memory or a convincing vision of memory-justice in relation to the attacks.

4.4 Analogising justice after 9/11: Guantánamo, Nuremberg, Abu Ghraib

Like the extra-legal modes of retaliation analysed above, the pursuit of juridical retribution for 9/11 has been a highly politicised process. The prosecution of those accused of planning and executing the September 11 attacks has engendered a (re)nationalisation of justice, which has marginalised legal precedents that have underscored international jurisprudence since the aftermath of World War II (notably, the foundations of international law and the Geneva Conventions on Human Rights). Yet, even as their juridical legacy has been undermined, the American-led Nuremberg trials, held in Germany from 1945–6, have been widely conscripted as an analogy for the pursuit of justice after 9/11. Replicating the tendencies seen in the Americanisation of the Holocaust analysed in Chapter 3, such comparisons invoke the memory of Nuremberg in order to validate the troubled military commissions at Guantánamo Bay. However, as will become clear, this interpretation has not always proven easy to impose, and those in charge of the hearings have struggled to distance their proceedings from the spectre of an altogether more troubling event from the recent past – the torture of prisoners in American custody at Abu Ghraib. Caught between two oppositional frames of memory – Nuremberg and its claim to justice, Abu Ghraib and its stain of injustice – the attempt to construct a coherent legal memory for 9/11 has been undermined by the need to secure a positive legacy for Guantánamo Bay.

The aftermath of the Holocaust transformed the way juridical processes sought to reckon with historical atrocity. Hannah Arendt famously argued that the genocide had exploded 'the limits of the law' (Arendt 1992, 54), 'overstepping and shattering any and all legal systems' (Arendt 1992, 54). Accordingly, as Felman contends, the proceedings that followed the end of the Second World War were responsible for establishing a 'precedent and a new paradigm of trial' in which 'the law was challenged to address the causes and consequences of historical traumas' (Felman 2002, 1). These precedents laid the foundations for contemporary models of jurisprudence. Mark Osiel argues that the postwar proceedings represented 'the serious beginning of the construction of international criminal courts in the fight against grave humanitarian law (HL) and human rights (HR) violations' (Osiel 2012, 89), whilst Levy and Sznaider similarly contend that the Nuremberg trials created 'a new cosmopolitan law' that marked the beginnings of a 'new transnational world' (Levy and Sznaider 2010, 71).

Despite the (contemporary and retrospective) criticisms levelled at these proceedings,[18] the post-Holocaust trials entered the popular imagination as a triumph of memory, law, and justice. As Douglas comments, these proceedings are generally upheld as 'powerful, imaginative, and socially necessary responses to extreme crimes' in which 'the law, formally conceived, emerged victorious' (Douglas 2001, 5). In the United States, the Holocaust trials have engendered a vocabulary of victimhood and perpetration that (as analysed in the previous chapter) has subsequently been deployed to frame the (cultural, political, and juridical) interpretation of other events. As Levy and Snzaider contend:

> The American understanding of the Holocaust, which framed the Nuremberg trials, was originally universalistic [. . .]. Even though, or perhaps precisely because, the Holocaust and the fate of the Jews remained a neglected aspect of the Nuremberg trials, it formed the backdrop for its universalistic message. The struggle at Nuremberg was seen as one between civilisation and barbarism. Civilisation was the victim, Nazi barbarism the perpetrator (Levy and Sznaider 2010, 73–4).

In the aftermath of 9/11, the Bush Administration sought to capitalise on this vision by harnessing the problematic – and fitful – process of justice at Guantánamo Bay to the Nuremberg precedent.[19]

Comparisons between Guantánamo and Nuremberg peaked in the run-up to the 2008 election, as government officials attempted to secure a positive legacy at the end of their time in office. As Jeffrey Toobin, former assistant United States attorney and senior legal analyst for CNN commented in April 2008, in this period, '[t]he Bush Administration, instead of closing Guantánamo, [was] trying to rebrand it — as a successor to Nuremberg rather than as a twin of Abu Ghraib' (Toobin 2008). In June 2008, Brigadier General Thomas W. Hartmann, legal adviser to the Office of Military Commissions, described the court at Guantánamo as a 'modern Nuremberg' (Horton 2008). Policy statements aimed to enshrine a similar perspective. In December 2008, the State Department issued a memorandum to US embassies, stating that American ambassadors should defend the decision to seek the death penalty for the September 11 accused 'by recalling the executions of Nazi war criminals after World War II' (Associated Press 2008). As an Associated Press report states:

> the department advises American diplomats to refer to Nuremberg if asked by foreign governments or media about the legality of capital punishment in the 9/11 cases.
>
> 'International Humanitarian Law contemplates the use of the death penalty for serious violations of the laws of war,' says the cable, which was written by the office of the department's legal adviser, John Bellinger. 'The most serious war criminals sentenced at Nuremberg were executed for their actions' (Associated Press 2008).

Despite the frequency with which the Nuremberg analogy was deployed by Bush Administration officials, however, the discourses surrounding the 2008 election also exemplify the ambiguous hermeneutics of memory. As Jack Goldsmith, a Harvard law professor and assistant attorney general under the Bush Administration remarks, 'Pentagon officials like to compare the Guantánamo process to the Nuremberg tribunals that convicted top Nazi war criminals at the end of World War II. But critics say the Nuremberg analogy actually highlights the shortcomings of military justice at the U.S. Naval base' (Goldsmith 2012). In June 2008, then Senator Obama invoked the Nuremberg precedent to argue against the decision to deny the right to habeas corpus to prisoners at Guantánamo Bay on the grounds that it overturned the balance of fairness and accountability necessary to ensure the integrity and authority of the court. Obama commented:

> During the Nuremberg trials, part of what made us different was even after these Nazis had performed atrocities that no one had ever seen

before, we still gave them a day in court, and that taught the entire world about who we are but also the basic principles of rule of law (Goldsmith 2012).

Colonel Morris Davis, the former chief prosecutor of the military commissions at Guantánamo (who resigned from his post in 2007, believing that defendants would not be offered the right to a fair trial), contended in a 2008 interview with *Harper's Magazine* that, from the start, the proceedings had been 'manipulated by administration appointees in an attempt to foreclose the possibility of acquittal' (Horton 2008). Davis's indictment of the Guantánamo commissions was buttressed by a comparison to Nuremberg – he contended, 'even at Nuremberg there had been some acquittals, something that had lent great credibility to the proceedings' (Horton 2008).[20]

These critiques subvert the connection between Nuremberg and Guantánamo, established by the Bush Administration, rendering the twenty-first-century military commissions the antithesis, rather than the mirror, of the post-war trials. In so doing, they raise the spectre of an altogether less positive memorative analogue for the prison. In an interview with *Time* magazine, navy captain Prescott Prince, chief military counsel to Khalid Sheik Mohammed (the most prominent of the 9/11 accused), argued that the analogisation of Guantánamo and Nuremberg was invalidated by the torture of detainees in American captivity. He asserted: '[t]here is no comparison, because none of the top Nazi defendants faced torture, or waterboarding, or other forms of 'enhanced interrogation' — or had to be concerned that information elicited under torture might be used against them in a court of law' (Zagorin 2008). Prince thus connected the military tribunals with the worst excesses of the War on Terror. In so doing, he implicitly tied the construction of legal memory at Guantánamo to the memory of the extra-legal measures deployed at black site prisons, Bagram Airbase, and, most famously, Abu Ghraib after 9/11.

Whilst the torture of detainees elsewhere has remained an open, but invisible, secret, the abuse of prisoners at Abu Ghraib is notable for its exposure.[21] As W. T. J. Mitchell comments, the infamous images that have circulated in the global public sphere since 2004 are 'imprinted on collective memory' (Mitchell 2011, 114) by dint of their hypervisibility.[22] For David Simpson, the 'radical turbulence' of the Abu Ghraib images has the effect of destabilising the very 'distinctions between them and us, between civilisation and barbarism' (Simpson 2006, 110) that the Bush Administration sought to impose (and which it aimed to instil through its repeated references to Nuremberg). The photographs undermine this heroic vision of the nation by recalling troubling moments from the American past. Simpson comments that, upon seeing the pictures, the public was 'reminded of the darker moments in our own national history – such as those lynching postcards – which are after all not simply to be consigned to a barbaric past from which we have emerged' (Simpson 2006, 110), whilst Mitchell contends that 'the images seem to keep coming back to haunt the nation in whose name they were produced, while eliciting screen memories of lynching photographs, martyrdoms, and scenes of torture' (Mitchell 2011, 116).

For all their subversive potential, however, critics remain uncertain about the political and ethical efficacy of the Abu Ghraib images. Susan Sontag (2004) famously critiqued the 'analgesic' effect of such photographs, arguing that contemporary culture is 'weakened by the expectations brought to images, disseminated by the media, whose leaching out of content contributes most to the deadening of feeling' (Sontag 2003, 95). Stephen F. Eisenman similarly noted that the pictures formed part of 'the long Western history of the representation of torture that has helped inscribe an oppressive ideology of master and slave on our bodies and brains, enabling (especially at times of fear) a moral forgetfulness or even paralysis to set in – an "Abu Ghraib effect"' (Eisenman 2007, 99). Considering the lack of high-profile prosecutions, and the relatively minor impact the release of the photographs appeared to have on government or military policy, Mitchell contends, 'it is difficult to think of another image in the contemporary mediasphere that does so many things while seeming to accomplish so little. This is why its only guarantee is memorability, and its only power is to awaken the desire for a justice to come' (Mitchell 2011, 122).

Mitchell suggests that, whilst their immediate effect may have been slight, the legacy of the Abu Ghraib photographs lies in their memorative potency. These images, he asserts, will 'haunt all attempts to understand [the post-9/11] period' (Mitchell 2011, 118). This haunting is 'most evident in the continued effort to disavow, quarantine, and "disappear" the images' (Mitchell 2011, 118) by successive US governments.[23] However, he continues, 'every effort to make the image of the enemy vanish, or (more precisely) of what has been done to the enemy in our name, has sparked a new revival of its circulation' (Mitchell 2011, 118).

It is here that the resonance between the Abu Ghraib images and the Guantánamo trials becomes clear. The torture of detainees in American custody is the connection that links Abu Ghraib to Guantánamo Bay in the public imagination.[24] The abuse of prisoners threatens to transform Guantánamo Bay from a forum of law and justice to a space of lawlessness and injustice as the memory of torture destabilises the clear-cut boundaries between civilisation and barbarism, innocence and guilt, victimhood and perpetration, upon which the authority of the court (and its judgement regarding the events of 9/11 and their aftermath) depends.

Accordingly, those in charge of the military tribunals, under both Bush and Obama Administrations, have attempted to expunge all references to torture from the legal (and historical) record. Ironically, however, the very measures intended to protect the integrity of the court have done most to undermine its claim to Nuremberg's inheritance. Many of the precautions taken to preserve the image of national exceptionalism transgress the juridical principles established in the aftermath of World War II. Under the Bush Administration, those in charge of Guantánamo Bay have undermined the Geneva Conventions (by refusing to grant detainees the right to habeas corpus), marginalised human rights (through the use of 'enhanced interrogation techniques' tantamount to torture), subverted international and American law (by neglecting to try prisoners in civil courts and adopting instead the legally precarious, and problematic, model of military tribunals),[25] and occluded a cosmopolitan model of justice in favour of a unilateral, and highly nationalistic, legal process.[26] Many of these procedures have ceased under the Obama Administration, however, the government has continued to construct a veil of secrecy around the court, which stands in direct contravention of the (relatively) open and transparent pursuit of justice at Nuremberg at the end of World War II.

Although the military commissions established by Obama to try the September 11 accused look set to proceed to trial (unlike the proceedings inaugurated under the Bush Administration), the pre-trial hearings have been dogged by numerous complications. Debates have arisen over attorney-client privileges,[27] the defence's ability to call witnesses,[28] the applicability of the Constitution to the defendants,[29] whether secret sessions can be held in the absence of the accused,[30] and, most recurrently, government censorship of the proceedings.[31] Whilst Guantánamo's official motto celebrates 'Safe, Transparent, and Legal Detention' (Rosenberg 2014), the flow of information and material leaving the camp is strictly limited. No cameras are allowed into the courtroom and the closed sessions are fed, with a forty-second delay, into viewing rooms provided for victims' families and representatives of the press. Although this delay is officially intended to allow the judge to block any information deemed dangerous to national security, the device also limits the information available to watching reporters.[32]

Critics of the proceedings contend that these measures represent an attempt to sanitise legal memory by forestalling any discussion of the detainees' treatment in US captivity. Clive Stafford Smith, director of the charity Reprieve and an attorney for several of the Guantánamo detainees, remarks:

> the courtroom has the sealed-off press section [. . . because a]ll they care about is the evidence of the accused being tortured. They keep saying that the accused will see all the evidence, but the accused already knows he's been tortured. The point is to make sure that the media and the public don't see the evidence of torture (Toobin 2008).

Defense lawyers argue that the decision to 'presumptively classify' aspects of their clients' testimonies relating to their treatment in American custody deliberately invalidates their 'memories and experiences' (Rosenthal 2012). However, as Caroll Bogert of Human Rights Watch remarks:

> Torture is Guantánamo's Original Sin. It is both invisible and omnipresent. The U.S. government wants coverage of the 9/11 attacks, but not the waterboarding, sleep deprivation, prolonged standing and other forms of torture that the CIA applied to the defendants. It's tricky, prosecuting the 9/11 case while trying to keep torture out of the public eye. 'Torture is the thread running through all of this,' one of the detainees' psychiatrists told me. 'You can't tell the story without it' (Bogert 2014).

Whilst the government and the prosecution have moderated the release of information from the Guantánamo courtroom, they have been less successful in suppressing the memory of torture elsewhere in the American legal system. The military commissions have been recurrently undermined by their imbrication in a wider network of cases concerning the abuse of prisoners (including and exceeding the September 11 accused). Since enemy combatants arrived at Guantánamo Bay in 2002, a series of civil cases relating to conditions in American custody have been heard in the district, federal, and supreme courts of the United States.[33] The first detainee case to reach the supreme court was *Rasul v. Bush* in April 2004, which marked the culmination of two separate actions, the first involving twelve Kuwaiti nationals, the second two British citizens and an Australian, all of whom had been imprisoned at Guantánamo Bay since 2002, all of whom had been denied access to lawyers or the courts.

The case coincided with the release of the first pictures of torture from Abu Ghraib. As Jonathan Hafetz argues, the circulation of these images 'validated the concern [. . .] that by exempting the president's sweeping claims of executive power from habeas corpus review, the Court would insulate the worst forms of illegal detention and abuse from judicial scrutiny' (Hafetz 2011, 117). The debate surrounding the defendants' rights to habeas corpus is thus inherently, if implicitly, linked to the controversy over torture – and the *Rasul* judgement reflects this connection. Whilst earlier hearings in district and appellate courts had ruled against the detainees, arguing with the government that foreign nationals held outside the mainland United States could not claim habeas review, this ruling held that detainees could seek judicial redress under the federal habeas corpus statute, underscoring as Hafetz notes, 'the importance of habeas corpus as a check against illegal executive action' (Hafetz 2011, 119).[34]

Despite the cessation of enhanced interrogation techniques from 2009, the spectre of torture continues to inform institutional struggles over the authority to determine the treatment and rights of detainees. In a federal court hearing in February 2014, six former Guantánamo detainees brought litigation against Donald Rumsfeld, seeking compensation for the torture they endured at Guantánamo Bay. As the Center for Constitutional Rights notes, this suit had initially been dismissed by a lower court in 2013, because 'the law in the federal courts left it unclear whether torture and religious abuse were prohibited at the time' (Center for Constitutional Rights 2014). However, whilst the supreme court has declined to hear torture cases from other prisoners who were mistreated at Guantánamo on the grounds that 'immunity doctrines apply to shield the actions of government officials who abused detainees while they were suspected of being enemy combatants' (Center for Constitutional Rights 2014), this case differs because the torture of the claimants continued even after they had been cleared for release. Noel Brinkerhoff contends that, as a result, 'Guantánamo Bay could become the focus of multiple lawsuits by detainees who have won the right to sue in federal court over the conditions of their confinement' (Brinkerhoff 2014).

Whilst these cases reveal the ways in which the interruptive memory of torture has continued to concern the diverse institutions of the US legal system, two recent developments suggest that it may yet exert an even more immediate impact upon the court's eventual judgement in the September 11 hearings. In November 2013, the wife of David Hicks, an Australian convicted of material support for terrorism under the Bush

Administration, filed a federal lawsuit to overturn her husband's verdict on the grounds that the charge for which he was convicted was not a war crime (and thus could not be tried in a military court),[35] and the evidence used against Hicks, including his confession, had been obtained under torture.[36] As the court documents filed by his attorney state:

> Over the course of more than five years, Mr Hicks was repeatedly beaten, sexually assaulted, threatened with deadly violence, injected with unknown substances and subjected to an entire arsenal of psychological gambits, ploys and subterfuges that had as their aim the destruction of his personality. [. . .] Unless the word has simply lost its meaning in this new day, the abuse he endured constitutes torture (O'Brien 2013).

The Hicks hearings raise doubts about whether the eventual verdict of the September 11 Commissions will withstand future scrutiny. Lawyers for the 9/11 defendants argue that, should their clients be found guilty, the death penalty should not be imposed because the jury's judgement will necessarily be based on evidence obtained under torture. Although prosecution officials have assembled 'clean teams' of investigators not involved in interrogations to assemble their case against the defendants, their attorneys contend that such provisions are insufficient. As Stafford Smith remarks, 'The clean teams are a joke [. . .]. It's impossible to "unhear" what they said when they were tortured' (Toobin 2008).

Whilst the Hicks case threatens to undermine the eventual judgement of the court, the second recent development places the entire legitimacy of the commissions in doubt. In March 2014 the Senate released a report into the treatment of detainees in American custody under the Bush Administration. Whilst the full contents of the document have not yet been made public, Intelligence Committee chairwoman Senator Dianne Feinstein contends that it 'includes details of each detainee in CIA custody, the conditions under which they were detained, how they were interrogated, the intelligence they actually provided and the accuracy – or inaccuracy – of CIA descriptions about the program to the White House, Department of Justice, Congress and others' (Feinstein 2012). Given that many of the delays that have occurred during the pre-trial hearings at Guantánamo have revolved around the need to conceal classified information about the detainees' treatment in American custody, as Army Major Jason Wright, defense attorney for Khalid Sheikh Mohammed argues, whilst the 'U.S. government has gone to great lengths to classify evidence of crimes – crimes committed by U.S.

actors', '[w]ere this information in this Senate report to be revealed [. . .] it would completely gut the classification architecture currently in place before the commissions' (Leopold 2014). In a motion filed to obtain an unredacted copy of this material, Richard Kammen, defense attorney for Abd al-Rahim al-Nashiri (accused of planning the bombing of the USS Cole in 2000, and currently under trial in a separate military commission at Guantánamo Bay) comments that the report 'will be central to the accused's defense [. . .] in impeaching the credibility of the evidence against him and in mitigation of the death sentence the government is seeking to impose' (Leopold 2014). Furthermore, he asserts, the publication of this material 'would really eliminate the "need" for military commissions, which are in my view mainly a vehicle to have what will look like trials but will keep whatever evidence of torture the judge ultimately allows secret from or sanitised to the public' (Leopold 2014).

The shadow of torture thus threatens to undermine the commission's integrity as an architect of memory, an arbiter of justice, and an instrument of the law. Saby Ghoshray argues that torture manifests 'a tear in the legal fabric, a constitutional black hole covered by the shadow of imperial sovereignty' (Ghosray 2007, 81), and McClintock similarly concludes that the tribunals ultimately represent little more than a *'theater of judicial semblance'*, a 'simulacrum of legality where none exists' (McClintock 2011, 104–5). Whilst the release of the CIA report appears to signal the slow emergence of the official memory of the abuses that took place in American custody after 9/11, Sarat and Hussain question whether 'without some measure of [official] accountability for crimes, particularly torture, such overtures may be insufficient' (Sarat and Hussain 2010, 19). It seems unlikely that any attempt to reckon with this legacy will be American-led. As Hajjar notes, 'Congress's record on the issue of international law violations over the last decade displays a pattern of sanctioning official impunity' (Hajjar 2010, 111). Such comments are borne out by a host of legislative rulings from the 2002 American Service-Members' Protection Act (which authorises the president to override the authority of the International Criminal Court in its attempts to detain or prosecute members of the US armed forces), to the 2003 Universal Jurisdiction Rejection Act (which argues that the notion of universal jurisdiction is a threat to the sovereignty of the United States), and the 2006 Military Commissions Act (which granted retrospective immunity for American breaches of the Geneva Conventions back to 1997).

In the aftermath of 9/11, the institutions of the juridico-political sphere have recurrently worked to shield Americans from prosecution.

However, as Scot Horton (an attorney responsible for pursuing the international prosecution of Americans in relation to these cases) notes, if 'U.S. courts and prosecutors will not address the matter [. . .] foreign courts appear only too happy to step in' (Horton 2008). Over the past few years, there have been several attempts to prosecute American officials for the rendition and torture of European citizens from Spain, Italy, and Germany, among others.[37] Cases have also been brought against foreign states and nationals for their role in the abuse of terror suspects. In December 2013, Guantánamo detainees al-Nashiri and Abu Zubaydah filed a lawsuit against the Polish government for its role in facilitating the establishment of the CIA black site prison where, they allege, they were tortured by American operatives. Their claim builds upon the lawsuit of Khaled al-Masri, a Lebanese-born German citizen. Having repeatedly tried to hold the US accountable for his torture and rendition by the CIA, al-Masri successfully sued the Macedonian government for $82,000 in the European Court of Human Rights for its role in aiding and abetting his abuse.[38]

One might argue that together these trials offer a tentative mode of juridical cosmopolitanism that upholds the transnational pursuit of justice in the face of the engrained reluctance of the American juridico-political sphere to hold US officials accountable for their actions. Whilst their mistreatment in American custody does not, of course, exonerate the September 11 accused of their (self-confessed) roles in the planning and execution of the attacks, the way in which the narrative of torture has haunted the Guantánamo tribunals, supplanting the Nuremberg analogy with the spectre of Abu Ghraib, suggests that the frame of legal memory is perhaps more complex, and certainly less stable, than it might first appear. The tensions and inconsistences exhibited by the agendas of political and juridical institutions, across the different branches of the American government, through the varying courts of the US legal system, and beyond, underscore the multifarious construction of juridical redress. Taking these considerations into account, the final section of this chapter considers the ways in which the nexus of memory, law, and justice might be reframed as a constantly evolving montage unfolding across legal, political, cultural, and national borders.

4.5 Reframing memory, law, and justice

Felman suggests that the 'law [. . .] is responsible not just for the recording but for the censorship of history' (Felman 2002, 83–4). Legal processes attempt to 'mark at once what history *remembers* and what history *forgets*, at once what is pragmatically included in and what is programmatically excluded from collective memory' (Felman 2002, 84). Alert to these sanitising tendencies, Osiel contends that, in seeking justice for historical atrocities, we should be 'wary of the potential for political manipulation, injustice to defendants, distortion of the historical record, and fostering dangerous delusions of purity and grandeur' (Osiel 2012, 294). As this chapter has sought to demonstrate, juridical discourses relating to 9/11 have repeatedly mobilised the master-narratives of American memorial culture to protect the historic image of American innocence: Judge Hellerstein has deployed the rhetoric of trauma to eschew the need for a public judgement upon the failings of US corporations in civil cases relating to the attacks; the presidential addresses of Bush and Obama have instrumentalised the paradigms of the jeremiad in order to legitimise contentious extra-legal modes of retribution; and legal and political officials have repeatedly invoked analogies to the Nuremberg trials as a means of validating the military commissions at Guantánamo Bay and eliding the troubling memory of torture. However, whilst these frames of memory have done much to underscore the impression of American innocence in wider memorial culture, they have been destabilised by their instrumentalisation in the US legal system. The self-evidence they assume elsewhere is problematised, their central claims unsettled, and their ability to act as stabilising frameworks for the representation of attacks undermined by the contingencies of justice.

The juridical afterlife of 9/11 has been messy and complex, calling into conflict the branches of American government, criminal and military justice systems, district and supreme courts, and American and international law. Legal and extra-legal forms of reckoning (from financial settlements to civil trials, military tribunals to covert assassinations) have assigned different degrees of responsibility (corporate negligence, criminal guilt, sponsorship of terrorism, war crimes) to disparate parties (individuals, corporations, terrorist organisations, nation-states) on behalf of diverse complainants (victims' families, rescue workers, corporations, the nation), impelling divergent modes of redress (financial recompense, public accountability, imprisonment, death). Although these vicissitudes of accountability are not morally, politically, or indeed, legally equivalent to each other, they exemplify the fact that the work of historical reckoning comprises a complicated assemblage of diverse practices, policies, and proceedings from the (national and international) institutions of the juridico-political sphere.

As Osiel argues, there are 'two very different ways' in which the law might contribute to the construction of memory-justice in the wake of historical atrocity:

> The first views legal proceedings as drawing upon an already-existing consensus within a country regarding its first principles and as employing that consensus to fuse a single, shared interpretation of its recent past. [. . .] The second view does not expect legal proceedings to draw upon, nor even necessarily to produce any society-wide consensus on such matters. [. . .] The proceedings are founded on civil dissensus. They produce the kind of solidarity embodied in the increasingly respectful way that citizens can come to acknowledge the differing views of their fellows (Osiel 2012, 22–3).

Whilst the master-narratives analysed throughout this book have been mobilised to give the impression of a consensual approach to the legal memory of 9/11, both their inability to maintain an interpretative hegemony in juridico-political discourse, and the wide range of (conflicting) proceedings relating to the attacks, expose the inherently dissensual nature of memory-justice. Major disasters impel multifarious modes of redress and their legal afterlife is long and complicated. Broadening the historical and geographical lens through which we approach the work of historical reckoning facilitates a recalibration, not only of the *frames* of memory, law, and justice, but of their respective *scales* as well. This process engenders five key developments, which I will briefly outline by way of conclusion.

Firstly, as intimated above, it is necessary to acknowledge the montaged nature of the law itself. Accordingly, I contend that the interests of justice are best served by accommodating memorative dissensus (to adopt Osiel's terminology) to generate a legal discourse that allows for divergent approaches to the past. The legal memories constructed by disparate proceedings need not produce a coherent narrative, rather, each nuances and mediates our understanding of past events. As Douglas argues, '[i]ndividual trials must be staged to reach closure; yet the discourse of legal judgement and the historical understanding it contain remains fluid and can be completely revised' (Douglas 2001, 4).

Secondly, I suggest that, in a rapidly globalising age, the work of justice assumes an international dimension. Treating 9/11 in this way would make it necessary to acknowledge the narratives of Guantánamo and Abu Ghraib, the earlier al Qaeda attacks on US embassies and assets, subsequent bombings in Bali, Madrid, and London, the events of the Arab Spring, the spread of Islamism to Africa and the Arabian Peninsula, and the lives lost as 'collateral damage' in the ongoing War on Terror, as tangential but essential parts of the narrative of the attacks (an even longer focus might confront the history of Western involvement in the Middle East and the divisive legacy of centuries of imperialism and invasion). Such thinking should not relativise the horrific events of September 11 2001, or mitigate the guilt of those responsible for the attacks, but hold the juridical record open to the complexity of history. As Osiel asserts, in moving towards a legal memory founded upon dissensus, the law should 'treat easy cases as if they were hard ones', 'make debate within the courtroom be made to resonate with the public debate beyond the courtroom', offering a 'circuitous route to judgement' that is 'vulnerable to contextualising historical arguments' (Osiel 2012, 296).

Thirdly, I argue that, without losing sight of the specificities of each process of reckoning, it is important to remain aware of legal precedents that might inform present visions of justice. Whilst it is undoubtedly true that catastrophe forces the law to innovate, it is dangerous to allow the uncertainty of aftermath to override valuable lessons that have been learned from past proceedings. Whilst all models of justice are necessarily imperfect and incomplete, important precedents have been marginalised after 9/11. As Peter Judson Richards argues, '[a]t a time when calls for global American intervention alternate with cries against American imperialist overreaching, examples from the historical experience of once-similarly situated Western forebearers and allies, allowing for differences occasioned by the passage of time, deliver an illuminating prospect' (Richards 2007, 10). Yet, 'American understanding of the practices to which international law applies often lingers under the fog of a more general historical and cultural amnesia' (Richards 2007, 9).

Fourthly, given the shortcomings of the juridical processes analysed throughout this chapter, I suggest that to presume the law's fidelity to memory and justice is to ignore the fact that, without careful self-reflexion, this fragile triumvirate can disintegrate into oppositional forces. As Levy and Sznaider contend, whilst '[l]egal procedures institutionalize remembering and forgetting [. . .], trials have to proclaim truth and justice, which often do not correspond to memory' (Levy and Sznaider 2010, 19). Despite their apparent similarities, in many ways, the ideals of law and memory rely on antithetical foundations: whilst the law aims to pass judgement on the past, memory opens it up to contrasting interpretations; whilst the law simplifies historical events to their barest fundamentals (innocence and guilt), memory acknowledges their complexity; whilst the law seeks objective truth, memory admits the coexistence of numerous perspectives. Accordingly, I argue, we might most profitably consider the law as one medium of collective memory among many: its judgement one of multiple interpretations of history; its vision of justice one of myriad modes of redress.

Finally, I hope that this *cultural interdiscursivity* might be paralleled by increasing *critical interdisciplinarity* across the social sciences and humanities. Savelsberg laments the lack of dialogue between the fields of criminology, war, and genocide studies, contending that 'such segmentation of knowledge has problematic consequences for our understanding of atrocities and crime generally' (Savelsberg 2010, 40). Emerging scholarship in this area has begun to recognise the shared interests of memory studies, human rights, and law, yet there is more scope for development, particularly in bringing together the complementary fields of transcultural memory and comparative justice to think critically about the intersections of diverse forms of historical reckoning in an increasingly globalised age. This process demands reflexivity from theorists about their entanglement with the hegemonic discourses of the public sphere and their own roles in establishing, maintaining, and critiquing the frames of memory, law, and justice.

Ultimately, I argue that a montaged approach to memory, law, and justice would acknowledge the dissensus within and across these three discourses, conceiving each as a multifaceted and open-ended process of which contradiction and incoherence are inherent and necessary properties. To recognise the montaged nature of this triumvirate – in practice and in theory – is to embrace the complexities of history and the messy vicissitudes of accountability it engenders. Finally, then, I turn to the Conclusion to consider how the *transcendental* frames of memory critiqued throughout this book might be reworked to provide a *montaged* culture of memory, tolerant of diversity and attentive to difference, both inside and outside national boundaries.

Conclusion

Over the course of this book, I have examined the ways in which frames of memory acquire hegemonic dominance when mobilised by the discourses of the public-political sphere, calling for more attention to the biases naturalised by such paradigms through their repetition over time, arguing for greater reflexivity in the relationship between memorative practice and theory, and urging the development of a more diverse culture of memory that seeks to open up, rather than delimit, dialogue and debate about the past. The preceding chapters foreground three frames of memory that have mediated representations of 9/11 across cultural, critical, political, and juridical discourses over the past thirteen years – the rhetoric of trauma, the tropes of the jeremiad, and Americanised Holocaust memory. These *transcendental* paradigms underscore the simultaneous ubiquity and uniqueness of American suffering by collectivising trauma, nationalising victimhood, and exceptionalising the attacks. In so doing, such templates (implicitly or explicitly) mask other losses from view, perpetuating an introspective and exclusionary memorial culture that is reluctant to acknowledge any mode of contextualising historicity. Accordingly, I suggest that we might productively move towards a *montaged* memorial culture that is inclusive of a variety of perspectives, agendas, and interpretations, and global in its orientation. In so doing, I argue for more attention to the political and ethical implications of frame-setting, and call for greater reflexivity from practitioners and theorists of memory about the ways in which their narratives intersect with and relate to the hegemonic discourses of the public-political sphere.

The politics of framing has received significant critical attention in the aftermath of 9/11, most notably, perhaps, in the work of Nancy Fraser and Judith Butler. Both Butler and Fraser are alert to the hegemonic implications of frame-setting, critiquing the ways in which such processes exacerbate the perpetuation of injustice through the creation of what Fraser describes as 'non-persons' (Fraser 2008, 19) and Butler conceptualises as the inequitable hierarchies of life that designate some individuals and collectives as 'grievable' and others as 'barely human' (Butler 2004, 32). Whilst Fraser argues for a process of *re*framing to 'change the deep grammar of frame-setting in a globalising world' (Fraser 2008, 23) and conceive of justice from an international perspective, Butler calls for a *de*framing of war and violence that allows for 'a loosening of the mechanism of control, and with it, a new trajectory of affect' and empathy (Butler 2009, 11). Both of these processes have significant implications for the future montaging of memory.

Fraser contends that 'frame-setting is among the most consequential of political decisions' (Fraser 2008, 19). At its extremity, she argues, misframing results in a kind of 'political death' through which individuals and groups become 'non-persons with respect to justice' (Fraser 2008, 20). Attentive to the normative dimensions of framing, Fraser aims to resist the 'meta-political misrepresentation' that arises when states 'monopolize the activity of frame-setting, denying voice to those who may be harmed in the process, and blocking creation of democratic arenas where the latter's crimes can be vetted and redressed' (Fraser 2008, 26). In so doing, she attempts to challenge the 'Keynesian-Westphalian' framework that has dominated political and legal culture in the post-1945 era, urging 'transnational social movements [to] contest the national frame within which justice conflicts have historically been situated and seek to re-map the bounds of justice on a broader scale' (Fraser 2008, 1).

Such contentions resonate closely with my call to montage the memory of September 11. Without negating the devastating impact of the attacks upon those whose lives were most immediately affected, I suggest that we need to position 9/11 and its aftermath as *global* events with far-reaching causes and consequences to destabilise the highly nationalistic frames through which these occurrences have been interpreted. Such ambitions have informed a number of critical and cultural counter-narratives that have emerged in the American public sphere over the past thirteen years, challenging the hegemonic frames of memory that have dominated the commemoration of September 11. Whilst it is impossible to do justice to the complexity and heterogeneity of these discourses here, in order to begin the work of montaging the memorial culture of 9/11, it seems pertinent to offer an overview of some of the most significant counter-memories to have emerged following the attacks.

From the immediate aftermath of 9/11, prominent American scholars such as Noam Chomsky (2001 and 2011) and Fredric Jameson (2003) sought to develop a critical strand of 'dissent from the homeland' (Hauerwas and Lentricchia 2003). Recent years have seen more specific attempts to destabilise the frames of memory analysed throughout this book (sometimes with direct reference to their circulation after September 11, sometimes in relation to the longer cultural history of these paradigms) – from Michael Rothberg's (2009b) critique of the introspective tropes of 9/11 trauma fiction to Donald Pease's (2009) interrogation of the resurgent American exceptionalism that followed the attacks, Norman Finkelstein's (2003) polemic on the US Holocaust industry to Lisa Hajjar's (2010) attempt to disrupt the pervasive nationalisation of juridical processes since 2001. Faced with a growing corpus of critical literature dedicated to exposing the commodification (Heller 2005; Sturken 2007), politicisation (Faludi 2008), mediatisation (Grusin 2010; Mitchell 2011), and hierachisation (Butler 2004 and 2009) of American memorial culture, a number of theorists have subsequently argued for a rethinking (Sherman and Nardin 2006; Birkenstein, Froula, and Randell 2010) of the popular and political discourses surrounding the attacks.

These sentiments have, in turn, been reflected by efforts within memorial practice that have sought to facilitate a globally oriented frame of memory that resists the introspective allure of the nationalised cosmopolitanism analysed in Chapter 3. Many of these endeavours attempt to reconceptualise the problematic process of commemoration at Ground Zero. Krzysztof Wodiczko's *City of Refuge*, for example, is conceived as 'as a project parallel and supplemental' to Arad and Walker's *Reflecting Absence* (see Chapter 2), which aims:

> to create a place for a more active, critical, and discursive memory of the September 11 attack, examined in its historical and political context, in the light of the military action taken in its wake, and its domestic and international fallout. The memorial will be a place for operative memory, memory in action. It will be an interrogative and 'agnostic', not antagonistic, institute of memory, a public forum and base from which to initiate new transformative projects (Wodiczko 2009, 12).[1]

Amy Waldman's (2011) novel *The Submission* similarly seeks to reimagine the memorial process at Ground Zero by exposing the hegemonic and deeply politicised concerns that have informed the commemoration of the attacks, highlighting the deep divisions such dynamics reveal in American society.[2] In so doing, the text exemplifies the heightened prominence of memorative discourses in the public-political sphere after 9/11 and foregrounds the way in which the debates surrounding commemoration have often acquired exclusionary and intolerant dimensions.

Literary culture has been central to the attempt to admit alternative perspectives on the attacks. Ulrich Baer's *110 Stories* brings together 110 writers (representing the number of floors in each of the Twin Towers) to reflect on 9/11. Asserting that 'there will be no single story to contain the event' (Baer 2002, 5), Baer encourages a multiplicity of perspectives to emerge on the understanding that '[t]he simple date *September 11* must be unraveled to reveal and spell out the many stories it contains – not all compatible, not all easy to absorb, not all welcomed by everyone, but neither morose nor sentimental' (Baer 2002, 3).[3] This move to montage the memory of 9/11 has subsequently been developed and extended by other authors. Perhaps surprisingly, the genre of teenage fiction offered the first significant body of work that attempted to dispel the exclusionary frameworks of hegemonic memorial culture, examining the ways in which September 11 affected the lives of Muslims both inside and outside the US. This welcome willingness to address the 'Other' can be seen in a number of texts aimed at the young adult market, including: Shaila Abudallah's (2009) *Saffron Dreams*, Firyal Alshalabi and Sam Drexler's (2003) *The Sky Changed Forever*, Neesha Meminger's (2009) *Shine, Coconut Moon*, and Catherine Stine's (2005) *Refugees*. Assuming a pedagogic mandate, these novels seek to encourage greater awareness of other cultures and belief systems and foster tolerance in their audience.

For adult readers, more recent novels like Mohsin Hamid's (2007) *The Reluctant Fundamentalist* also attempt to reframe the narrative of the attacks by establishing what Richard Gray describes as an 'interstitial perspective' (Gray 2011, 103) in order to challenge normative readings of the post-9/11 world as a 'clash of civilisations' and reposition identity and culture as hybrid constructions that exceed the bounds of nationality.[4] Teju Cole's (2011) *Open City* develops this transcultural dimension further by situating the events of 9/11 within a global chronicle of suffering and loss, tracing memorative trajectories from the streets of Manhattan to the Biafran Wars in Nigeria, the spectre of the Holocaust, and the legacies of Western colonialism.[5] There have also, of course, been a number of post-9/11 novels published outside the United States that seek to recontextualise the attacks within longer histories of exclusion and invasion. In so doing, these texts attempt (some more successfully than others) to destabilise the absolutist binaries of victimhood and perpetration that have informed much memory work relating to September 11 by nuancing the narrative of the recent past.[6]

Acknowledging the ways in which American memorial culture is imbricated in a global assemblage of texts and discourses is a crucial facet of the attempt to montage memory. Over the past thirteen years, a number of important cultural and critical interventions have been made in the narrative of 9/11 from outside the US. These include the 2002 film

11'09"01, which features a series of short works by directors from as far afield as Bosnia, Israel, Japan, Iran, Burkina Faso, providing very different interpretations of the September 11 attacks. That same year saw the publication of the seminal Verso trilogy by continental philosophers Slavoj Žižek, Jean Baudrillard, and Paul Virilo, who collectively contend that the system of Western capitalism is deeply implicated in the history of the attacks.[7] These works were followed by the somewhat less polemic dialogue between Jürgen Habermas and Jacques Derrida (Borradori 2003) and Habermas's (2006) more lengthy monograph on *Philosophy in a Time of Terror*,[8] both of which argue for a more cosmopolitan approach to contemporary politics and government.

Whilst the above examples highlight the ways in which memorative practices are founded upon the circulation and exchange of ideas between different individuals, collectives, institutions, and nations, the global dispersal of objects reclaimed from Ground Zero in the aftermath of the attacks exemplifies the material mobilities of memory. Previously archived in Hangar 17 at JFK airport, since 2008, over 1,500 artefacts have been made publically available to individuals and communities wishing to erect memorials to 9/11.[9] Parts of the Twin Towers have now been dispatched to every state in the US, as well as to international destinations including Canada, France, the UK, Afghanistan, and New Zealand. As I have commented elsewhere,[10] these objects have been transformed, both physically and figuratively, by their travels; the pieces of steel have been melted down, carved up, or assimilated with different materials. Some have been placed in complex memorative constellations with other events and experiences.[11] Others have been mobilised as symbols of political, empathic, or cultural affinities between individuals and collectives.[12] The resulting memorials are intended to serve widely different purposes for very divergent communities.[13] They are also imbricated in a wider cultural and critical discourse that includes the photographic archive taken by Francesc Torres (2011), who documented the materials stored at Hangar 17, a travelling museum exhibit relating to Torres's work, newspaper reports on the installation of the memorials, and critical accounts of these endeavours (including, of course, my own).

Each of these elements intersects in the international network of remembrance that surrounds the events of September 11 2001. In attempting to reframe the memorial culture of 9/11 as a global concern, it is crucial to remain reflexive about the multifaceted agendas that inform and impel the work of memory, and to recognise that any act of framing, however well intentioned, has the potential to become a hegemonic endeavour. As Fraser argues, it is important not to replace the Keynesian-Westphalian (nation-centric) paradigm with a 'single all-encompassing global frame' (Fraser 2008, 43), which will reproduce the inequitable dynamics of its predecessor. In order to avoid replicating these tendencies, Fraser asserts that the process of framing must remain continually in dispute, resulting in 'a set of multiple, functionally defined frames, corresponding to the multiple, functionally defined "whos" that emerge through such debates and are judged entitled to consideration with respect to various issues' (Fraser 2008, 43). For Fraser, therefore, every frame, once established, must continually be challenged and contested – every frame must exist as part of a montage of other templates of representation and interpretation.

Such considerations point towards the model of *de*framing outlined by Butler. Arguing that frames (of memory, justice, war, experience, and so on) are always partial and partisan, Butler contends that 'to call the frame into question is to show that the frame never quite contained the scene it was meant to limn, that something was already outside. [. . .] Something exceeds the frame that troubles our sense of reality; in other words, something occurs that does not conform to our established understanding of these things' (Butler 2009, 9). Alert to the ways in which frames are transferred across time and space, Butler points to moments when it is possible to challenge the authority and legitimacy of established constructions of perception and experience. She remarks:

> The frame that seeks to contain, convey, and determine what is seen (and sometimes, for a stretch, succeeds in doing precisely that) depends upon the conditions of reproducibility in order to succeed. And yet, this very reproducibility entails a constant breaking from context, a constant delimitation of new context, which means that the 'frame' does not quite contain what it conveys, but breaks apart every time it seeks to give definitive organisation to its content. In other words, the frame does not hold anything together in one place, but itself becomes a kind of perpetual breakage, subject to a temporal logic by which it moves from place to place. [. . .] This leads us to a different way of understanding of both the frame's efficacy and its vulnerability to reversal, to subversion, even to critical instrumentalisation (Butler 2009, 10).

Butler asserts that moments of 'breaking out' (Butler 2009, 11) occur when dominant frames of representation are challenged by events that threaten normative understandings of the reality. She highlights two particular examples from the post-9/11 period: the dissemination of the Abu Ghraib images in 2004 (see Chapter 4) and the publication of a volume entitled *Poems from Guantánamo: The Detainees Speak* (Falkoff 2007). For Butler, these events manifest a challenge to visual and narrative frames of the American public-political sphere, allowing alternative constructions of history to become visible.[14] In the aftermath of 9/11, several memorial practitioners have sought to mobilise the spectres of Abu Ghraib and Guantánamo to destabilise the dominant frameworks into which the events of September 11 have been conscripted. A number of former Guantánamo detainees have produced memoirs (some ghost-written) of their abuse in American custody, exposing practices that official memory has been slow to acknowledge[15]; current prisoners have published letters and testimonial accounts in international newspapers and media outlets[16]; and lawyers and human rights activists have circulated accounts of their visits to the site.[17] In turn, journalists have sought to encourage greater transparency from the Guantánamo commissions by publishing narrative and visual commentary on the proceedings[18]; and a number of plays, novels, exhibitions, and films have attempted to intercede in the framing of Guantánamo.[19] Although produced by multiple parties with heterogeneous agendas,[20] some of which (such as the memoirs of Khalid Sheikh Mohammed published by *The Huffington Post* in 2014) may well seem offensive and unethical, such endeavours collectively open up the tightly controlled discourses that surround the prison.

In recent years, a number of critical interventions have also aimed to extend the geographical and historical reach of Guantánamo Bay in the public imaginary. Karen J. Greenberg positions the prison as the place where multiple narratives of the War on Terror converge:

> the focal point for the innumerable controversies that have surrounded the American responses to terrorism – from protests over U.S. detention policies and interrogation techniques, to pragmatic and philosophical concerns over the viability of military commissions, to diplomatic relations with the detainees' countries of origin. The issues that coalesce at Guantánamo are symbolic of the range of moral, legal, and policy questions that have persisted throughout the ongoing War on Terror (Greenberg 2013, 169).

Linking Guantánamo to the hidden sites – and largely unacknowledged locations – that formed the post-9/11 network of black site prisons, Jonathan Hafetz contends:

> [f]or too long [. . .], Guantánamo has been viewed in isolation, overshadowing other abuses and concealing broader shifts in America's

national policy since September 11, 2001. Guantánamo was never secretly a prison, nor was it hermetically sealed. Rather, Guantánamo was part of a larger, interconnected global detention system that included other military prisons such as Bagram Airbase in Afghanistan, secret CIA jails, and the transfer of prisoners to other countries for torture. [. . .] Guantánamo, in short, was like an island in an archipelago of U.S. detention operations: the most visible example of a larger prison system designated to operate outside the law (Hafetz 2011, 1).

For Greenberg and Hafetz, the memory of Guantánamo is inherently montaged, signalling trajectories to globally dispersed sites of suffering that, as yet, find articulation only in their absence and resistance to recall.

Such readings suggest that, when deframed, this isolated, extra-national locale is revealed as the fulcrum for multidirectional paths of memory, to use Michael Rothberg's (2009a) phrase, functioning as a palimpsest of history and experience. As those curating the Guantánamo Public Memory Project (and the related film, *Memories of Guantánamo*) demonstrate, these trajectories reveal the site's imbrication in a longer chronicle of nationhood, power, and exclusion, implicating vast numbers of Cuban and Haitian asylum seekers who were detained at the centre by the US in the late twentieth century. Overseen by a conglomerate of academic and NGO institutions (chiefly Columbia University and International Sites of Conscience), this project underscores the multifaceted work of memory, combining archival research with a vast collection of testimonies (from former detainees, prosecutors, CIA operatives, attorneys, and politicians), a travelling museum exhibit, educational initiatives, and an activist wing striving to end the perpetuation of injustice at the site. Combining the work of academics, NGOs, educators, filmmakers, photographers, and journalists, the Guantánamo Public Memory Project highlights the ways in which, when critically and reflexively construed, the work of theorists and practitioners of memory can be mutually productive.

In linking Guantánamo's past to the present prison and its future legacy, this project resonates strongly with Butler's call for memorative practices that shift the 'temporal dimension of the frame' to set the conditions for the 'astonishment, outrage, revulsion, admiration, and discovery' (Butler 2009, 10–11) that follow when the 'non-figurable and, to some extent, non-intentional operation of power' becomes visible (Butler 2009, 73–4). This interventionist approach to memory is exemplified by the recent protest of the Witness Against Torture group. On

11 January 2014 (the twelfth anniversary of the opening of the camp), 150 activists, dressed in the orange jumpsuits and black hoods that exemplify the public image of Guantánamo detainees, created an unofficial 'living exhibit' at the National Museum of American History on the National Mall in Washington, DC. Adopting stress positions (their hands behind their back, their heads down, either standing or kneeling), protesters occupied the space in front of a display entitled 'The Price of Freedom: Americans at War' in order to challenge the historical narrative constructed by the museum.[21]

As Carmen Trotta, one of the protesters, remarked to *The National Catholic Reporter*, the Smithsonian 'lacks the history of the last 12 years and the so-called global war on terror' (Fincher 2014). Thus, in a gesture of memorative redress, Witness Against Torture occupied multiple spaces within the museum over the course of their two-hour intervention, giving lectures, singing songs, and unfurling a banner that read 'Make Guantánamo History' from the atrium balcony.[22]

One of the most interesting aspects of this event was the way in which the museum's security guards cooperated with the activists. As Megan Fincher reports:

> To everyone's surprise, the decision came from the head of security to re-open [The Price of Freedom] exhibit without removing the Guantánamo exhibit. He made them promise to leave when the museum closed, and told them that they could have 'no fliers, no banners, no standing on or interfering with exhibits, and voices must be moderate,' Trotta said (Fincher 2014).

The unofficial exhibit was consequently allowed to exist, temporarily, as the dark shadow of the official display: the unfreedom of Guantánamo Bay framing the narrative of freedom celebrated by the Smithsonian. Whilst the protest clearly manifested an attempt to disrupt orthodox readings of American history by colonising the sites of official memorial culture, the complicity of the museum guards testifies to the contingency of hegemonic representations of the past, revealing the ways in which exclusionary frames of memory may be appropriated and subverted by interventions that resist the attempt to delimit the visible, the sayable, and the grievable.

Both Fraser's conception of reframing and Butler's consideration of deframing have implications for the future of memory after 9/11. Whilst Fraser's analysis aims to move beyond the Keynesian-Westphalian template that privileges the nation-state as the central coordinate of contemporary experience, urging us to position the events of 9/11 and their aftermath in a global framework, Butler's work suggests that practitioners and theorists of memory might productively take interventionist measures to disrupt memorial culture whenever the dominant frames of memory become unreflexive and delimiting. The montaging of memory is thus dependent on the simultaneous reframing and deframing of memory: opening up memorial culture to a broad range of perspectives and attitudes, including those dismissed as 'Other' or deviant by the hegemonic public sphere and facilitating an ongoing challenge to transcendental and exclusionary frames of memory as and when they are asserted.

Neither the frames of memory discussed throughout the proceeding chapters, nor the brief overview of counter-memories outlined above, offers an exhaustive chronicle of the memorial culture of 9/11. That is not the intention of this book; rather, I have drawn upon diverse media across multiple discourses in order to highlight patterns of articulation and mediation in the American public sphere, and places or moments at which these frames might be countered and destabilised.

In closing, it seems pertinent to consider one final example that illuminates the trajectory American memorial culture has taken since the horrific events of September 11 2001. In the week this book was completed, the National September 11 Museum opened at Ground Zero. As the most visible commemorative centre for the attacks, the inauguration of this institution offers an apt moment to consider the evolution of commemorative discourse over the past thirteen years.

In his address at the dedication ceremony, President Obama replicated the central tropes of the frames of memory analysed throughout this book, calling upon the exhibits to bear witness to the sacredness of the site, the strength of national unity, and the exceptionalism of the American nation. Yoking together the familiar discourses of trauma and triumphalism, Obama declared the museum 'a sacred place of healing and hope', which would 'reaffirm the true spirit of 9/11' and 'enshrine it forever in the heart of our nation' (Obama 2014). He positioned Ground Zero as a connective space where visitors might encounter the victims of the attacks:

> Here, at this memorial, this museum, we come together. We stand in the footprints of two mighty towers, graced by the rush of eternal waters. We look into the faces of nearly 3,000 innocent souls – men and women and children of every race, every creed, and every corner of the world. We can touch their names and hear their voices and

glimpse the small items that speak to the beauty of their lives. A wedding ring. A dusty helmet. A shining badge (Obama 2014).

However, even while evoking the diversity of the victims, Obama conscripted their memory into symbols of 'a nation that stands tall and united and unafraid – because no act of terror can match the strength or the character of our country [. . .], nothing can ever break us; nothing can change who we are as Americans' (Obama 2014).

Although Obama's speech did little to move beyond the narratives that have previously informed the commemoration of 9/11 in official memorial culture, the media coverage of the opening of the museum was instructive for its willingness to critique and decentre these frames. In its discussion of the dedication ceremony, *The New York Times* took care to contextualise its reading of the attacks, moving beyond the rhetoric of incomprehensibility and trauma to describe the events of September 11 as 'the worst foreign attack on American soil, one that shocked the world and ushered in a new era of fear, war, determination and clashes of values while redefining America's place in the world' (Baker and Farrell 2014). Without marginalising the memory of the victims, or negating the horror of 9/11, the *Times* positions the National September 11 Museum as one element of the wider history of September 11 and its aftermath, commenting on the problematic legacies of the War on Terror, Guantánamo Bay, drone strikes, and surveillance, and illustrating the ways in which they continue to haunt contemporary politics at home and abroad. Most importantly, however, the paper's reportage highlights the fact that none of these issues was mentioned in Obama's speech. This attention to the occlusions in official memory suggests that the commentators have become alert to the silences and absences inherent in hegemonic renditions of history – and, in turn, to the media's role in shaping and intervening in the construction of exclusionary frames of memory.

A similarly critical attitude has been evidenced by tabloid coverage of the museum's shop, which sells a number of rather tasteless artefacts, including dog coats and leads, 9/11 jewellery, World Trade Center–themed clothing, and replicas of the Twin Towers. Whilst much of this merchandise has been on sale at various outlets at Ground Zero for a number of years (firstly, in the preview site on Vesey Street, and secondly in the shop of the National September 11 Memorial, which opened in 2011), the controversy surrounding these items has been interesting for the way in which it has exposed the media's willingness to critique the newly opened museum, undermining its official representation as the sacred site of national memory and the protector of American exceptionalism.[23] As Chip Colwell-Chanthaphonh contends in *The Huffington Post*, "since its opening, the National September 11 Memorial Museum has garnered daily headlines. From the exclusive opening ceremonies to architectural critiques to indignation over merchandise sold in the gift shop, Ground Zero has again become the most talked about place of memory in America" (Colwell-Chanthaphonh 2014).[24]

Thirteen years after the attacks, Ground Zero remains a site of controversy and contestation, implicated in a vast montage of memorative texts and discourses, and shadowed by the vociferous debates that have surrounded the plans for reconstruction and remembrance since the immediate aftermath of 9/11. However, one unforeseen consequence of the preoccupation with memory in the American public sphere after September 11 seems to be the emergence of an enhanced memorative literacy, exemplified by the foregrounding of commemorative politics in cultural narratives such as Waldman's *The Submission*, the reflexive collaboration of memorative practitioners and theorists in endeavours like the Guantánamo Public Memory Project, a renewed sense that members of the public, like Witness Against Torture, have the right to participate in memorial culture and the ability to intervene when they feel that particular voices are being excluded or certain perspectives marginalised, and the media's willingness to challenge the absences and elisions in official memory. Whilst there can be no redeeming the catastrophic events of September 11 2001, and no adequate atonement for the losses suffered on that day, it is just possible that a more careful attention to the ethics and politics of memory in the global public sphere might yet prove an important legacy of the afterlife of 9/11.

Notes

Preface

1 These words, taken from a poem entitled 'Trio' by Thomas Moore, form the epigraph of the official guide to Arlington. See Atkinson (2007).

Introduction

1 See Olick and Robbins (1998); Klein (2000); Kansteiner (2002); Erll and Nünning (2008); Crownshaw (2010); Erll (2011a). It should also be noted that recent studies by Astrid Erll (2011b) and Susannah Radstone (2011) have argued that more attention should be paid to the distinct national contexts in which memory studies has emerged rather than the broad conditions of its evolution.

2 See Niven (2006).

3 See Nora (1989) and Huyssen (1995 and 2003).

4 See Nora (1989).

5 Olick and Robbins point out that the notion of collective processes of remembrance had found earlier mention across disciplines in the work of literary critic Lev Vygotsky (1929), psychologist F. C. Bartlett (1932), and sociologist G. H. Mead (1932).

6 See Kansteiner (2002); Huyssen (2003); Radstone (2005); Kansteiner and Weilnböck (2008).

7 Nora argues that, in the modern world, *lieux de memoire* (sites of memory) have replaced *milieu de memoire* ('real environments of memory'). Positing a *lieu de memoire* as 'a turning point where consciousness of a break with the past is bound up with the sense that memory has been torn' (Nora 1989, 7), Nora suggests that such materialisations of memory reveal a debased reification of a past we can no longer relate to.

8 Radstone defines 'mediation' as the difference between events and their representation and 'articulation' as the practices and processes that shape these representations – 'the linkages between (perhaps contradictory) discourses and the mapping of their relation to the institutions of the public sphere' (Radstone 2005, 134).

9 Michael Rothberg (2009a) challenges such a 'zero-sum' conceptualisation of memory (in both theory and practice), arguing for a more democratic, 'multidirectional' public sphere able to accommodate contrasting memories from divergent social, political, religious, or ethnic groups.

10 See Rothberg (2003; 2008; 2009b), Simpson (2006), and Sturken (2007).

11 Having said this, whilst the recent transcultural turn in memory studies (outlined in Chapter 3) would seem to have been motivated by concerns very

pertinent to the volatile geopolitical climate of the post-9/11 world (addressing the need for greater international solidarity and an ability to recognise the humanity of the 'Other'), none of the seminal works in this field interrogate the events of September 11 and their aftermath in any detail.

12 This concomitancy of practice and theory is perhaps best exemplified by Young's role as a judge on the panel for the National September 11 Memorial at Ground Zero, revisiting his earlier advisory capacity on the Memorial to the Murdered Jews of Europe in Berlin.

13 In this sense, one might see this project as akin to Hayden White's (1975 and 1987) seminal discussion of historiography. White's analysis of history as the 'content' of a particular 'form' certainly informs my interest in the mediating effects of narrative frameworks. He approaches historical texts as acts of literary *emplotment*, in which 'the events, agents, and agencies represented in the chronicle [...] can be apprehended as elements of specific story types' (White 1987, 45). White identifies four major modes of emplotment (tragedy, comedy, romance, and satire), each of which he aligns with a corresponding ideological thrust (radical, conservative, and so on). Whilst my approach to memory is not as prescribed as White's reading of history (I would not reify the narrative frameworks through which memories are articulated to so few established or inflexible modes), I do argue for a similar means of emplotment, with a related attention to the political or ideological implications of each form.

Chapter 1

1 As will be discussed in the Conclusion, there are, of course, many exceptions to this paradigm. From the American canon alone, these include novels like Philip Roth's (2005) *The Plot Against America*, Mohsin Hamid's (2007) *The Reluctant Fundamentalist,* Dave Eggers's (2009) *Zeitoun*, and Amy Waldman's (2011) *The Submission*.

2 See Gray (2008 and 2011) and Rothberg (2009b).

3 For a full analysis of this evolution, see Leys (2000) and Luckhurst (2008).

4 See Freud (1961).

5 Caruth here conflates structural and historical trauma, blurring the distinction between a general referential failure and the specific pathological consequences of discrete historical events. LaCapra contends that such thinking propagates a confusion between (structural) absence and (historical) loss that engenders 'the conflation of a putatively transhistorical condition of abjection with the specific problem of victimisation, thereby both adding to the allure of victimhood and obscuring the status of discrete historical victims', facilitating 'the confusion of the imaginary or vicarious experiential identification with certain events and the belief that one actually lived through them' (LaCapra 2004, 117–18).

6 As Amy Hungerford argues in her important critique of Felman and Caruth, in these accounts, 'actual history – the things that happen in the world – is either excluded from the discussion or reduced to a kind of trace, just as actual trauma [...] is also excluded' (Hungerford 2004, 114). In consequence, experience becomes dehistoricised and transferrable as it is 'cut free of the person to whom the trauma happens' (Hungerford 2004, 114).

7   See Schwartz (2005), Foer (2006), DeLillo (2007).

8   See Kingsbury (2003), Haskell (2005), DeLillo (2007).

9   See Rozan (2008).

10   Glass (2007).

11   In his analysis of *Falling Man*, Peter Boxall suggests that something of this half-formed character pertains to 9/11 fiction itself. Boxall argues that, displaced by the events of September 11, the 'elements of the novel hang estranged from themselves and from each other, waiting for a form to emerge in which their new alignment might find itself spoken, and embodied' (Boxall 2009, 194).

12   See NCITF (2003).

13   This impossible erasure of 9/11 is a textual device we also see in the desire of Foer's Oskar to reverse the events of the day so that 'Dad would've left his [final answerphone] messages backward until the machine was empty, and the plane would've flown backward away from him, all the way to Boston' (Foer 2006, 325).

14   Whereas traumatic memory is destined to repeat the past outside of conscious recall and mastery, narrative memory allows 'the person to associate the happening with the other events of his life', facilitating 'an inward reaction through the words we address to ourselves, through the organisation of the recital of the events to others and to ourselves, and through the putting of this recital in its place as one of the chapters in our personal history' (Janet 1925, 273).

15   Abbott repeatedly returns to this confused issue of perpetration, whilst Marks (2004) and Nissenson (2005) somewhat inaccurately (or at least, simplistically) attribute 9/11 as an outcome of the Israeli-Palestinian conflict.

16   Despite the romanticisation of the home seen in Abbott's work, the domestic settings that dominate the corpus of 9/11 trauma fiction are characterised by fragmented or 'atypical' familial arrangements, suitable to a broken world. The texts of Friedman, Julia Glass, Kalfus, Prose, and Joseph O'Neill are peopled by families where the parents have divorced or separated. The novels of Abbott, DeLillo, McInerney, Messud, and Schulman deal with issues of adultery and infidelity, whilst those of Foer, Kingsbury, Maynard, and Reynolds Price (2006) portray marital reunions and homecomings. These are families familiar with pain, households for whom 9/11 will occasion a tightening of bonds and a communal working through of loss.

17   Despite ironically exploiting the narrative of 9/11 as an analogy for her divorce, Kalfus's protagonist, Joyce, manages to understand that such a personalisation of the attacks is inherently narcissistic (and works only at a symbolic level). She comments:

> *Every* American felt that he had been personally attacked by the terrorists, and that was the patriotic thing of course, but patriotic metaphors aside, wasn't the belief a bit delusional? There was a difference between being killed and not being killed. Was everyone walking around America thinking they had been intimately, self-importantly, involved in the destruction of the World Trade Center? (Kalfus 2006, 78)

18   Although Gray *is* right to note (as I myself have done) that many novels 'accommodate the claim that things have fundamentally changed since the terrorist attacks, [but] their forms do not necessarily register or bear witness to that change' (Gray 2011, 51), the complaint that '[w]hat is acknowledged

is not always enacted' (Gray 2011, 51) problematises his analysis. Gray's belief that '[n]ew events generate new forms of consciousness requiring new structures of [...] imagination to assimilate and express them' (Gray 2011, 29) is not borne out by his emphasis on trauma as an exemplary framework for representation. As we have seen throughout this chapter, trauma is not a new concept, but has long roots in psychoanalytic and literary theory, not to mention its more recent predominance in cultural practice. Gray's analysis itself might thus arguably be indicted, on its own terms, for having 'assimilated [9/11] into conventional structures and a series of tropes' that 'familiarise the unfamiliar' (Gray 2011, 51), as he suggests of the novels of this corpus.

19 The notion of mediatised trauma was, understandably, a concept that gained traction in the aftermath of the attacks – an event which many people 'witnessed' on television. In their study of 'Psychological Reactions to 9/11 across the United States', Brow and Silver cite instances of traumatisation far from the attack sites, arguing:

> the terrorist attacks were acutely felt nationwide and psychological symptoms that were not limited to those who lost someone close to them or experienced or witnessed the attacks directly. Media, and television in particular, were undoubtedly responsible for transmitting the psychological impact of the 9/11 attacks across the country (Brow and Silver 2009, 39).

I do not necessarily take issue with these claims, but I would contend that not all psychological or emotional responses to the attacks should be classified as trauma, which is, after all, a distinct pathology with particular symptoms.

20 As Kaplan notes in her discussion of the media coverage of Iraq and Rwanda, 'media traumatisation' has complex ethical and political implications, acting as both an empathic conduit to engagement with the suffering of others ('pro-social') and a mode of deflection, a generator of 'empty empathy'. See Kaplan (2005, 87–100).

21 Drawing upon surveys carried out in New York at various intervals following the attacks, for example, DiGrande et al. assert that, whilst 7.5 per cent of New Yorkers exhibited symptoms of PTSD one month after the attacks, by four months this figure had fallen to 1.7 per cent, and 6 months on less than 1 per cent (DiGrande et al. 2009, 54).

22 Janoff-Bulman and Usoof-Thowfeek note a similar 'national shift in moral orientation in the immediate aftermath of 9/11' (Janoff-Bulman and Usoof-Thowfeek 2009, 82), a move to the right which intensified this personalisation of politics. They argue that the years following 9/11 were noteworthy not only for the country's elevated concern with national security, but for 'a parallel emphasis on a socially conservative agenda, where abortion and gay rights rather than foreign terrorists became the threats to contain as a nation' (Janoff-Bulman and Usoof-Thowfeek 2009, 85). The state's enhanced interest in essentially private matters (conservatives' insistent invoking of 'family values', coupled with a determined demonisation of feminism, homosexuality, abortionists, and stem-cell advocates) represents exactly the form of the 'antipolitical politics' identified by Berlant.

23 Unlike the more ambiguous texts analysed above, Patrick McGrath's 'Ground Zero' explicitly parodies this infantilisation of citizens. McGrath's short story focuses upon the unhealthy relationship between a New York therapist and her

patient in the aftermath of 9/11. From the outset, the therapist is determined to view her subject, Dan, as a child. With the therapist as his (increasingly unreliable) narrator, McGrath depicts the breakdown in the characters' personal and professional relationship, as Dan begins a love affair that threatens to displace his therapist from her privileged 'maternal' role. Terrified of his new independence, the therapist attempts to manipulate the rhetoric of trauma to return Dan to the position of child. In a moment of wilful self-delusion, she comments that 'so destructive had been the impact of the terror attacks on Dan's psyche, they had in effect pushed him back to a more primitive stage of libidinal organisation' (McGrath 2005, 192–3). Desperate to refute the authenticity of his love affair, the narrator describes Dan's separation from her as a 'kind of suicidal infantilism, a primal unthinking embrace of the death instinct' (MacGrath 2005, 213–14), maintaining that 'he is, at this moment, a child. At this moment he has regained the childish aspect of his nature' (McGrath 2005, 198).

Chapter 2

1 There are, of course, important distinctions between these concepts, which will be developed over the course of this chapter.

2 For a more detailed critique of this notion, see Huyssen (1995 and 2003).

3 It is important to note that the nature of American exceptionalism has altered over time. As Pease contends, '[t]he *American* dimension of American exceptionalism has undergone decisive shifts in its self-representation from the City on the Hill in the sixteenth century to the Conqueror of the World's Markets in the twentieth century' (Pease 2009, 8).

4 It should be noted that Rose presents a slightly different reading of fantasy to either Pease or myself. Arguing for both its hegemonic and counter-hegemonic dimensions, she contends that whilst the modern state 'relies on fantasy for an authority it can ultimately neither secure nor justify' (Rose 1998, 10), fantasy can also be an unsettling form of 'transgenerational haunting' (Rose 1998, 5), a testament to troubling pasts that should be seen as 'threatening political composure' (Rose 1998, 7). Thus, 'if fantasy can give us the inner measure of statehood, it might also help to prise open the space in the mind where the worst of modern statehood loses its conviction, falters, and starts to let go' (Rose 1998, 15).

5 Whilst I accept Rose's assertion that 'fantasy – far from being the antagonist to public, social being – plays a central, constitutive role in the modern world of states and nations' (Rose 1998, 4), I remain sceptical of any unproblematic collectivisation of pathological symptoms, and Pease at times fails to clearly define the dynamics of psychosocial phenomena such as 'national traumas' or the 'national psyche' throughout his otherwise compelling analysis. Over the course of what follows, therefore, my understanding of fantasy refers to a cultural(-ideologico) construct: the product of a 'cultural imaginary' (the networking of diverse representational media) rather than an 'American psyche' (a collective pathology).

6 As Meyer (2001) argues, the very shape of the nation's capital was defined by its foundational political documents – DC's ten-miles-squared original layout was laid out in Article One of the Constitution. In his formative plan for the

city (1791), Pierre L'Enfant aimed to ensure that Washington would represent the imaginative, as well as the political, centre of the United States.

7 See Young (1993).

8 The memorial has been met with a mixed reaction from critics, veterans, politicians, and members of the public – appearing both as a dark 'gash of shame' in the nation's symbolic centre (a 'feminising' demasculinisation of the heroic vision of the nation enshrined by the two presidential monuments to which the walls of Lin's memorial open in a trajectory that disrupts the smooth historical narrative of triumphalism), and a suitably sombre tribute to a difficult and divisive conflict that provides a place to both remember and reflect. In response to what some felt were the detrimental anti-heroic qualities of Lin's abstract memorial, two figurative sculptures have since been added to the site. The first (erected in 1984) comprises a statue of three multi-ethnic soldiers by Frederick Hart, the second (erected in 1993) is the Vietnam Women's Memorial by Glenna Goodacre. For more detail on the memorial's conception and reception see Sturken (1997).

9 See Mills (2004) for more on the controversies surrounding the construction of the memorial.

10 Bush's dichotomous moral universe is admirably critiqued by Peter Singer (2005). Singer comments that 'George W. Bush [was] not only America's president, but also its most prominent moralist. No other president in living memory has spoken so often about good and evil, right and wrong' (Singer 2005, 1). He further notes that Bush had 'spoken about evil in [...] about 30 percent of all the speeches he gave between the time he took office and June 16 2003' (Singer 2005, 2).

11 Beamer died on United 93 and the now infamous words 'let's roll' have been attributed to him, making him one of the heroes of 9/11 in popular culture.

12 This explicit nationalism has been countered somewhat by the Obama Administration, which (in conjunction with various 9/11 organisations) in April 2009 passed the 'Edward M. Kennedy Serve America Act', declaring September 11 the National Day of Service and Remembrance. Although still retaining its status as a national day, the latter Act repositions citizens' duties from patriotism to service in the local community, partially returning the act of remembrance to a vernacular level.

13 On 2 January 2011, President Obama signed the James Zadroga 9/11 Health and Compensation Act to provide $4.3 billion dollars of medical treatment for responders made ill by breathing in toxins and dust at Ground Zero. This Act is subject to ongoing debate over its lack of coverage for cancer treatments.

14 The Act officially mandates the state's support for the memorials at Ground Zero, the Pentagon, and Shanksville, underlining their status as part of official memory culture. None of the three central memorial projects have been federally funded, but have been financed by money raised by the National September 11 Museum and Memorial, the Pentagon Memorial Fund, and the National Park Service (in the case of the Flight 93 National Memorial) respectively. It is also worth noting that, although the memorials at Ground Zero and Shanksville have been officially designated as 'national' sites, the Pentagon memorial has not.

15 See http://www.9-11heroes.us for examples of similar heroic narratives.

16　The implications of the elevation of firefighters in the national imaginary can perhaps be seen most clearly in the debate over the naming of victims in Arad and Walker's memorial at Ground Zero. Whilst it was originally intended to set the names of people who died in the line of duty apart from 'ordinary' casualties, many victims' families have felt that to do so would create a hierarchy of victimhood. Eventually a compromise was reached to separate out the emergency service officials and to list other victims, not in alphabetical order but with loosely associative connections. See Salazar (2011).

17　343 firefighters were killed in the attacks, whilst 23 NYPD officers and 37 Port Authority police officers lost their lives.

18　Interestingly, the exhibition on 9/11 in the New York City Fire Museum resists this discourse of heroism, and instead offers a display (over two small rooms on the ground floor) that concentrates on documenting the events of the day in a sombre and sensitive fashion. The exhibition contains many small memorials to individual firehouses or firemen, as well as a number of the commemorative tokens left by the public in the immediate aftermath of the attacks, but it refuses to be drawn into the overarching, sentimentalised narrative into which firefighters have widely been co-opted.

19　For an excellent analysis of the broader dynamics of the post-9/11 graphic novel, see Jenkins (2006).

20　The whole collection portrays a sense of masculine strength in comparison to female vulnerability in ways that resonate strongly with Faludi's (2008) analysis of the reversion to traditional gender stereotypes in the aftermath of the attacks.

21　Thomas Foster contends that 'the events of 9/11 charge Captain America with the affect and vulnerability he previously lacked – more accurately, the narrowly patriotic sentiments that characterised practically his entire affective repertoire' (Foster 2005, 262). Captain America thus becomes the ideal figurehead for the dominant response to 9/11 – a symbol that 'reproduces the logics of American exceptionalism and individualism, as well as the reassertion that complex historical dynamics can be understood in the simplest moral terms' (Foster 2005, 270).

22　Produced and published by a public institution, *Portraits of Grief* arguably forms part of official memorial culture as defined by Burgoyne whilst, as a private endeavour with public circulation, Doctorow's *Lamentation* and Skomal's *Heroes* seem to occupy a space between official and vernacular forums of memory.

23　Begun in San Francisco in 1987, the NAMES Project AIDS Memorial Quilt has since toured the United States extensively, and now features more than 44,000 panels (made by friends, family members, and partners), each commemorating the life of someone who has died from AIDS. For more detail on this powerful counter-memorial, see Sturken (1997) and The NAMES Project Foundation, at http://www.aidsquilt.org/about/the-aids-memorial-quilt.

24　The process of mending is intended to create associative contexts for the attacks, reframing them as part of the chronicle of American history. Accordingly, the 'honor of stitching' has been carried out by:

> soldiers and schoolchildren who survived the shooting at Ft. Hood, Texas, by World War II veterans on the deck of the USS Missouri in Pearl Harbor, by the family of

Martin Luther King Jr., and by thousands of everyday service heroes nationwide. On President Lincoln's Birthday, a piece of the flag that Abraham Lincoln was laid on when he was shot at Ford's Theater was stitched into the fabric (New York Says Thank you Foundation 2011).

25 The shop of the National September 11 Memorial and Museum, for instance, stocks a range of merchandise inscribed with the legend 'in the darkness we shine brightest'.

26 In an interview with Cathy Caruth, Geoffrey Hartman (1996) suggests that sites of extreme atrocity (particularly Holocaust camps) lose their ability to function as 'memory places' because they are stripped of their symbolic – and narrativising – dimension by the traumatic events that occurred therein. They thus become 'non-places', unclaimed sites (to return to Caruth's own terminology), awaiting hermeneutic seizure.

27 Alongside the Lower Manhattan Development Corporation, the Port Authority, the leaseholder, Larry Silverstein, the state administrations of New York and New Jersey, the City of New York, and the federal government, private interest groups involving themselves in the redevelopment process included: the Coalition of 9/11 Families, September's Mission, the Battery Park Residents Association, Tribeca Residents Association, the Civic Alliance, WTC Families for Proper Burial, the Manhattan Institute, the World Trade Center Restoration Movement, Team Twin Towers, and many other interested parties.

28 See Stephens, Luna, and Broadhurst (2004), Goldberger (2005), and Nobel (2005) for a fuller account of the competition process, the individual designs, and the controversial construction period that followed.

29 See Stephens, Luna, and Broadhurst (2004).

30 In summer 2003, Libeskind's credibility was dealt a blow when New York architect Eli Attia, a staunch critic of his design, demonstrated that the sun would not shine uninterrupted into the Wedge of Light between 08:46 and 10:28.

31 See Goldberger (2005) and Nobel (2005).

32 When the eight finalists of the competition were announced in November 2003, each of these projects seemed somewhat derivate, comprising a series of repeated tropes (light, water, healing) and familiar commemorative ideas. As Goldberger argues, the designs had a 'somewhat generic quality, as if they were more concerned with encouraging feelings of warmth rather than emotions more directly concerned to the trade-center tragedy' (Goldberger 2005, 255).

33 Because the entrance to the memorial is located close to the footprint of the South Tower, it feels very much as though the northern portion of the site (and the victims named within it) have been marginalised.

34 As Yifat Gutman argues in her study of the development of Ground Zero, from the earliest days after the attacks, the site was divided into two 'spatial realities' – a 'street site' and an 'official site' (Gutman 2009, 60). The official site comprised the space for commercial and memorial redevelopment, bordered by information boards that separated Ground Zero from the street. Gutman argues that the text and images on this fence represented 'a nationalised trajectory from the site's past to its future' (Gutman 2009, 60). The paving area directly in front of the display fences was subject to

strict regulations (no flyering, no rollerblading, no pets, no commercial use, no bicycles), but on the opposite side of the street, more heterogeneous behaviours occurred. Here, anti-war protesters mixed with victims' associations demonstrating against the planned memorial, and conspiracy activists alongside tourists and street performers. The street site was also home to an impromptu series of memorials that augmented and, in some cases, challenged the official history laid out on the fence. However, with the onset of building works in March 2009, the personal memorials were removed and the spatial narratives closed down.

35 Nobel echoes this contention in slightly different terms, arguing that the memorial elides confrontation with the loss of life that occurred on 9/11 by mourning instead the loss of the Twin Towers. Fetishising the footprints, he claims ensures that:

> the absences will still be there, exactly as big as the buildings, and to a visitor confronting the memorial, so much bigger at that moment than the memory of those who died all around. How will the dead compete with all this reverence for lost construction? Even if it communicates nothing else, the design will immortalize the Twin Towers and the fact that they once really did stand (Nobel 2005, 255).

Chapter 3

1 For a more detailed critique of the diverse narrative frameworks that inform different modes of transcultural memory, see Bond (2014).

2 Quotes transcribed on visit, 30 March 2011.

3 Such acritical techniques are replicated throughout the opening exhibits. Displays such as 'Condoning Terrorism, Condemning Terrorism' offer brief aphorisms from those either 'for' or 'against' terrorist action. This feature comprises revolving blocks with a quote ('anti-terror') on one side in green, and another ('pro-terror') in red. As the parties from whom the quotes are derived are not linked in any way, and neither the sentiments nor the speakers are contextualised, this seems to be a rather empty exercise that verges upon familiar tendencies to reductively divide the post-9/11 world into 'good' and 'evil' entities. However, the second half of the CELL does offer a more critical engagement with terrorism. Exhibit five (entitled 'Protecting Liberty, Protecting Lives – a delicate balance'), for example, produces a well-nuanced discussion of 'the critical balance between security and civil liberties, intelligence gathering and privacy right, and the relationship between democratic societies and the governments they elect' in the post-9/11 world. The sixth exhibit provides a simplistic but well-thought-out overview of 'Myths or Facts' relating to terrorism, balancing what had been a very 9/11-centric display with a broader international perspective.

4 For an excellent analysis of the museum and memorial processes at the OCNM, see Linenthal (1995).

5 See Novick (1999).

6 I do not have space to comment in more detail on the interpretative decisions made during the design of the USHMM, or upon the various controversies that have embroiled the museum over issues of authenticity,

commodification, and ideologisation. For a critique of these issues, see Novick (1999) and Finkelstein (2003); for a more sympathetic, yet insightful reading of the USHMM, see Rothberg (2000); and for a detailed description of the museum's genesis, see Weinberg and Elieli (1995) and Linenthal (1995).

7 See Young (1993), Andrea Liss (1998), and Jane Caplan (2000).

8 See Rothberg's (2009) introduction for an excellent summary of the issues at stake here – most notably the debate surrounding the presence of the USHMM near the Mall in the absence of a museum to slavery.

9 A notable exception to this trend is Art Spiegelman (2004), whose response to 9/11 attempts to disconnect traumatic experience from the triumphalist narratives of the Bush Administration, partially through intertextual references to his earlier work on the Holocaust. See *In the Shadow of No Towers* (2004) and *The Complete Maus* (2003).

10 See Suson (2002) for a record of the photographs taken by Suson at Ground Zero when working with the FDNY.

11 As Hilene Flanzbaum argues, mobilised in American memorial culture, *The Diary of Anne Frank* has been interpreted as 'a story of universal appeal, about unfailing optimism and the strength of the human spirit as manifested in the face of terrible deprivations' (Flanzbaum 1999, 3).

12 Prior to 9/11, Libeskind was best known for his design for the Jewish Museum in Berlin (an extension to the larger Berlin Museum). This building is noticeable for its translation of historical trauma into affective architectural experience. The design does not aim to replace a horrific past with a heroic future. As Andrew Benjamin comments, the Jewish Museum 'works around and includes a productive void, a void space that is always charged with absence', generating a 'structure of mourning' that is shaped by vigilance (Benjamin 1997, 116). As suggested in the previous chapter, however, in his proposal for Ground Zero, Libeskind appears to eschew this critical approach, translating the same architectural figures (shards, voids, contortions) into 'healing' symbols.

13 The links between the future of Ground Zero, September 11, and the war in Iraq were made much of during this period. At a pro-war rally at Ground Zero, attended by 25,000 construction workers, New York governor George Pataki suggested that the statue of Saddam Hussein infamously toppled in Baghdad (and for a brief moment ill-advisedly swathed in an American flag) should be melted down into beams for the Freedom Tower. He urged, '[l]et's melt it down. Let's bring it to New York and let's put it in one of the girdles that's going to rise over here as a symbol of the rebuilding of New York and the rebuilding of America' (in Nobel 2005, 208).

14 As Brown comments:

> guidance is built into the installations themselves. More than being guided, the visitor's very experience of the museum is orchestrated by the media installations; so, too, almost all the thinking about tolerance, bigotry, and prejudice is undertaken by the museum, notwithstanding the frequent injunction to the visitor to 'think' (Brown 2006, 115).

15 See Rothstein (2011) for a critique of the dehistoricising properties of the MOTNY's curation.

16 For a more detailed account of the connection between American Holocaust memory and the pro-Israeli Jewish lobby in the United States, see Finkelstein (2003); for a divergent opinion, see Novick (2000).

17 The conflict in the former Yugoslavia highlighted the numerous (ethical, juridical, and political) issues at stake in attempting to read the present as a re-enactment of the past, which are summarised admirably in Steve Coll's (1994) account of the parallels drawn between Serbian 'ethnic cleansing' and the Holocaust.

18 Although Krauthammer originally coined the term 'Bush Doctrine' in relation to the administration's decision to withdraw from the Kyoto treaty in June 2001, it is most commonly associated with the state's military policies after 9/11. Perhaps the clearest definition of the Bush Doctrine's generally accepted meaning was given in the *National Security Strategy of the United States* (2002).

19 Freud characterises screen memories as 'mnemic residues' in which an (often traumatic) early event is hidden by a later memory. In his essay of the same name, Freud argues that the screen memory 'owes its value as memory not to its intrinsic content, but to the relation obtaining between this content and some other, which has been oppressed' (Freud 1899, 19).

20 In his thoughtful account of contemporary memorial culture, Richard Stamelman comments on the speed with which the events of 9/11 have been commemorated, contending that, whilst the 'metamorphosis of a locus of history into a site of memory usually requires [...] the passage of decades, generations, even centuries', what 'is most interesting about the World Trade Center disaster is [...] that the event itself and the landscape of the event have so rapidly been transformed into a memory site' (Stamelman 2003, 15). Indeed, in contrast with his earlier statement, Laub also concedes that:

> The landscape around the destruction of the Twin Towers continues to be humane, filled with people attempting to comfort and to restore. This is completely different from the landscape of the Holocaust, in which the surrounding world was dumbfounded by the extraordinary impact of death or stood back and let it happen' (Laub 2003, 207).

21 Whilst there are clearly some connections between the United States' support of Israel and anti-American sentiments in the Middle East, it seems dangerous to equate 9/11 unproblematically with the extremely convoluted relationship between Israel and Palestine for fear of occluding complexity and simplifying – politically and ethically – complicated dynamics.

22 For more on the complexity of recent discourses surrounding victimhood and perpetration, see Niven (2006).

23 More nuanced comparisons have been drawn between 9/11 and other histories in literary and critical culture. Whilst I am wary of their unreflexive subscription to the paradigms of trauma culture, the post-9/11 novels of Foer (2006) and Price (2006) attempt to destabilise the exceptionalist discourse that accompanies the Holocaust analogy by contextualising the attacks within the histories of the US bombing of Dresden during the Second World War and the long narrative of slavery and racism in the American South.

Pease also makes an interesting observation when he contends that the events of September 11 opened hidden trajectories of remembrance, revealing 'the suppressed historical knowledge of the United States' origins in the devastation of native people's homelands' (Pease 2009, 161) and the ongoing marginalisation of Native communities throughout succeeding centuries. He further contends that the attacks thus served to destabilise the myth of the United States as a perpetually innocent 'Virgin Land' – an abundant Eden, unmarked by the fractures and frictions of history.

Chapter 4

1 See, among others, Teitel (2000); Booth (2001); Cohen (2001); Douglas (2001); Misztal (2001); Felman (2002); Sarat and Kearns (2002); Douglas, Sarat, and Umphrey (2007); Kardstedt (2009); Hazan and de Stadelhofen (2010); Levy and Sznaider (2010); Stonebridge (2011); Savelsberg and King (2011); Osiel (2012); Lessa (2013).

2 For a genealogy of justice and its many cultural, historical, and philosophical permutations, see Sandel (2007).

3 Whilst I find Felman's theory useful for her outline of the connection between trial and trauma, I am more skeptical of her tendency to position the court itself (and the law more generally) as a traumatised forum, subject to the irruption of repressed collective memories. Although (as sections three and four of this chapter make clear) I am interested in the ways in which legal processes may screen and unscreen other events, I interpret these mechanisms as political rather than psychical phenomena.

4 See Edelman (2007); Weiser (2010).

5 See US Department of Justice (2013).

6 Whilst there is not room to consider the implications of Daniels's case in any detail, it seems pertinent to offer a brief overview of the trial. In August 2002, 600 relatives of 9/11 victims registered a $1 trillion lawsuit against defendants including Saudi Arabia and the Taliban for their roles in supporting terrorism. Saudi Arabia was eventually removed from the litigation and a revised case came to trial in December 2011. Daniels ruled that individuals (including Osama bin Laden, by then deceased, and Ayatollah Khameni), corporations (including Iran Airlines and the National Bank of Iran), terrorist organisations (Hezbollah and the Taliban), and the state of Iran were guilty of providing material support to al Qaeda – yet, as the Associated Press note, '[i]t would be near impossible to collect any damages, especially from the Taliban or al-Qaida' (AP foreign 2011). The case thus raises questions about the efficacy of juridical justice in this context.

7 In June 2014, as this book was going to print, the Second US Circuit Court of Appeals overturned Hellerstein's decision to award a $55 million bonus to rescue workers on the grounds that his ruling was premature as it had not taken into account an ambiguity in the 2010 settlement over the amount of compensation for which the litigants were eligible (see Stempel 2014). None of the hearings pertaining to these cases will be dealt with in detail here, however, they form an important part of the juridical afterlife of the attacks. For more detail on restitutive lawsuits relating to responders at Ground Zero,

including the subsequent passing of the Zagroda Health and Compensation Act, see Hellerstein, Henderson, and Twerski (2012).

8   See Navarro (2011).

9   See Weiser (2011a).

10   See Weiser (2009 and 2011b).

11   See Ferguson (2007).

12   In recent years, such concerns have seen both legal and scholarly practice turn away from the paradigm of the trauma trial. Discussing this 'recent epistemic shift in international law', Eyal Weizman notes a change 'in emphasis from human testimony to material evidence' that is 'indicative of larger cultural and political transformations' (Weizman 2011, 103) by those wary of 'the quasi-religious dialectics of victims and perpetrators' (Weizman 2001, 37) that define the culture of the trauma trial.

13   See Chapter 2 for a detailed analysis of this speech.

14   These criticisms particularly related to the controversial detention centre at Guantánamo Bay: Bush's speech was televised from the White House following the supreme court's ruling that the military commissions the administration had established at Guantánamo were unconstitutional; Obama's 2009 address was delivered in the National Archives the day after Congress refused his request for $80 million to close the prison; and his 2013 talk was given to the National Defense Academy in the midst of intense controversy over the treatment of detainees on hunger strike.

15   Echoing Bush's defence of torture and black site prisons, Obama supports the use of drones on a number of grounds, arguing, firstly, that 'our actions are effective'; secondly, that 'these strikes have saved lives'; and thirdly, that 'America's actions are legal' (Obama 2013).

16   See Junod (2012) and Gardner (2013) for more on the legal and ethical issues surrounding Obama's use of drone warfare.

17   The prescience of these anxieties was affirmed in a rather unexpected manner during the delivery of this speech. Obama was recurrently interrupted by an audience member protesting the ongoing detention of prisoners cleared for release from Guantánamo Bay, and the treatment of the 102 detainees then on hunger strike. Her remarks were stymied by the president, who cautioned, 'free speech is you being able to speak, but also, you listening and me being able to speak' (Obama 2013). However, at no stage did Obama attempt to listen to his interlocutor, and their interchange suggests much about the operation of power, the limits of transparency, and the silencing of particular voices in the public sphere. This unscripted incident reveals the irruptive quality of memories that will not stay silent, but continue to intrude on the carefully controlled discourses of the public sphere.

18   As a number of commentators have remarked, in the absence of a legal category able to recognise and prosecute the crime of genocide, these trials mediated and marginalised the memory of the Holocaust in rather problematic ways. See Douglas (2001), Bloxham (2003), Sarat, Douglas, and Umphrey (2007), Levy and Sznaider (2010), and Stonebridge (2011).

19   The establishment of the military commissions has been difficult from the start. Whilst the Bush Administration first authorised proceedings in November 2001, these trials were invalidated by a supreme court ruling in 2006 on the grounds that they were unconstitutional, before being

re-established, in revised form, later the same year under the Military Commissions Act (MCA). The MCA upheld the use of physical coercion during interrogations and denied the right of habeas corpus to any non-citizen held as an 'enemy combatant' by the United States. Upon taking office in 2009, Obama declared that Khalid Sheikh Mohammed (the alleged master planner of 9/11) and four co-conspirators would be tried in a civil court in Manhattan. However, after strong opposition from the City of New York and Congressional Republicans, in January 2010 the White House announced it would relinquish plans for a criminal trial and reinstate military tribunals at Guantánamo. With the arraignment of the defendants in May 2012, the pre-trial hearings began. See Hafetz (2011) and Foster (2012) for more on this complicated process.

20 Commentators have contended that, faced with indefinite detention without trial, one of the only ways out of Guantánamo for detainees was, ironically, to plead guilty to a relatively minor offence and hope for a sentence commuted to time already served. Such comments suggest a preconstruction of legal memory based upon a biased mode of memory-justice. See Tuttle (2008).

21 On 28 April 2004, the American CBS news programme *Sixty Minutes II* broadcast the first public images of abuse of Iraqi detainees by American soldiers from the 800th Military Police Brigade at Abu Ghraib Prison. These photographs represented just a fraction of the images in the possession of the US administration. According to the 2006 report of the US Army's Criminal Investigation Command, the full Abu Ghraib archive submitted to the American authorities revealed:

> a total of 1,325 images of suspected detainee abuse, 93 video files of suspected detainee abuse, 660 images of adult pornography, 546 images of suspected dead Iraqi detainees, 29 images of soldiers in simulated sex acts, 20 images of a soldier with a swastika drawn between his eyes, 37 images of Military Working Dogs being used in abuse of detainees and 125 images of questionable acts (Eisenman 2007, 123–4).

See Simpson (2006), Eisenman (2007), and Mitchell (2011).

22 Mitchell's comments were, strangely, prefigured by Donald Rumsfeld's attempts to mitigate the scandal. Speaking in 2004, Rumsfeld argued that it was only the photos that gave 'these incidents a vividness, indeed a horror, in the eyes of the world' (Rajiva 2005, 38). Rajiva notes that in his references to the events at Abu Ghraib, Rumsfeld remained 'strikingly focused on the perception of the abuse rather than the substance as though, absent the photos, the incidents did not warrant the highest priority' (Rajiva 2005, 41).

23 As Mitchell notes, whilst the Bush Administration did everything in its power to prevent the images entering the public sphere by declaring an 'amnesty' on the photographs, the Obama regime continues to suppress photographs, along with pictures of torture at Guantánamo Bay, Bagram, and other black site prisons.

24 Despite significant differences between the two prisons, these symbolic connections are also underscored by procedural and personnel links. As Mitchell remarks, both officers and prisoners at Abu Ghraib were subjected to a process of 'Gitmoizing', exemplified by the fact that 'Major General Geoffrey

Miller, the commander of the Guantánamo Bay detention facility, had been sent to Abu Ghraib with the authority of the secretary of defense behind him to "get tough" on the prisoners being dragged in by the hundreds during nightly raids' (Mitchell 2011, 125–6).

25   Peter Judson Richards comments that 'ambiguity clings to the notion of a "military tribunal"' (Richards 2007, 5); granted latitudes unavailable to the normal court of law (less rigorous procedures, a foreshortened trial process, a lower burden of proof), these 'quasi-judicial' institutions (Richards 2007, 5) operate a form of extraordinary justice demanded – and justified – by a state of emergency. Military tribunals are not bound by established protocol, but formulated to address the specifics of the situation for which they are required. Conceptually, procedurally, and doctrinally indeterminate, legitimated by no stable authority (hearings may be held under the auspices of both national and international law), tribunals in different historical and cultural settings may bear very little relation to one another.

26   As Lisa Hajjar notes, the United States has used international law 'selectively, advancing interpretations that defy international consensus and asserting the legality of state practices that foreign governments and international organisations classify as violations' (Hajjar 2003).

27   Having previously complained about limited access to their clients, and lack of translators, lawyers for the prosecution stalled pre-trial hearings in February 2013 over fears that their conversations were being monitored. During the same session, guards seized (previously cleared) legal documents from defendants' rooms whilst they were in court (Savage 2013b).

28   Defence attorneys must ask permission from the prosecution to offer witness testimony (MacGreal 2013).

29   Judge James Pohl has repeatedly refused to rule on this issue, announcing that he prefers to consider individual issues as and when they arise (Eviatar 2012).

30   The matters that can be discussed in the court are currently decided in closed hearings without either defendants or spectators present. Judge Pohl has yet to rule on whether the accused will also be removed from the courtroom whilst classified information relating to their detention and treatment in black site prisons and Guantánamo is considered. See Sutton (2012).

31   In a chaotic session in January 2013, the live feed from the court was cut off by third parties not in the room. The judge subsequently ruled that he alone had jurisdiction over censoring the proceedings (Savage 2013a).

32   See Sanchez (2012).

33   The hearings discussed here represent only a small sample of the numerous cases that relate to the treatment of detainees after 9/11. For a much more detailed discussion, see Hafetz (2011).

34   The contradictory perspectives expressed in the various *Rasul* rulings exemplify the manner in which the juridical afterlife of 9/11 has seen recurrent struggles between political and judicial institutions. In response to *Rasul* (and the later judgement of *Hasul v. Rumsfeld*), the passing of the Detainee Treatment Act sought to prevent further habeas hearings in federal courts, placing the authority for constructing legal memory firmly in the hands of the executive and the military. This Act was in turn challenged by the supreme court in *Hamdan v. Rumsfeld*, which invalidated the president's military commissions and argued that the Geneva Conventions must apply to detainees

in American custody. Pursuant to this ruling, the Military Commissions Act of 2006 restored proceedings at Guantánamo Bay, whilst the landmark supreme court hearing of *Boumediene v Bush* offered the decisive judgement on the matter of habeas corpus, rejecting the government's claims that the provisions of the Constitution were limited to American citizens. See Hafetz (2011) for more on these decisions.

35 Several of the cases brought before tribunals under the Bush Administration have subsequently been overturned on the grounds the charges levelled against the defendants could not be tried in military court as they did not qualify as crimes under the laws of war. In 2013, the US court of appeal dismissed a similar conviction relating to Abd al Hadi al Iraqi, on charges of conspiracy, against the advice of the Obama government. See Savage (2014).

36 See O'Brien (2013) and Savage (2014) for more information.

37 In 2009, for example, an Italian court indicted a number of CIA agents for the kidnapping of Abu Omar from Milan, none of whom have since been extradited – partly because the Berlusconi government refused to enforce the court's ruling. See Hajjar (2010) for details.

38 See Lennard (2013). Other cases are currently ongoing in Lithuania and France. See Saytas (2014) and FIDH (2014) respectively.

Conclusion

1 Building upon a Levinasian framework, Wodiczko seeks to resist the securitisation, politicisation, and militarisation that characterised the cultural, political, and to some extent, topographical landscapes of America in the aftermath of September 11. Placing 9/11 in a global network of suffering and loss, he calls for Americans to consider themselves as 'ethical exiles', to resist 'the fantasies and ideologies behind the present-day Homeland Security measures', in order to 'transform New York City into an international refuge' (Wodiczko 2009, 21). Whilst both his project and his speculative design for a memorial are rather, perhaps deliberately, idealistic, Wodiczko's work is notable for the way in which his manifesto includes critiques of this endeavour from scholars and critics. In this sense, it manifests an interesting, and promisingly reflexive, relationship between memorative theory and practice.

2 Foregrounding the divisive culture of memory that surrounded the redevelopment of Ground Zero, Waldman imagines what would have happened had a Muslim architect won the tender to design the September 11 memorial. In so doing, she not only highlights the resurgent Islamophobia that surfaced in the aftermath of the attacks, but suggests that it is impossible to conceive of memory outside political frameworks because our perception of the past, and our opinions about the most suitable means of its representation, are always mediated by the discourses of the public sphere.

3 In his introduction to the collection, Baer suggests that the volume was intended to challenge the frames of memory critiqued throughout this book. Asserting 'the need for narrative in the wake of a disaster', he refuses the descent into traumatised aporia, calling for stories 'that explore the possibilities of language in the face of gaping loss, and register that words might be all that's left for the task of finding meaning' (Baer 2002, 1). In so doing,

Baer resists the triumphalist discourses that surrounded the attacks in early memorial cultural, rejecting 'the arrogant and foolish certainty of having the correct response to a severe collective trauma' (Baer 2002, 2) in order to 'confront reality without promising wholeness or denying absence, shock, and loss' (Baer 2002, 6). It is thus not so much the individual stories in the collection as Baer's philosophy that interests me. In many ways, his methodology appears to comprise a succinct model for the ethical montaging of memory in the wake of catastrophe.

4 The notion of the 'clash of civilisations' was originally found in the work of conservative American historian Samuel Huntington. Following the fall of the Soviet Union, Huntington argued that 'the fundamental source of conflict in this new world will not be primarily ideological or primarily economic. The great divisions among humankind and the dominating source of conflict will be cultural', noting, in particular, that 'Islam has bloody borders' (Huntington 1996). Hamid's novel challenges this reductive assessment of contemporary history by emphasising the hybrid nature of identity. The second-person narration also attempts to problematise the binaries of 'us' and 'them' (Christianity and Islam, West and East, freedom and tyranny) so forcibly asserted in Bush's political rhetoric, implicating readers in the narrative and encouraging them to challenge their own preconceptions and stereotypes.

5 Cole's novel reveals the palimpsestic nature of New York, examining (in a Sebaldian fashion) the hidden pasts that lie buried beneath the surface of the city. In so doing, he exposes history as an ongoing narrative of dispossession and dislocation. Accordingly, as Pieter Vermeulen (2013) argues, whilst the novel appears to represent an exemplary mode of literary cosmopolitanism through the way in which it brings disparate experiences and memories together, it is perhaps most profitably read as a negative or failed cosmopolitanism that highlights the inevitable pain and isolation of human beings, rather than generating productive or empathic connections between communities of suffering.

6 See Hacker (2007), Hosseini (2007), and Shamsie (2009) for examples.

7 Baudrillard, Žižek, and Virilio all portray terrorism as the dark underside of contemporary capitalism. Although the trilogy does interesting work in terms of nuancing the binaries of victimhood and perpetration established by the Bush Administration, it is rather problematic for the way in which it verges, at times, on negating the genuine suffering engendered by 9/11.

8 Opposing the hegemonic grammar that underscores the clash of civilisations narrative, Habermas calls for 'an egalitarian universalism that requires the decentering of one's own perspective', demanding 'that one relativise one's own views to the perspective of equally situated and equally entitled others' (Habermas 2006, 35). In so doing, his work resonates with, and informs, Fraser's call for a transnational model of justice. However, whilst there is no doubt that the notion of a reflexive international community engaged in a dialogical process of juridical exegesis is seductive, various critics have noted (see Butler [2004] and Stonebridge [2011]) that, in its current incarnation, international law tends to reinscribe Western-oriented hierarchies of power and life. Although I thus find Habermas's faith in the egalitarian possibilities of a reconfigured international law to be idealistic at times, I am sympathetic

to the claim that 'non-Western cultures must appropriate the universalistic content of human rights with their own resources and in their own interpretation, one that establishes a convincing connection to local experiences and interests' (Habermas 2006, 35).

9 See Torres (2011) for more on the reclamation and archiving of this material.

10 See Bond and Rapson (2014).

11 For example, the Trade Center steel at the Caen Memorial for Peace in France (which places 9/11 in a commemorative constellation with other major events from Western history, such as the fall of the Berlin Wall) or the structure at the International Peace Garden in Canada (which utilises the steel as a means of calling for a more harmonious global future).

12 Such as the German-American firefighters memorial in Bavaria (which was created as a gesture of solidarity between firefighters), or the steel erected at Babi Park in Denver (which forms part of a new Memorial to the Victims of World Terrorism), and Daniel Libeskind's *Memoria e Luce* in Padua, Italy (intended as an empathic link between Italy and the USA).

13 For example, the highly personal memorial in Tucson, Arizona, to Christina Taylor-Green (who was killed in the 2011 shootings in the city), compared to the militarisation of memory represented by the steel incorporated into the hull of the *USS New York*.

14 As intimated in the previous chapter, the torture of detainees at Abu Ghraib and Guantánamo challenges the juridical, political, and moral economy of American exceptionalism.

15 See Begg (2006); Shephard (2008); Worthington (2007).

16 Whilst each of these documents testifies to the media's power to circulate the testimonies of those without a public voice, it is important to note that these accounts offer extremely different perspectives from those detained in the prison. Some manifest attempts to expose the injustice of their ongoing detention without charge or trial, such as the letter from the British detainee Shaker Aamer published by *The Guardian* in 2014 (see Aamer 2014), the testimony of Emad Hassan, a Yemini prisoner cleared for release in 2010 but still held at the camp, which was made available by *Middle East Monitor* in 2014 (see Worthington 2014), or the commentary of hunger striker Moath Al-Alwi, who protested against his force-feeding in *The Nation* in 2014 (Al-Alwi 2014). Others seek to justify and reinforce militant Islamism, such as the diaries of Abu Zubaydah, which were made public by Al Jazeera in 2013 (see Barker 2013) and the memoirs of Khalid Sheikh Mohammed, architect of the 9/11 attacks, which were controversially published by *The Huffington Post* in 2014 (see Reilly 2014).

17 See Stafford Smith (2007a) and (2007b); Khan (2009).

18 Carol Rosenberg of the *Miami Herald*, for example, is an almost constant presence at the hearings, whilst courtroom artist Janet Hamlin published her sketches of the proceedings. See Hamlin (2013).

19 In 2004, the Tricycle Theatre in London produced *Guantánamo: Honour Bound to Defend Freedom,* which dramatised a selection of documentary and archive material relating to the prison and later transferred to New York. Anna Perera's (2009) novel *Guantánamo Boy* considers the rendition and torture of a fictional innocent British minor brought from Pakistan to Guantánamo. In 2012, American artist Molly Crabapple produced a series of sketches and

paintings of Guantánamo based on her observations when visiting the camp (see Crabapple 2014), whilst in 2013 *Harper's Magazine* published a series of drawings by Steve Mumford, which were later exhibited in New York. *The Road to Guantánamo*, a docu-drama depicting the journey of three British Muslims imprisoned in Guantánamo before being freed without charge was released in 2006, and *Camp X-Ray*, a fictional film about a relationship between a female guard at Guantánamo and a male guard, came out in 2014.

20 The restrictive conditions imposed on reporting from Guantánamo has ensured that only a few journalists access the camp with any regularity, giving these individuals an unusual influence in mediating public opinions of the prison and the commission. Furthermore, as demonstrated by Hamlin's sketches (which are subject to censorship and revision), representations of the camp are inevitably partial and, in all likelihood, partisan.

21 See Fincher (2014).

22 See Fincher (2014).

23 See Prendergast (2014).

24 Colwell-Chanthaphonh further highlights the dissatisfaction of certain of the victims' family members over the ways in which their relatives' remains have been contained and curated at the museum. He comments:

> On May 10 [2014], a small motorcade quietly transferred nearly 8,000 pouches containing the fragments of the unidentified remains to the new 9/11 museum complex. They will reside there in a room open only to family members, until, it is hoped, the day the Chief Medical Examiner can link the tissue fragments to known victims. Some families clearly expressed gratitude for the move. But just as clearly, others expressed outrage. They are upset that rather than being placed in an above ground Tomb of the Unknown the remains are now below ground, accessible through the museum building; they are upset that a quote by Virgil and plaques were designed as part of the paid visitor experience (at $24 per person) to draw attention to the unidentified remains on the other side of the wall; they are upset that some of the artifacts in the museum's collection called "composites" (crushed WTC floors compressed together) have still not been exhaustively searched for remains. [...] What museums have learned in recent decades is that the ethical care of human remains requires consent and consultation – to seek the participation of kin in the decision-making process through open and meaningful dialogue. The 9/11 museum has failed on both counts. The new museum took nine years and a reported $700 million to build, yet administrators found neither the resources nor the time to meaningfully and transparently consult with all of the victims' kin about the management of the unidentified remains (Colwell-Chanthaphonh 2014).

Bibliography

Aamer, Shaker. 2014. 'In Guantánamo "national security" rides roughshod over human rights'. *The Guardian*, January 5. Accessed March 20, 2014. http://www.theguardian.com/commentisfree/2014/jan/05/ Guantánamo -national-security-human-rights-us-military-constitution.

Abbott, Shirley. 2008. *The Future of Love*. New York: Algonquin Books.

Abudallah, Shaila. 2009. *Saffron Dreams*. Ann Arbor: Modern History Press.

Al-Alwi, Moath. 2014. 'A letter from Guantánamo: "Nobody can truly understand how we suffer"'. *Aljazeera,* March 13. Accessed March 30, 2014. http://www.aljazeera.com/indepth/opinion/2014/03/letter-from-Guantánamo-nobody-c-201431385642747154.html.

Alshalabi, Firyal, and Sam Drexler. 2003. *The Sky Changed Forever*. Boulder: Aunt Strawberry Books.

American Psychological Association. 2001. *Coping with Terrorism*. Accessed December 13, 2009. www.apa.org/helpcenter/terrorism.aspx.

American Psychological Association. 2004. *Diagnostic and Statistical Manual of Mental Disorders*. Washington, D.C.: American Psychiatric Press.

Anne Frank Museum. 2012. Accessed January 6, 2012. http://www.annefrank.org/.

AP Foreign. 2011. 'NY judge: Iran, Taliban, al-Qaida liable for 9/11'. *The Guardian,* December 23. Accessed December 26, 2011. http://www.guardian.co.uk/world/feedarticle/10008684.

Arendt, Hannah. 1992. Letter to Karl Jaspers, 17 August 1946. In *Hannah Arendt Karl Jaspers correspondence 1926–1969*, edited by Lotte Kohler and Hans Saner. New York: Harcourt Brace.

Assmann, Jan. 2008. 'Communicative and cultural memory'. In *Cultural Memory Studies: An International and Interdisciplinary Handbook*, edited by Astrid Erll and Ansgar Nünning, 109–88. Berlin and New York: Walter de Gruyter.

Associated Press. 2008. 'U.S. compares 9/11 cases to nuremberg trials'. *NBC News,* February 2. Accessed on June 14, 2013. http://www.nbcnews.com/id/23132293/ns/world_news-terrorism/t/us-compares-cases-nuremberg-trials/#.U4HpX9xN1uY.

Atkinson, Rick, ed. 2007. *Where Valor Rests: Arlington National Cemetery*. Washington, D.C.: National Geographic.

Auster, Paul. 2008. *Man in the Dark*. London: Faber and Faber.

Ax, Joseph. 2013. 'American Air, Cantor Fitzgerald settle 9/11 suit for $135mln'. *Reuters,* December 13. Accessed on April 30, 2014. http://in.reuters.com/article/2013/12/17/americanairlines-cantor-idINL2N0JW1SB20131217.

Baer, Elizabeth. 2003. 'Fallout of various kinds'. In *Trauma at Home*, edited by Judith Greenberg, 158–67. Lincoln and London: University of Nebraska Press.

Baer, Ulrich, ed. 2002. *110 Stories – New York Writes After September 11*. New York: New York University Press.

Baker, Peter and Stephen Farrell. 2014. 'Obama Dedicates 9/11 Memorial Museum'. *The New York Times*, May 15. Accessed May 16, 2014. http://www.nytimes.com/2014/05/16/nyregion/obama-dedicates-9-11-memorial-museum.html?_r=1.

Barker, Memphis. 2013. 'The diaries of Abu Zubaydah are not what you expect from a jihadist'. *The Independent*, November 11. Accessed February 10, 2014. http://www.independent.co.uk/voices/comment/the-diaries-of-abu-zubaydah-are-not-what-you-would-expect-from-a-jihadist-8933316.html.

Bartlett, F. C. 1932. *Remembering: A Study in Experimental and Social Psychology*. Cambridge: Cambridge University Press.

Bassin, Donna. 2003. 'A not so temporary occupation inside Ground Zero'. In *Trauma at Home*, edited by Judith Greenberg, 195–203. Lincoln and London: University of Nebraska Press.

Baudrillard, Jean. 1988. *America*. Translated by Chris Turner. London and New York: Verso.

Baudrillard, Jean. 2002. *The Spirit of Terrorism*. Translated by Chris Turner. London and New York: Verso.

Bavis Family. 2011. 'Litigation in the name of Mark L. Bavis comes to an end'. Accessed February 1, 2013. http://www.prnewswire.com/news-releases/litigation-in-the-name-of-mark-l-bavis-comes-to-an-end-130258678.html.

Begg, Moazzam. 2006. *Enemy Combatant: a British Muslim's Journey to Guantánamo and Back*. London: Simon and Schuster.

Bell, Duncan S. A. 2003. 'Mythscapes: Memory, mythology, and national identity'. *British Journal of Sociology* 54.1: 63–81.

Benjamin, Andrew. 1997. *Present Hope: Philosophy, Architecture, Judaism*. London and New York: Routledge.

Benjamin, Walter. 1968. 'The work of art in the age of mechanical reproduction'. Translated by Harry Zohn. In *Illuminations*, edited by Hannah Arendt, 219–54. New York: Harcourt Brace & World.

Bercovitch, Sacvan, and Myra Jehlen. 1986. *Ideology and Classic American Literature*. Cambridge: Cambridge University Press.

Bercovitch, Sacvan. 1978. *The American Jeremiad*. Wisconsin and London: University of Wisconsin Press.

Bercovitch, Sacvan. 1981. 'The ideological context of the American Renaissance'. In *Forms and Functions of History in American Literature: Essays in Honour of Ursula Brumm*, edited by Winfried Fluck, Jürgen Peper, and Willi Paul Adams, 1–20. Berlin: Schmidt.

Berger, James. 2003. 'There's no backhand to this'. In *Trauma at Home*, edited by Judith Greenberg, 52–9. Lincoln and London: University of Nebraska Press.

Bergman, Jay. 1987. 'The perils of historical analogy: Leon Trotsky on the French Revolution'. *Journal of the History of Ideas* 48.1: 73–98.

Berlant, Lauren. 1991. *The Anatomy of National Fantasy: Hawthorne, Utopia, and Everyday Life*. Chicago and London: University of Chicago Press.

Berlant, Lauren. 1997. *The Queen of America Goes to Washington City*. Durham and London: Duke University Press.

Bernard-Donals, Michael. 2005. 'Conflations of memory, or what they saw at the USHMM after 9/11'. *New Centennial Review* 5.2: 73–106.

Birkenstein, Jeff, Anna Froula, and Karen Randell, eds. 2010. *Reframing 9/11: Film, Popular Culture and the 'War on Terror'*. New York and London: Continuum.

Blight, David W. 2011. 'Will it ever rise?' *Memory Remains: 9/11 Artifacts at Hangar 17*, edited by Franscec Torres, 92–5. Washington, D.C.: National Geographic.

Bloxham, Donald. 2003. *Genocide on Trial: War Crimes Trials and the Formation of Holocaust History and Memory*. Oxford: Oxford University Press.

Bogert, Carroll. 2014. 'There's something you need to see at Guantánamo Bay'. *Human Rights Watch*, February 4. Accessed March 30, 2014. http://www.hrw.org/news/2014/02/04/theres-something-you-need-see-Guantánamo-bay.

Bond, Lucy and Jessica Rapson, eds. 2014. *The Transcultural Turn: Interrogating Memory Between and Beyond Borders*. Berlin: Walter de Gruyter.

Bond, Lucy. 2014. 'Types of transculturality: Narrative frameworks and the commemoration of 9/11'. In *The Transcultural Turn: Interrogating Memory Between and Beyond Borders*, edited by Lucy Bond and Jessica Rapson, 61–81. Berlin: Walter de Gruyter.

Booth, W. James. 2001. 'The unforgotten: Memories of justice'. *The American Political Science Review*. 95.4: 777–91.

Borger, Julian and Richard Norton-Taylor. 2002. 'Rumsfeld steps up Iraq war talk'. *The Guardian*, August 21. Accessed August 30, 2011. http://www.guardian.co.uk/world/2002/aug/21/iraq.richardnortontaylor.

Borradori, Giovanna. 2003. *Philosophy in a Time of Terror: Dialogues with Jürgen Habermas and Jacques Derrida*. Chicago and London: University of Chicago Press.

Boxall, Peter. 2009. *Since Beckett: Contemporary Writing in the Wake of Modernism*. London: Continuum.

Brinkerhoff, Noel. 2014. 'Court rules judges may oversee prison conditions at Guantánamo, opening door to detainee lawsuits'. *All Gov*, February 13. Accessed April 1, 2014. http://www.allgov.com/news/top-stories/court-rules-judges-may-oversee-prison-conditions-at-guantánamo-opening-door-to-detainee-lawsuits-140213?news=852427.

Brow, Marnie and Roxanne Cohen Silver. 2009. 'Coping with a collective trauma: Psychological reactions to 9/11 across the United States'. In *The Impact of 9/11 on Psychology and Education: The Day That Changed Everything?*, edited by Matthew J. Morgan, 37–48. New York: Palgrave Macmillan.

Brown, Wendy. 2006. *Regulating Aversion: Tolerance in the Age of Identity and Empire*. Princeton and Oxford: Princeton University Press.

Burgoyne, Robert. 2006. 'From contested to consensual memory: The Rock and Roll Hall of Fame and Museum'. In *Memory, History, Nation: Contested Pasts*, edited by Katherine Hodgkin and Susannah Radstone, 208–20. New Brunswick and London: Transaction Publishers.

Burke, Jason. 2011. *The 9/11 Wars*. London: Allen Lane.

Bush, George. W. 2001a. '9/11 address to the nation', September 11. Accessed July 2, 2011. http://www.americanrhetoric.com/rhetoricofterrorism.html.

Bush, George W. 2001b. 'Remarks at National Day of Prayer and Remembrance'. September 14. Accessed July 2, 2011. http://www.americanrhetoric.com/rhetoricofterrorism.html.

Bush, George W. 2001c. 'National Day of Prayer and Remembrance for the victims of the terrorist attacks, a proclamation'. September 13. Accessed July 2, 2011. http://www.americanrhetoric.com/rhetoricofterrorism.html.

Bush, George W. 2001d. 'President's address from cabinet room'. September 12. Accessed July 2, 2011. http://www.americanrhetoric.com/rhetoricofterrorism.html.

Bush, George W. 2001e. 'First address to United Nations General Assembly'. November 10. Accessed July 2, 2011. http://www.americanrhetoric.com/rhetoricofterrorism.html.

Bush, George W. 2001f. 'Remarks at Barksdale Air Force Base'. September 11. Accessed July 2, 2011. http://www.americanrhetoric.com/rhetoricofterrorism.html.

Bush, George W. 2001g. 'Address to Congress'. September 20. Accessed July 2, 2011. http://www.washingtonpost.com/wpsrv/nation/specials/attacked/transcripts/bushaddress_092001.html.

Bush, George W. 2001h. 'Remarks at Emma Brooker Elementary School'. September 11. Accessed July 2, 2011. http://www.americanrhetoric.com/rhetoricofterrorism.html.

Bush, George W. 2002. '2002 State of the Union Address'. January 29. Accessed July 2, 2011. http://www.americanrhetoric.com/rhetoricofterrorism.html.

Bush, George W. 2003. 'Full text: Bush's speech'. *The Guardian*, March 18. Accessed November 17, 2011. http://www.guardian.co.uk/world/2003/mar/18/usa.iraq.

Bush, George. 2006. 'President Bush's speech on terrorism'. *The New York Times*, September 6. Accessed April 27, 2014. http://www.nytimes.com/2006/09/06/washington/06bush_transcript.html?pagewanted=all&_r=0.

Butler, Judith. 2004. *Precarious Life: The Powers of Mourning and Violence*. London: Verso.

Caplan, Jane. 2000. 'Reflections on the reception of Goldhagen in the United States'. In *The 'Goldhagen Effect': History, Memory, Nazism – Facing the German Past*, edited by Geoff Eley, 151–63. Ann Arbor: University of Michigan Press.

Caruth, Cathy, and Geoffrey Hartman. 1996. 'An interview with Geoffrey Hartman'. *Studies in Romanticism* 35.4: 630–52.

Caruth, Cathy. 1995. *Trauma: Explorations in Memory*. Baltimore and London: Johns Hopkins University Press.

Caruth, Cathy. 1996. *Unclaimed Experience: Trauma, Narrative and History*. Baltimore and London: Johns Hopkins University Press.

Center for Constitutional Rights. 2014. 'Court hears appeal from former Guantánamo detainees in damages case'. February 21. Accessed March 28, 2014. http://www.ccrjustice.org/newsroom/press-releases/court-hears-appeal-former-guantánamo-detainees-damages-case.

Center for Empowered Living and Learning. 2011. Visitor leaflet.

Center for Empowered Living and Learning. 2012. Accessed May 5, 2011. http://www.thecell.org/.

Chanin, Clifford. 2006. '9/11 and the American landscape'. In *9/11 and the American Landscape: photographs by Jonathan Hyman*, 8–9. New York: World Trade Center Memorial Foundation.

Cheong, Soi. 2013. 'American Airlines to pay $135m settlement over 9-11 terrorist attack to firm that had 658 workers killed'. *The Associated Press*, December 17. Accessed on April 30, 2014. http://www.syracuse.com/news/index.ssf/2013/12/american_airlines_to_pay_135m_settlement_over_9-11_terrorist_attack_to_firm_that.html.

Chomsky, Noam. 2001. 'A quick reaction'. *Counterpunch*, September 12. Accessed July 1, 2010. http://humanities.psydeshow.org/political/chomsky-1.htm.

Chomsky, Noam. 2011. *9-11: Was There an Alternative?* New York: Seven Stories Press.

Clark, Rebecca. 2006. *A Museum Walking Tour*. The Oklahoma City National Memorial Foundation.

Clarke, Richard A. 2009. 'The trauma of 9/11 is no excuse'. *The Washington Post*, May 31. Accessed on June 2, 2009. http://www.washingtonpost.com/wp-dyn/content/article/2009/05/29/AR2009052901560.html.

Coates, Susan W., Daniel S. Schechter, and Elsa First. 2003. 'Brief interventions with traumatized children and families after September 11'. In *September 11: Trauma and Human Bonds*, edited by Susan W. Coates, Jane L. Rosenthal, and Daniel S. Schechter, 23–49. London: The Analytic Press.

Coates, Susan W., Jane L. Rosenthal, and Daniel S. Schechter, eds. 2003. *September 11: Trauma and Human Bonds*. London: The Analytic Press.

Cohen, Richard. 1993. 'It's not a holocaust: Rhetoric and reality in Bosnia'. *The Washington Post*, February 28.

Cohen, Richard. 1999. 'A look into the void: Kosovo as Holocaust analogy'. *The Washington Post*, 16 April.

Cohen, Richard. 2010. 'Obama muddles his mosque message'. *The Washington Post*, August 17. Accessed July 17, 2011. http://www.washingtonpost.com/wpdyn/content/article/2010/08/16/AR2010081603169.html.

Cohen, Stanley. 2001. *States of Denial: Knowing About Atrocities and Suffering*. Cambridge: Polity.

Cole, Teju. 2011. *Open City*. London: Faber and Faber.

Coll, Steve. 1994. 'In the shadow of the Holocaust'. *The Washington Post Magazine*, September 25.

Colwell-Chanthaphonh, Chip. 2014. 'Forgetting the 9/11 victims'. *The Huffington Post*, June 10. Accessed June 11, 2014. http://www.huffingtonpost.com/american-anthropological-association/forgetting-the-911-memorial-victim_b_5447250.html.

Crabapple, Molly. 2014. 'Today marks the 12th anniversary of America's Guantánamo prison disgrace'. *The Guardian*, January 11. Accessed April 17, 2014. http://www.theguardian.com/commentisfree/2014/jan/11/Guantánamo-american-disgrace-never-happen-again.

Crockatt, Richard. 2003. *America Embattled: September 11, Anti-Americanism and the Global Order*. London and New York: Routledge.

Crownshaw, Richard. 2010. *The Afterlife of Holocaust Memory in Contemporary Literature and Culture*. Basingstoke: Palgrave Macmillan.

Cvetkovich, Ann. 2003. 'Trauma ongoing'. In *Trauma at Home After 9/11*, edited by Judith Greenberg, 60–8. Lincoln and London: University of Nebraska Press.

Davis, Walter A. 2009. 'Trauma and tragic transformation: Why we learned nothing from 9/11'. In *The Impact of 9/11 on Psychology and Education: The Day That Changed Everything?*, edited by Matthew J. Morgan, 139–50. New York: Palgrave Macmillan.

Dean, Carolyn J. 2003. 'Empathy, pornography, and suffering'. *Differences* 14.1: 88–124.

DeLillo, Don. 2001. 'In the Ruins of the Future'. *The Guardian*, December 22. Accessed November 27, 2007. http://www.guardian.co.uk/books/2001/dec/22/fiction.dondelillo.

DeLillo, Don. 2007. *Falling Man*. Basingstoke and Oxford: Picador.

Derrida, Jacques. 1990. 'Force of law: The "mystical foundation of authority"'. Translated by Mary Quaintance, *Cardozo Law Review*. 11.5/6: 919–1046.

Desch, Michael C. 2006. 'The myth of abandonment: The use and abuse of the holocaust analogy'. *Security Studies* 15.1: 106–45.

DiGrande, Laura, Rachel Fox, and Yuval Neria. 2009. 'Posttraumatic stress after the 9/11 attacks: an examination of national, local, and special population studies'. In *The Impact of 9/11 on Psychology and Education: The Day That Changed Everything?*, edited by Matthew J. Morgan, 49–63. New York: Palgrave Macmillan.

Dobnik, Verena. 2005. 'Museum goes inside Ground Zero'. *New York Times,* August 27.

Doctorow, E. L. 2002. *Lamentation 9/11*. New York: Ruder Finn Press.

Dolan, Frederick M. 1994. *Allegories of America: Narratives, Metaphysics, Politics.* Ithaca and London: Cornell University Press.

Donadio, Rachel. 2005. 'The irascible prophet: V. S. Naipaul at home'. *The Guardian*, August 7.

Douglas, Lawrence. 2001. *The Memory of Judgment: Making Law and History in the Trials of the Holocaust.* New Haven and London: Yale University Press.

Dunlap, David W. 2006. 'A hands-on tribute to the pain and valor of 9/11.' *The New York Times,* June 11. Accessed July 7, 2011. http://www.nytimes.com/2006/06/11/nyregion/11memorial.html.

Eaglestone, Robert. 2004. *The Holocaust and the Postmodern.* Oxford: Oxford University Press.

Edelman, Susan. 2007. 'Families fume at "callous" judge'. *New York Post,* September 9. Accessed on January 21, 2013. Http://www.nypost.com/p/news/regional/item_AA5dv35yzjcIifNgKSBMhK.

Edkins, Jenny. 2003. *Trauma and the Memory of Politics.* Cambridge: Cambridge University Press.

Eggers, Dave. 2009. *Zeitoun*. London: Penguin Books.

Eisenman, Stephen F. 2007. *The Abu Ghraib Effect.* London: Reaktion Books.

Erll, Astrid, and Ann Rigney, eds. 2009. *Mediation, Remediation, and the Dynamics of Cultural Memory.* Berlin and New York: Walter de Gruyter.

Erll, Astrid and Ansgar Nünning, eds. 2008. *Cultural Memory Studies: an International and Interdisciplinary Handbook.* New York and Berlin: Walter de Gruyter.

Erll, Astrid. 2009. 'Remembering across time, space and cultures: Premediation, remediation and the Indian mutiny'. In *Mediation, Remediation, and the Dynamics of Cultural Memory,* edited by Astrid Erll and Ann Rigney, 109–38. Berlin and New York: Walter de Gruyter.

Erll, Astrid. 2011a. *Memory in Culture.* Translated by Sara B. Young. Basingstoke: Palgrave Macmillan.

Erll, Astrid. 2011b. 'Travelling memory'. *Parallax* 17.4: 4–18.

Eviatar, Daphne. 2012. 'Does the US Constitution apply to the 9/11 trial? Maybe'. *The Huffington Post,* October 18. Accessed December 1, 2012. http://www.huffingtonpost.com/daphne-eviatar/does-the-us-constitution_b_1981735.html.

Falkoff, Marc. 2007. *Poems from Guantánamo: The Detainees Speak.* Iowa City: University of Iowa Press.

Faludi, Susan. 2008. *The Terror Dream.* London: Atlantic Books.

FDIH (International Federation for Human Rights). 2014. 'Former Guantánamo detainees urge French judge to subpoena Guantánamo commander for role in detainee torture'. February 26. Accessed April 6, 2014. http://www.fidh.org/en/europe/france/14782-former-Guantánamo-detainees-urge-french-judge-to-subpoena-former.

Feinberg, Kenneth. 2004. 'Closing statement from the special master, Mr. Kenneth R. Feinberg, on the shutdown of the September 11 Victim Compensation Fund'. U.S. Department of Justice. Accessed March 3, 2010. http://www.justice.gov/archive/victimcompensation/closingstatement.pdf.

Feinstein, Dianne. 2012. 'Feinstein statement on CIA detention, interrogation report'. December 13. Accessed April 4, 2014. http://www.feinstein.senate.gov/public/index.cfm/press-releases?ID=46c0b685-a392-4400-a9a3-5e058d29e635.

Feldman, Jeffrey D. 2003. 'One tragedy in reference to another: September 11 and the obligations of museum commemoration'. *American Anthropologist* 105.4: 839 – 43.

Felman, Shoshana, and Dori Laub. 1992. *Testimony: Crises of Witnessing in Literature, Psychoanalysis and History*. New York and London: Routledge.

Felman, Shoshana. 1992. 'Education and crisis, or the vicissitudes of teaching'. In *Testimony: Crises of Witnessing in Literature, Psychoanalysis, and History*, edited by Shoshana Felman and Dori Laub, 1–56. New York and London: Routledge.

Felman, Shoshana. 2002. *The Juridical Imagination: Trials and Traumas in the Twentieth Century.* Cambridge and London: Harvard University Press.

Ferguson, Robert A. 1984. *Law And Letters in American Culture.* Cambridge and London: Harvard University Press.

Ferguson, Robert A. 2007. *The Trial in American Life.* Chicago: University of Chicago Press.

Fincher, Megan. 2014. 'Living Guantánamo exhibit in D.C. museum'. *National Catholic Reporter,* January 17. Accessed February 14, 2014. http://ncronline.org/social-tags/Guantánamo-bay-detention-camp.

Finkelstein, Norman G. 2003. *The Holocaust Industry.* London and New York: Verso.

Flanzbaum, Hilene, ed. 1999. *The Americanization of the Holocaust.* Baltimore and London: Johns Hopkins University Press.

Foer, Jonathan Safran. 2006. *Extremely Loud and Incredibly Close.* London: Penguin Books.

Foote, Kenneth E. 2003. *Shadowed Ground: America's Landscapes of Violence and Tragedy.* Austin: University of Texas Press.

Foster, Peter. 2012. 'Guantánamo Bay 9/11 trial "could go on for years"'. *The Telegraph,* May 6. Accessed October 11, 2012. http://www.telegraph.co.uk/news/worldnews/al-qaeda/9249436/Guantánamo-Bay-911-trial-could-go-on-for-years.html.

Foster, Thomas. 2005. 'Cynical nationalism'. In *The Selling of 9/11,* edited by Dana Heller, 254–87. New York: Palgrave Macmillan.

Francois-Cerrah, Myriam, Ryan Grim, and Ryan J. Reilly. 2014. 'Mastermind of the Sept. 11 attacks wants to convert his captors'. *The Huffington Post,* January 14. Accessed on March 17, 2014. http://www.huffingtonpost.com/2014/01/14/khalid-sheikh-mohammed-manifesto_n_4591298.html.

Franzen, Jonathan. 2001. 'The talk of the town.' *The New Yorker,* September 24. Accessed June 11, 2010. http://www.newyorker.com/archive/2001/09/24/010924ta_talk_wtc.

Fraser, Nancy. 2008. *Scales of Justice: Reimagining Political Space in a Globalizing World.* Cambridge and Malden: Polity Press.

Freud, S. 1914. 'Remembering', 'Repeating', and 'Working-through'. *The Standard Edition of the Complete Psychological Works of Sigmund Freud,* Volume XII (1911–1913): 145–56. London: Hogarth Publishing Company.

Freud, Sigmund. 1899. 'Screen memories', *Standard Edition 3*. Translated by James Strachey, 301–22. London: The Hogarth Press.

Freud, Sigmund. 1961. *Beyond the Pleasure Principle*. E, edited by James Strachey. New York: W. W. Norton & Company.

Friedlander, Saul. 1992. *Probing the Limits of Representation*. Cambridge: Harvard University Press.

Friedman, Dina. 2006. *Playing Dad's Song*. New York: Farrar, Straus and Giroux.

Frum, David, and Daniel Perle. 2004. *An End to Evil: How to Win the War on Terror*. New York: Random House.

Gardner, Lloyd C. *Killing Machine: The American Presidency in the Age of Drone Warfare*. New York and London: The New Press.

Glass, Julia. 2007. *The Whole World Over*. London: Arrow Books.

Goldberger, Paul. 2005. *Up From Zero: Politics, Architecture, and the Rebuilding of New York*. New York: Random House.

Goldsmith, Jack. 2012. 'The shadow of Nuremberg'. *The New York Times*, January 20. Accessed September 7, 2012. http://www.nytimes.com/2012/01/22/books/review/justice-and-the-enemy-nuremberg-9-11-and-the-trial-of-khalid-sheikh-mohammed-by-william-shawcross-book-review.html.

Goshray, Saby. 2007. 'On the judicial treatment of Guantánamo detainees within the context of international law'. In *Guantánamo Bay and the Judicial-Moral Treatment of the Other*, edited by Clark Butler, 80–116. West Lafayette: Purdue University Press.

Gourevitch, Philip. 1993. 'Behold now behemoth: The Holocaust Memorial Museum: One more American theme park'. *Harper's*, July: 55–62.

Gradstein, Linda. 2006. 'Israel debates site for tolerance museum'. *NPR*, February 24. Accessed May 1, 2014. http://www.npr.org/templates/story/story.php?storyId=5231827.

Gray, Richard. 2008. 'Open doors, closed minds: American prose writing at a time of crisis'. *American Literature History* 21.1: 128–51.

Gray, Richard. 2011. *After the Fall: American Literature Since 9/11*. Oxford: Wiley-Blackwell.

Greenberg, Judith. 2003. 'Wounded New York'. In *Trauma at Home*, edited by Judith Greenberg, 21–38. Lincoln and London: University of Nebraska Press.

Greenberg, Karen J. 2013. 'Afterword'. In *Sketching Guantánamo: Court Sketches of the Military Tribunals: 2006–2013*, edited by Janet Hamlin. Washington: Fantagraphics Books.

Greenwald, Alice. 2006. 'Director's foreword'. In *9/11 and the American Landscape: photographs by Jonathan Hyman*, 4–5. New York: World Trade Center Memorial Foundation.

Ground Zero Museum Workshop. 2011. Accessed October 17, 2011. http://www.groundzeromuseum.com/.

Grusin, Richard. 2010. *Premediation: Affect and Mediality after 9/11*. Basingstoke and New York: Palgrave Macmillan.

Gutman, Yifat. 2009. 'Where do we go from here: The pasts, presents and futures of Ground Zero'. *Memory Studies* 2.1: 55–70.

Haberman, Clyde. 2009. 'A trauma that rippled outward'. *New York Times*, September 10. Accessed September 11, 2009. http://www.nytimes.com/2009/09/11/nyregion/11nyc.html.

Habermas, Jürgen. 2006. *The Divided West*. Translated by Ciaran Cronin. Cambridge: Polity Press.

Hacker, Katharina. 2007. *The Have-Nots*. Translated by Helen Atkins. New York: Europa Editions.

Hafetz, Jonathan. 2011. *Habeas Corpus After 9/11: Confronting America's New Global Detention System*. New York and London: New York University Press.

Hajjar, Lisa. 2003. 'From Nuremberg to Guantánamo: International law and American power politics'. *Middle East Research and Information Project* 229. Accessed December 14, 2013. http://www.merip.org/mer/mer229/nuremberg-Guantánamo.

Hajjar, Lisa. 2010. 'Universal jurisprudence as praxis: An option to pursue legal accountability for superpower torturers'. In *When Governments Break the Law*, edited by Austin Sarat and Nasser Hussain, 87–120. New York: New York University Press.

Halbwachs, Maurice. 1992. *On Collective Memory*. Translated by Lewis A. Coser. Chicago and London: University of Chicago Press.

Hamid, Mohsin. 2007. *The Reluctant Fundamentalist*. London: Penguin Books.

Hamill, Peter. 2006. 'September song'. In *9/11 and the American Landscape: photographs by Jonathan Hyman*, 6–7. New York: World Trade Center Memorial Foundation.

Hamlin, Janet. 2013. *Sketching Guantánamo: Court Sketches of the Military Tribunals 2006–2013*. Washington: Fantagraphics Books.

Hammad, Suheir. 2003. 'First writing since'. In *Trauma at Home*, edited by Judith Greenberg, 139–46. Lincoln and London: University of Nebraska Press.

Hartman, Geoffrey. 2003. 'On that day'. In *Trauma at Home*, edited by Judith Greenberg, 5–10. Lincoln and London: University of Nebraska Press.

Hartocollis, Anemona. 2007. '"Evidence in 9/11 damages case is restricted'. *The New York Times*. October 18. Accessed December 5, 2012. http://www.nytimes.com/2007/10/18/nyregion/18suit.html?ref=alvinkhellerstein&_r=0.

Haskell, John. 2005. *American Purgatorio*. Edinburgh and New York: Canongate.

Hauerwas, Stanley, and Frank Lentricchia, eds. 2003. *Dissent From the Homeland: essays after September 11*. Durham and London: Duke University Press.

Hazan, Pierre, and Sarah De Stadelhofen. 2010. *Judging War, Judging History: Behind Truth and Reconciliation*. Stanford: Stanford University Press.

Heller, Dana. 2005. 'Introduction: Consuming 9/11'. In *The Selling of 9/11*, edited by Dana Heller, 1–26. New York: Palgrave Macmillan.

Hellerstein, Alvin K., James A. Henderson Jr., and Aaron Twerski. 2012. 'Managerial judging: The 9/11 responders' tort litigation'. *Cornell Law Review* 98.1: 128–80.

Hier, Marvin. 2001. 'A message from Rabbi Marvin Hier'.

Hirsch, Marianne. 1997. *Family Frames: Photography, Narrative and Postmemory*. Cambridge: Harvard University Press.

Hirsch, Marianne. 2003. 'I took pictures: September 11, 2001 and beyond'. In *Trauma at Home*, edited by Judith Greenberg, 69–86. Lincoln and London: University of Nebraska Press.

Hodgkin, Katherine, and Susannah Radstone, eds. 2006. *Memory, History, Nation: Contested Pasts*. New Brunswick and London: Transaction Publishers.

Horton, Scott. 2008. 'Justice after Bush: Prosecuting an outlaw administration'. *Harper's Magazine*. December. Accessed May 20, 2013. http://harpers.org/archive/2008/12/justice-after-bush/.

Hosseini, Khalid. 2007. *A Thousand Splendid Suns*. London: Bloomsbury.

HR 1057. 2005. 'The True American Heroes Act'. Accessed January 21, 2009. http://www.opencongress.org/bill/109-h1057/show.

HR 3421. 2012. 'The Fallen Heroes of 9/11 Act'. Accessed November 14, 2011. http://www.opencongress.org/bill/112-h3421/show.

Huehls, Mitchum. 2008. 'Foer, Spiegelman, and 9/11's timely traumas'. In *Literature After 9/11*, edited by Ann Keniston and Jeanne Follansbee Quinn, 42–59. New York and London: Routledge.

Hughes, Richard T. 2004. *Myths America Lives By*. Urbana and Chicago: University of Illinois Press.

Hungerford, Amy. 2003. *The Holocaust of Texts – Genocide, Literature, Personification*. Chicago: University of Chicago Press.

Huntington, Samuel. 1996. *The Clash of Civilizations and the Remaking of the World Order*. New York: Simon and Schuster.

Huyssen, Andreas. 1995. *Twilight Memories: Marking Times in a Culture of Amnesia*. New York and London: Routledge.

Huyssen, Andreas. 2003. *Present Pasts: Urban Palimpsests and the Politics of Memory*. Stanford: Stanford University Press.

Hyman, Jonathan. 2006. *9/11 and the American Landscape*. New York: World Trade Center Memorial Foundation.

Jameson, Fredric. 2003. 'The dialectics of disaster'. In *Dissent from the Homeland: Essay after September 11*, edited by Stanley Hauerwas and Frank Lentricchia, 55–62. Durham and London: Duke University Press.

Janet, P. 1901. *The Mental State of Hystericals: A Study of Mental Stigma and Mental Accidents*. Translated by C. Corson. New York: Putnam.

Janet, P. 1925. *Psychological Healing: A Historical and Clinical Study*. Translated by Eden and Cedar Paul, two volumes. New York: Palgrave Macmillan.

Janoff-Bulman, Ronnie, and Ramila Usoof-Thowfeek. 2009. 'Shifting moralities: Post-9/11 responses to shattered national assumptions'. In *The Impact of 9/11 on Psychology and Education: The Day That Changed Everything?*, edited by Matthew J. Morgan, 81–96. New York: Palgrave Macmillan.

Jenkins, Henry. 2006. 'Captain America sheds his mighty tears: Comics and September 11'. In *Terror, Culture, Politics: Rethinking 9/11'*, edited by Daniel J. Sherman and Terry Nardin, 69–102. Bloomington and Indiana: Indiana University Press.

Junod, Tom. 2012. 'The lethal presidency of Barack Obama'. *Esquire*, July 9. Accessed December 11, 2012. http://www.esquire.com/features/obama-lethal-presidency-0812.

Kacades, Irene. 2003. '9/11/01 = 1/27/01: The changed posttraumatic self'. In *Trauma at Home*, edited by Judith Greenberg, 168–186 . Lincoln and London: University of Nebraska Press.

Kalfus, Ken. 2006. *A Disorder Peculiar to the Country*. London: Simon & Schuster.

Kansteiner, Wulf and Harald Weilnböck. 2008. 'Against the concept of cultural trauma'. In *Cultural Memory Studies: An International and Interdisciplinary Handbook*, edited by Astrid Erll and Ansgar Nünning, 229–40. Berlin and New York: Walter de Gruyter.

Kansteiner, Wulf. 2002. 'Finding meaning in memory: A methodological critique of collective memory studies'. *History and Theory* 41.2: 179–97.

Kaplan, E. Ann. 2005. *Trauma Culture: The Politics of Terror and Loss in Media and Literature*. New Brunswick: Rutgers University Press.

Karstedt, Susanne, ed. 2009. *Legal Institutions and Collective Memories*. Oxford: Hart Publishing.

Kennedy, Edward. 2001. 'Statement of Senator Edward M. Kennedy on the economic stimulus package', October 24. Accessed July 13, 2011. http://www.senate.gov/kennedy/statements/01/10/2001A25B49.html.

Khan, Mahvish. 2009. *My Guantánamo Diary: The Detainees and the Stories They Told Me*. New York: PublicAffairs.

Kingsbury, Karen and Gary Smalley. 2003. *Remember*. Wheaton: Tyndale House.

Klein, Kerwin Lee. 2000. 'On The Emergence of "Memory" in Historical Discourse'. *Representations* 69.4: 127–50.

Krauthammer, Charles. 2010. 'Sacrilege at Ground Zero'. *The Washington Post*, August 13. Accessed July 21, 2011. http://www.washingtonpost.com/wpdyn/content/article/2010/08/12/AR2010081204996.html.

LaCapra, Dominick. 2001. *Writing History, Writing Trauma*. Baltimore: Johns Hopkins University Press.

LaCapra, Dominick. 2004. *History in Transit: Experience, Identity, Critical Theory*. Ithaca and London: Cornell University Press.

Landsberg, Alison. 2004. *Prosthetic Memory: The Transformation of American Remembrance in the Age of Mass Culture*. New York: Columbia University Press.

Laub, Dori. 1992. 'Bearing witness, or the vicissitudes of listening'. In *Testimony: Crises of Witnessing in Literature, Psychoanalysis, and History*, edited by Shoshana Felman and Dori Laub, 57–74. New York and London: Routledge.

Laub, Dori. 2003. 'September 11, 2001 – An event without a voice'. In *Trauma at Home*, edited by Judith Greenberg, 204–15. Lincoln and London: University of Nebraska Press.

Lennard, Natasha. 2013. 'Gitmo detainees sue Poland over CIA rendition'. *The Salon*, December 3. Accessed February 12, 2014. http://www.salon.com/2013/12/03/gitmo_detainees_sue_poland_over_cia_rendition/.

Lessa, Francesca. 2013. *Memory and Transitional Justice in Argentina and Uruguay*. Basingstoke: Palgrave Macmillan.

Levy, Daniel and Natan Sznaider. 2006. *The Holocaust and Memory in the Global Age*. Translated by Assenka Oksiloff. Philadelphia: Temple University Press.

Levy, Daniel and Natan Sznaider. 2010. *Human Rights and Memory*. University Park, PA: University of Pennsylvania Press.

Lewis, Anthony. 1999. 'On a wing and a prayer'. *The New York Times*, May 15.

Leys, Ruth. 2000. *Trauma: a Genealogy*. Chicago and London: University of Chicago Press.

Libeskind, Daniel. 2004. *Breaking Ground: Adventures in Life and Architecture*. London: John Murray.

Lincoln, Abraham. 1861. 'Farewell speech'. Accessed July 10, 2011. http://www.historyplace.com/lincoln/farewell.html.

Linenthal, Edward T. 1993. *Sacred Ground: Americans and Their Battlefields*. Urbana and Chicago: University of Chicago Press.

Linenthal, Edward T. 1995. *Preserving Memory: The Struggle to Create America's Holocaust Museum*. New York: Viking.

Linenthal, Edward T. 2001. *The Unfinished Bombing: Oklahoma City in American Memory*. Oxford: Oxford University Press.

Lippman, Jonathan. 2004. 'Preserving safety and access to the courts'. *New York Law Journal* 83, April 30.

Liss, Andrea. 1998. *Trespassing through Shadows: memory, photography, and the Holocaust*. Minneapolis: University of Minnesota Press.

LoCicero, Alice, Allen J. Brown, and Samuel J. Sinclair. 2009. 'Fear across America in a post-9/11 world'. In *The Impact of 9/11 on Psychology and Education: The Day That Changed Everything?*, edited by Matthew J. Morgan, 97–114. New York: Palgrave Macmillan.

Lower Manhattan Development Corporation. 2001. 'Governor and mayor name Lower Manhattan redevelopment corporation'. November 29. Accessed November 18, 2009. www.renewnyc.com/listnews.aspx.

Luckhurst, Roger. 2003. 'Traumaculture'. *New Formations* 50.3: 28–47.

Luckhurst, Roger. 2008. *The Trauma Question*. London and New York: Routledge.

MacGreal, Chris. 2013. 'Lawyers for 9/11 suspects ask to be locked up at Guantánamo'. *The Guardian*, January 29. Accessed January 29, 2013. http://www.guardian.co.uk/world/2013/jan/29/lawyers-9-11-suspects-Guantánamo.

Makhmalbaf, Samira et al. 2002. *11'09»01*. Produced by Alain Brigand. Studio Canal.

Marks, Bridget. 2004. *September: a Novel*. Chicago: Volt Press.

Maynard, Joyce. 2003. *The Usual Rules*. New York: St Martin's Press.

McCarthy, Cormac. 2006. *The Road*. London: Picador.

McClintock, Anne. 2011. 'Paranoid empire: Spectres from Guantánamo and Abu Ghraib'. In *States of Emergency: The Object of American Studies*, edited by Russ Castronovo and Susan Gillman, 88–115. Chapel Hill: University of North Carolina Press.

McGrath, Patrick. 2005. 'Ground Zero'. In *Ghost Town*, 175–243. London: Bloomsbury Publishing.

McInerney, Jay. 2001. 'Brightness falls'. *The Guardian*, September 15. Accessed June 11, 2010. http://www.guardian.co.uk/books/2001/sep/15/september11.usa1.

McInerney, Jay. 2005. 'The uses of invention'. *The Guardian*, September 17. Accessed August 20, 2008. http://www.guardian.co.uk/books/2005/sep/17/fiction.vsnaipaul.

McInerney, Jay. 2007. *The Good Life*. London: Bloomsbury.

Mead, G. H. 1932. *The Philosophy of the Present*. La Salle: Open Court.

Meek, Alan. 2010. *Trauma and Media: Theories, Histories, and Images*. New York: Routledge.

Meminger, Neesha. 2009. *Shine, Coconut Moon*. New York: Margaret K. McElderry Books.

Messud, Claire. 2007. *The Emperor's Children*. London: Picador.

Meyer, Jeffrey F. 2001. *Myths in Stone: Religious Dimensions of Washington, D.C.* Berkley, Los Angeles, and London: University of California Press.

Meyerowitz, Joel. 2006. *Aftermath*. New York and London: Phaidon Press.

Miller, Nancy K. 2008. 'Portraits of grief: Telling details and the new genres of testimony'. In *Literature After 9/11*, edited by Ann Keniston and Jeanne Follansbee Quinn, 19–41. New York and London: Routledge.

Mills, Nicolaus. 2004. *Their Last Battle: The Fight for the National World War II Memorial*. New York: Basic Books.

Misztal, Barbara A. 2001. 'Legal attempts to construct collective memory'. *Polish Sociological Review*, 133.1: 61–77.

Mitchell, W. J. T. 2011. *Cloning Terror: The War of Images, 9/11 to the Present*. Chicago and London: University of Chicago Press.

Moore, Michael. 2004. *Fahrenheit 9/11*. Directed by Michael Moore. Dog Eat Dog Films.

Moses, A. Dirk and Michael Rothberg. 2014. 'A dialogue on the ethics and politics of transcultural memory'. In *The Transcultural Turn: Interrogating Memory Between and Beyond Borders*, edited by Lucy Bond and Jessica Rapson, 29–38. Berlin: Walter de Gruyter.

Moses, A. Dirk, ed. 2008. *Empire, colony, genocide: conquest, occupation, and subaltern resistance in world history*. New York and Oxford: Berghahn Books.

Museum of Tolerance New York. 2014. Accessed May 17, 2014. http://www.museumoftolerancenewyork.com.

Names Project Foundation. 2011. Accessed July 10, 2011. http://www.aidsquilt.org/.

Nash Smith, Henry. 1986. 'Symbol and idea in *Virgin Land*'. In *Ideology and Classic American Literature*, edited by Sacvan Bercovitch and Myra Jehlen, 21–25. Cambridge: Cambridge University Press.

National Center for Infants, Toddlers and Families. 2003. *Diagnostic Classification 0–3*. Washington, D.C.: Zero to Three.

National Park Service. 2005. 'Franklin Delano Roosevelt Memorial'. Washington, D.C.

National Park Service. 2011. 'National World War II Memorial'. Washington, D.C.

National Security Strategy of the United States of America. 2002. Accessed September 20, 2011. http://georgewbush-whitehouse.archives.gov/nsc/nss/2002/.

Navarro, Mireya. 2011. 'Payout rises for workers at 9/11 site'. *The New York Times,* September 12. Accessed December 13, 2012. http://www.nytimes.com/2011/09/13/nyregion/payout-rises-for-911-site-workers-but-not-lawyers.html?ref=alvinkhellerstein.

New York Says Thank You Foundation. 2011. Accessed July 10, 2014. http://national911flag.org.

New York Times. 2001. 'Among the missing'. Editorial, October 14. Accessed October 17, 2011. http://www.nytimes.com/2001/10/14/opinion/among-the-missing.html.

New York Times. 2003. *Portraits, 9/11/01: The Collected 'Portraits of Grief' from the New York Times*. Foreword by Howell Raines and introduction by Janny Scott. New York: Henry Holt.

Nissenson, Hugh. 2005. *The days of awe*. Naperville: Sourcebooks.

Niven, Bill, ed. 2006. *Germans as Victims: Remembering the Past in Contemporary Germany*. Basingstoke: Palgrave Macmillan.

Nobel, Philip. 2005. *Sixteen Acres: Architecture and the Outrageous Struggle for the Future of Ground Zero*. New York: Metropolitan Books.

Nora, Pierre. 1989. 'Between memory and history: *Les Lieux de Mémoire*'. *Representations*, 26.1: 7–25.

Novick, Peter. 1999. *The Holocaust in American Life*. Boston and New York: Mariner Books.

O'Brien, Natalie. 2014. 'David Hicks' wife sues FBI, US agencies over secrecy'. *The Sydney Morning Herald,* February 22. Accessed April 2, 2014. http://www.smh.com.au/national/david-hicks-wife-sues-fbi-us-agencies-over-secrecy-20140222-3396l.html#ixzz2yD13uQVfhttp:/.

O'Donnell, Deborah A., and Jessica Powers. 2009. 'How has terrorism impacted the American family?'. In *The Impact of 9/11 on Psychology and Education: The*

Day That Changed Everything?, edited by Matthew J. Morgan, 161–72. New York: Palgrave Macmillan.

O'Neill, Joseph. 2008. *Netherland*. London: Fourth Estate.

Obama, Barack. 2009a. 'Executive order – review and disposition of individuals detained at the Guantánamo Bay naval base and closure of detention facilities'. January 22. Accessed April 26, 2014. http://www.whitehouse.gov/the-press-office/closure-Guantánamo-detention-facilities.

Obama, Barack. 2009b. 'Obama National Archives Speech'. *The Huffington Post*, June 21. Accessed May 1, 2014. http://www.huffingtonpost.com/2009/05/21/obama-national-archives-s_n_206189.html.

Obama, Barack. 2012. 'State of the Union Address'. *The Guardian*, January 24. Accessed March 7, 2012. http://www.guardian.co.uk/world/2012/jan/25/state-of-the-union-address-full-text.

Obama, Barack. 2013. 'Remarks by the president at the National Defense University'. May 23. Accessed May 2, 2014. http://www.whitehouse.gov/the-press-office/2013/05/23/remarks-president-national-defense-university.

Obama, Barack. 2014. 'Transcript of Obama's remarks at 9/11 Museum dedication'. *The News-Gazette*, May 15. Accessed May 16, 2014. http://www.news-gazette.com/news/nationworld/2014-05-15/transcript-obamas-remarks-911-museum-dedication.html.

Olick, Jeffrey K. 1999. 'Genre memories and memory genres: A dialogical analysis of May 8, 1945, commemorations in the Federal Republic of Germany'. *American Sociological Review* 64.3: 381–402.

Olick, Jeffrey K. and Joyce Robbins. 1998. 'Social memory studies: From "collective memory" to the historical sociology of mnemonic practices'. *Annual Review of Sociology* 24: 105–40.

Osiel, Mark. 2012. *Mass Atrocity, Collective Memory, and the Law*. New Brunswick and London: Transaction Publishers.

Patel, Andrea. 2001. *On That Day: a Book of Hope for Children*. Berkley and Toronto: Tricycle Press.

Pease, Donald E. 2009. *The New American Exceptionalism*. Minneapolis and London: University of Minnesota Press.

Percival, Jenny. 2010. 'Barack Obama compares oil spill to 9/11'. *The Guardian*, June 14. Accessed on September 7, 2011. http://www.guardian.co.uk/environment/2010/jun/14/barack-obama-oil-spill-911.

Perera, Anna. 2009. *Guantánamo Boy*. London: Puffin Books.

Perle, Richard. 2002. 'Why the West must strike first against Saddam Hussein'. *The Telegraph*, August 9. Accessed July 3, 2011. http://www.telegraph.co.uk/comment/personal-view/3580181/Why-the-West-must-strike-first-against-Saddam-Hussein.html.

Powers, Richard. 2001. 'The way we live now: 9-23-01: Close reading: Elements of tragedy; The simile'. *The New York Times*, September 23. Accessed July 9, 2011. http://www.nytimes.com/2001/09/23/magazine/the-way-we-live-now-9-23-01-close-reading-elements-of-tragedy-the-simile.html.

Poza, Hernán. 2003. 'A letter from Brooklyn – September 11, 2001'. In *September 11: Trauma and Human Bonds*, edited by Susan W. Coates, Jane L. Rosenthal, and Daniel S. Schechter, 15–21. London: The Analytic Press.

Prendergast, Daniel. 2014. 'Politicians rip crass 9/11 museum gift shop'. *The New York Post*, May 19. Accessed May 20, 2014. http://nypost.com/2014/05/19/

politicans-angered-over-crass-911-museum-gift-shop/?utm_campaign=
SocialFlow&utm_source=NYPTwitter&utm_medium=SocialFlow.

Price, Reynolds. 2006. *The Good Priest's Son*. New York: Scribner.

Prose, Francine. 2007. *Bullyville*. New York: Harper Collins.

Quesada, Joe et al. 2001. *Heroes*. New York: Marvel.

Radstone, Susannah. 2005. 'Reconceiving binaries: The limits of memory'. *History Workshop Journal* 59.1: 134–50.

Radstone, Susannah. 2011. 'What place is this? Transcultural memory and the locations of memory studies'. *Parallax* 17.4: 109–23.

Rajiva, Lila. 2005. *The Language of Empire: Abu Ghraib and the American Media*. New York: Monthly Review Press.

Richards, Peter Judson. 2007. *Extraordinary Justice: Military Tribunals in Historical and International Context*. New York and London: New York University Press.

Ricks, Thomas E. 2003. 'Holding their ground; As critics zero in, Paul Wolfowitz is unflinching on Iraq'. *The Washington Post*, December 23.

Ricoeur, Paul. 2004. *Memory, History, Forgetting*. Translated by Kathleen Blamey and David Pellauer. Chicago and London: University of Chicago Press.

Roosevelt, F. D. 1941. 'Third inauguration'. Accessed July 10, 2011. http://avalon.law.yale.edu/20th_century/froos3.asp.

Rose, Jacqueline. 1998. *States of Fantasy*. Oxford: Oxford University Press.

Rosenberg, Carol. 2014. '"Transparent" detention at Guantánamo? Not anymore'. *The Miami Herald*, January 4. Accessed March 20, 2014. http://www.miamiherald.com/2014/01/04/3852565/transparent-detention-at-Guantánamo.html.

Rosenfeld, Gavriel D. 2009. 'A looming crash or a soft landing? Forecasting the future of the memory "industry"'. *Journal of Modern History* 81.1: 122–58.

Rosenthal, Andrew. 2012. 'Justice delayed, torture classified'. *The New York Times*, May 4. Accessed July 19, 2012. http://takingnote.blogs.nytimes.com/2012/05/04/justice-delayed-torture-classified/.

Roth, Philip. 2005. *The Plot Against America*. London: Vintage Books.

Roth, Susan L. 2001. *It's Still a Dog's New York: A Book of Healing*. Washington, D.C.: National Geographic Society.

Rothberg, Michael and Stefan Craps. 2011. 'Introduction: Transcultural negotiations of Holocaust memory'. *Criticism* 53.4: 517–21.

Rothberg, Michael. 2000. *Traumatic Realism*. Minneapolis: University of Minnesota Press.

Rothberg, Michael. 2003. '"There is no poetry in this": Writing, trauma, and home'. In Judith Greenberg, ed. *Trauma at Home*, 147–58. Lincoln and London: University of Nebraska Press. 147–58.

Rothberg, Michael. 2008. 'Seeing terror, feeling art: Public and private in post-9/11 literature'. In *Literature After 9/11*, edited by Ann Keniston and Jeanne Follansbee Quinn, 123–42. London: Routledge.

Rothberg, Michael. 2009a. *Multidirectional Memory: Remembering the Holocaust in the Age of Decolonization*. Stanford: Stanford University Press.

Rothberg, Michael. 2009b. 'A failure of the imagination: Diagnosing the post-9/11 novel: A response to Richard Gray'. *American Literary History* 21.1: 152–58.

Rothberg, Michael. 2011. 'From Gaza to Warsaw: Mapping multidirectional memory'. *Criticism* 53.4: 523–48.

Rozan, S. J. 2008. *Absent Friends*. New York: Bantam Dell.

Rozario, Kevin. 2007. *The Culture of Calamity: Disaster and the Making of Modern America*. Chicago and London: University of Chicago Press.

Salazar, Cristian. 2011. 'Arrangement of 9/11 victims' names on memorial upsets survivors'. *The Detroit Free Press*, May 5.

Sanchez, Raf. 2012. 'Judge orders Khalid Sheikh Mohammed lawyers not to discuss torture'. *The Telegraph*, October 15. Accessed October 19, 2012. http://www.telegraph.co.uk/news/worldnews/september-11-attacks/9610884/Guantánamo-judge-orders-Khalid-Sheikh-Mohammed-lawyers-not-to-discuss-torture.html.

Sandel, Michael J., ed. 2007. *Justice: A Reader*. Oxford: Oxford University Press.

Santer, Eric. 1992. 'History beyond the pleasure principle: Some thoughts on the representation of trauma'. In *Probing the Limits of Representation: Nazism and the 'Final Solution'*, edited by Saul Friedlander, 143–54. Cambridge and London: Harvard University Press.

Sarat, Austin and Nasser Hussain, eds. 2010. *When Governments Break the Law: The Rule of Law and the Prosecution of the Bush Administration*. New York and London: New York University Press.

Sarat, Austin and Thomas R. Kearns, eds. 2002. *History, Memory, and the Law*. Michigan: University of Michigan Press.

Sarat, Austin, Lawrence Douglas, and Marta Merrill Umphrey, eds. 2007. *Law and Catastrophe*. Stanford: Stanford University Press.

Sattler, Peter. 2014 *Camp X-Ray*. Directed by Peter Sattler. IFC Films.

Savage, Charlie. 2013a. 'Judge overrules censors in Guantánamo 9/11 hearing'. *The New York Times*, January 30. Accessed January 30, 2013. http://www.nytimes.com/2013/01/31/us/politics/transcript-of-Guantánamo-hearing-points-to-outside-censors.html.

Savage, Charlie. 2013b. 'Legal clashes at hearing for defendants in 9/11 case'. *The New York Times*, February 14. Accessed February 14, 2013. http://www.nytimes.com/2013/02/15/us/legal-clashes-at-hearing-for-defendants-in-9-11-case.html.

Savage, Charlie. 2014. 'Appeals court allows challenges by detainees at Guantánamo prison'. *The New York Times*, February 11. Accessed April 3, 2014. http://www.nytimes.com/2014/02/12/us/appeals-court-clears-way-for-Guantánamo-challenges.html.

Savelsberg, Joachim J., and Ryan D. King. 2011. *American Memories: Atrocities and the Law*. New York: Russell Sage Foundation.

Savelsberg, Joachim. 2010. *Crime and Human Rights: Criminology of Genocide and Atrocities*. London: Sage Publications.

Saytas, Andrius. 2014. 'Lithuania to investigate allegations of CIA rendition'. *The Star*, February 21. Accessed April 5, 2014. http://www.thestar.com.my/News/World/2014/02/21/Lithuania-to-investigate-allegations-of-CIA-rendition/.

Scanlon, Jennifer. 2005. ''Your flag decal won't get you into heaven anymore': U.S. consumers, Wal-Mart, and the commodification of patriotism'. In *The Selling of 9/11*, edited by Dana Heller, 174–99. New York: Palgrave Macmillan.

Schama, Simon. 2005. 'Sorry Mr President, Katrina is not 9/11'. *The Guardian*, September 12. Accessed May 15, 2010. http://www.guardian.co.uk/world/2005/sep/12/hurricanekatrina.september11.

Schnurr, Rosina G. 2002. *Terrorism: The Only Way Is Through – A Child's Story*. Ottawa: Anisior Publishing.

Schulman, Helen. 2007. *A Day at the Beach*. New York: Houghton Mifflin.

Schulze-Engler, Frank. 2009. 'Introduction'. In *Transcultural English Studies: Theories, Fictions, Realities,* edited by Frank Schulze-Engler and Sissy Helff, ix – xvi. Amsterdam and New York: Rodopi.

Schwartz, Lynne Sharon. 2005. *The Writing on the* Wall. New York: Counterpoint.

Seltzer, Mark. 1997. 'Wound culture'. *October* 80.1: 3–26.

Shamsie, Kamila. 2009. *Burnt Shadows.* London: Bloomsbury.

Shephard, Michelle. 2008. *Guantánamo's Child: The Untold Story of Omar Khadr.* Toronto: John Wiley and Sons.

Sherman, Daniel and Terry Nardin, eds. 2006. *Terror, Culture, Politics: Rethinking 9/11.* Bloomington and Indianapolis: Indiana University Press.

Sicher, Efraim. 2000. 'The future of the past: Countermemory and postmemory in contemporary American post-Holocaust narratives'. *History & Memory* 12.2: 56–91.

Simon Wiesenthal Center. 2014. Accessed May 5, 2014. http://www.wiesenthal. com.

Simpson, David. 2006. *9/11: The Culture of Commemoration.* Chicago and London: University of Chicago Press.

Singer, Peter. 2004. *The President of Good and Evil: The Ethics of George W. Bush.* New York and London: Dutton.

Skitka, Linda J., Benjamin Saunders, G. Scott Morgan, and Daniel Wisneski. 2009. 'Dark clouds and silver linings: Social responses to 9/11'. In *The Impact of 9/11 on Psychology and Education: The Day That Changed Everything?,* edited by Matthew J. Morgan, 63–81. New York: Palgrave Macmillan.

Skomal, Lenore. 2002. *Heroes.* Philadelphia and London: Running Press.

Slotkin, Richard. 1986. 'Myth and the production of history'. In *Ideology and Classic American Literature,* edited by Sacvan Bercovitch and Myra Jehlen, 70–90. Cambridge: Cambridge University Press.

Smith, Terry. 2006. *The Architecture of Aftermath.* Chicago and London: University of Chicago Press.

Solnit, Rebecca. 2011. 'Civil society at Ground Zero'. *CBS News,* November 22. Accessed November 23, 2011. http://www.huffingtonpost.com/rebecca-solnit/civil-society-at-ground-z_b_1108438.html.

Sontag, Susan. 2001. 'The talk of the town'. *The New Yorker,* September 24. Accessed June 11, 2010. http://www.newyorker.com/archive/2001/09/24/010924ta_talk_wtc.

Sontag, Susan. 2003. *Regarding the Pain of Others.* London: Penguin Books.

Sontag, Susan. 2004. 'Regarding the torture of others'. *The New York Times,* May 23. Accessed December 5, 2010. http://www.nytimes.com/2004/05/23/magazine/regarding-the-torture-of-others.html.

Spiegelman, Art. 2003. *The Complete Maus.* London: Penguin.

Spiegelman, Art. 2004. *In the Shadow of No Towers.* New York: Pantheon.

Stafford Smith, Clive. 2007a. *Bad Men: Guantánamo Bay and the Secret Prisons.* London: Weidenfeld and Nicolson.

Stafford Smith, Clive. 2007b. *Eight o' Clock Ferry to the Windward Side.* New York: Nation Books.

Stamelman, Richard. 2003. 'Between memory and history'. In *Trauma at Home After 9/11,* edited by Judith Greenberg, 11–20. Lincoln and London: University of Nebraska Press.

Steinberg, Jacques. 1993. 'In ceremony of remembrance, reminders of human courage'. *The New York Times*, April 19.

Stempel, Jonathan. 2014. 'Bonus payout for WTC site workers premature – U.S. court'. *Reuters*, June 9. Accessed June 10, 2014. http://uk.reuters.com/article/2014/06/09/worldtradecenter-payout-lawsuit-idUKL2N0OQ0YM20140609.

Stephens, Suzanne, Ian Luna, and Robert Broadhurst. 2004. *Imagining Ground Zero*. London: Thames and Hudson.

Stine, Catherine. 2005. *Refugees*. New York: Delacorte Press.

Stonebridge, Lyndsey. 2011. *The Judicial Imagination: Writing After Nuremberg*. Edinburgh: Edinburgh University Press.

Stow, Simon. 2008. 'Portraits 9/11/01: The *New York Times* and the Pornography of Grief'. In *Literature After 9/11*, edited by Ann Keniston and Jeanne Follansbee Quinn, 224–41. New York and London: Routledge.

Sturken, Marita. 1997. *Tangled Memories: The Vietnam War, the AIDS Epidemic, and the Politics of Remembering*. Berkley, Los Angeles, and London: University of California Press.

Sturken, Marita. 2007. *Tourists of History*. Durham and London: Duke University Press.

Suson, Gary. 2002. *Requiem: Images of Ground Zero*. New York: Barnes and Noble.

Sutton, Jane. 2013. '9/11 Suspects' testimony about treatment at secret CIA prisons kept secret after judge's order'. *The World Post*, December 12. Accessed February 14, 2014. http://www.huffingtonpost.com/2012/12/12/911-suspects-cia-prisons_n_2287160.html.

Tal, Kali. 1996. *Worlds of Hurt*. Cambridge: Cambridge University Press.

Teitel, Ruti G. 2000. *Transitional Justice*. Oxford: Oxford University Press.

Tomsky, Terri. 2011. 'From Sarajevo to 9/11: Travelling memory and the trauma economy'. *Parallax* 17.4: 49–60.

Toobin, Jeffrey. 2008. 'Annals of law: Camp Justice'. *The New Yorker*, April 14. Accessed May 20, 2013. http://www.newyorker.com/reporting/2008/04/14/080414fa_fact_toobin?currentPage=all.

Torres, Fransesc, ed. 2011. *Memory Remains: 9/11 Artifacts at Hangar 17*. Washington, D.C.: National Geographic.

Trimarco, James, and Molly Hurley Depret. 2005. 'Wounded nation, broken time'. In *The Selling of 9/11*, edited by Dana Heller, 27–53. New York: Palgrave Macmillan.

Tuttle, Ross. 2008. 'Rigged trials at Gitmo'. *The Nation*, March 3. Accessed January 21, 2014. http://www.thenation.com/article/rigged-trials-gitmo#.

US Department of Justice. 2013. 'September 11th Victim Compensation Fund of 2001'. Accessed on February 26, 2013. http://www.justice.gov/archive/victimcompensation/.

Vermeulen, Pieter. 2013. 'Flights of memory: Teju Cole's *Open City* and the limits of aesthetic cosmopolitanism'. *Journal of Modern Literature* 37.1: 40–57.

Vinitzky-Seroussi, Vered. 2009. *Yitzhak Rabin's Assassination and the Dilemmas of Commemoration*. New York: SUNY Press.

Virilio, Paul. 2002. *Ground Zero*. Translated by Chris Turner. London and New York: Verso.

Vygotsky, L. S. 1929. 'The problem of the cultural development of the child'. *Journal of Genetic Psychology* 36: 414–34.

Waldman, Amy. 2011. *The Submission*. London: William Heinemann.
Washington, George. 1789. 'First inaugural address'. Accessed July 10, 2011. http://gwpapers.virginia.edu/documents/inaugural/final.html.
Weinberg, Jeshajahu, and Rina Elieli. 1995. *The Holocaust Museum in Washington*. New York: Rizzoli.
Weiser, Benjamin. 2009. 'Value of suing over 9/11 deaths is still unsettled'. *The New York Times*, March 12. Accessed December 14, 2012. http://www.nytimes.com/2009/03/13/nyregion/13lawsuits.html?pagewanted=all.
Weiser, Benjamin. 2010. 'Among 9/11 families, a last holdout remains'. *The New York Times*, September 10. Accessed November 16, 2012. http://www.nytimes.com/2010/09/11/nyregion/11family.html?pagewanted=all.
Weiser, Benjamin. 2011a. 'At 9/11 trial lawyers will watch the clock'. *The New York Times*, April 27. Accessed October 17, 2012. http://www.nytimes.com/2011/04/28/nyregion/at-911-trial-lawyers-will-watch-the-clock.html.
Weiser, Benjamin. 2011b. 'Family and United Airlines settle last 9/11 wrongful-death lawsuit'. *The New York Times*, September 19. Accessed September 7, 2012. http://www.nytimes.com/2011/09/20/nyregion/last-911-wrongful-death-suit-is-settled.html.
Weizman, Eyal. 2011. *The Least of All Possible Evils*. London: Verso.
Welsch, Wolfgang. 1999. 'Transculturality – the puzzling form of cultures today'. In *Spaces of Culture: City, Nation, World*, edited by Mike Featherstone and Scott Lash, 194–213. London: Sage.
White, Hayden. 1975. *Metahistory: The Historical Imagination in Nineteenth-Century Europe*. Baltimore and London: Johns Hopkins University Press.
White, Hayden. 1980. 'The value of narrativity in the representation of reality'. *Critical Inquiry* 7.1: 5–27.
White, Hayden. 1987. *The Content of the Form*. Baltimore: Johns Hopkins University Press.
Whitecross, Mat, and Michael Winterbottom. 2006. *The Road to Guantánamo*. Directed by Mat Whitecross and Michael Winterbottom. Film4.
Whitehead, Anne. 2004. *Trauma Fiction*. Edinburgh: Edinburgh University Press.
Wiesel, Elie. 1982. *Night*. Translated by Stella Rodney. London: Bantam Books.
Wiesel, Elie. 1985. *Against Silence: The Voice and Vision of Elie* Wiesel. New York: Holocaust Library.
Wiesel, Elie. 2002. 'War is the only option'. *The Observer*, December 22.
Wigley, Mark. 2002. 'Insecurity by design'. In *After the World Trade Center*, edited by Michael Sorkin and Sharon Zukin, 69–86. New York and London: Routledge.
Williams, Paul. 2007. *Memorial Museums: The Global Rush to Commemorate Atrocities*. Oxford and New York: Berg.
Wodiczko, Krzysztof. 2009. *City of Refuge*. London: Black Dog Publishing.
Woodward, Bob. 2004. *Plan of Attack*. New York: Simon and Schuster.
Worthington, Andy. 2007. *The Guantánamo Files: The Stories of the 774 Detainees in America's Illegal Prison*. London: Pluto Press.
Worthington, Andy. 2014. 'The Guantánamo experience: a harrowing letter by Yemeni Prisoner Emad Hassan'. *Eurasia Review*, February 21. Accessed March 1, 2014. 0 http://www.eurasiareview.com/20022014-Guantánamo-experiment-harrowing-letter-yemeni-prisoner-emad-hassan-oped/.

WTC Tribute Center. 2010. Accessed June 14, 2010. http://www.tributewtc.org . Accessed 14th June, 2010.

Wyatt, Edward. 2010. '3 Republicans criticize Obama's endorsement of mosque'. *New York Times*, August 14. Accessed July 17, 2011. http://www.nytimes.com/2010/08/15/us/politics/15reaction.html.

Young, James E. 1993. *The Texture of Memory: Holocaust Memorials and Meaning*. New Haven: Yale University Press.

Young, James E. 1999. 'America's holocaust: Memory and the politics of identity'. In *The Americanization of the Holocaust*, edited by Hilene Flanzbaum, 68–82. Baltimore and London: Johns Hopkins University Press.

Young, James E. 2003. 'Remember life with life: The new World Trade Center'. In *Trauma at Home*, edited by Judith Greenberg, 216–32. Lincoln and London: University of Nebraska Press.

Zagorin, Adam. 2008. 'U.S. justice on trial at Gitmo'. *Time*, June 4. Accessed July 19, 2013. http://content.time.com/time/nation/article/0,8599,1811683,00.html.

Zaskin, Elliott and Phillip C. Chapman. 1974. 'The uses of metaphor and analogy: Toward a renewal of political language'. *Journal of Politics* 36.2: 290–326.

Zehfuss, Maja. 2003. 'Forget September 11'. *Third World Quarterly* 24.3: 513–28.

Zimmerman, Laurie. 2010. 'Rosh Hashanah, 5771 – Park 51 and Museum of Tolerance'. Accessed May 10, 2014. http://www.shamayim.org/index.php?page=rosh-hashanah-5771---park-51-and-museum-of-tolerance.

Žižek, Slavoj. 2002. *Welcome to the Desert of the Real*. London and New York: Verso.

Index

Printed in Great Britain
by Amazon